Constitutional Law in Russia

Constitutional Law in Russia

Second Edition

Irina Bogdanovskaia
Sergey Danilov
Tatiana Vassilieva

This book was originally published as a monograph in the International Encyclopaedia of Laws/Constitutional Law.

Founding Editor: Roger Blanpain
General Editor: Frank Hendrickx
Volume Editors: André Alen & David Haljan

Wolters Kluwer

Published by:
Kluwer Law International B.V.
PO Box 316
2400 AH Alphen aan den Rijn
The Netherlands
E-mail: international-sales@wolterskluwer.com
Website: lrus.wolterskluwer.com

Sold and distributed in North, Central and South America by:
Wolters Kluwer Legal & Regulatory U.S.
7201 McKinney Circle
Frederick, MD 21704
United States of America
Email: customer.service@wolterskluwer.com

Sold and distributed in all other countries by:
Air Business Subscriptions
Rockwood House
Haywards Heath
West Sussex
RH16 3DH
United Kingdom
Email: international-customerservice@wolterskluwer.com

Printed on acid-free paper

ISBN 978-94-035-1141-2

e-Book: ISBN 978-94-035-1173-3
web-PDF: ISBN 978-94-035-1174-0

Printed in the United Kingdom by CPI Group (UK) Ltd, Croydon, CR0 4YY.

The Authors

Irina Bogdanovskaia is a Doctor of Juridical Sciences and was a Senior Research Fellow at the Institute of State and Law, Russian Academy of Sciences. She is specialized in Comparative Law and Comparative Constitutional law. Irina is the author of two books and numerous articles in this sphere. As an Associate Professor, she taught courses on Jurisprudence, Comparative Law and Comparative Constitutional Law at the International Law Institute of the Ministry of Justice of the Russian Federation and at the Academic Law University of the Institute of State and Law. Now she is a Chief, International Laboratory for IT and IP and a Head, Chair of Information Law, National Research University Higher School of Economics under the Government of the Russian Federation. Among her publications are monographs *The Precedent Law* (two editions) and *Zakon v. angliyskom prave*. She is also an editor and co-author for collective analytical study *The Right for Information,* and editor-in-chief of the high-ranking legal quarterly, *Pravo. Zhurnal Vysshey shkoly ekonomiki.*

Sergey Danilov for years worked as a Junior Research Fellow, Senior Research Fellow and Leading Researcher and Consultant at the Russian Academy of Sciences, where he received his Candidate and Doctor degrees in Historical Sciences, and at International Legal University under the Justice Ministry of Russia. At present he is Professor and Director, Center of Comparative Law at the National Research University Higher School of Economics. His main fields of interest and studies are Modern History and Comparative Constitutional Law. Among his publications are The *Foreign Constitutional Law in Schemes* (two editions), *Constitutional Economics Abroad* (two editions), *The Essays in Russian History and the Evolution of Canadian Federalism.* He is a member of the Editorial Board, *Annals of Social Sciences and Management Studies Journal* (ASM).

The Authors

Tatiana Vassilieva is Leading Researcher and Acting Head, Department of Comparative Law at the Institute of State and Law, Russian Academy of Sciences. She is a former Research Fellow of the Law Faculty of the Moscow State University, a consultant at the State Legal Department of the President of the Russian Federation. She is an author of numerous publications in the fields of the Comparative Constitutional Law and the Constitutional Law of Russia.

Table of Contents

List of Abbreviations

BMD	*Biulleten' mezhdunarodnykh dogovorov*
Bul. CEC	*Biulleten' Tsentral'noi izbiratel'noi komissii Russian Federation*
CIS	Commonwealth of Independent States
CPSU	Communist Party of the Soviet Union
RG	*Rossiiskaia gazeta*
RSFSR	Russian Soviet Federative Socialist Republic
SAPP	*Sobranie aktov Prezidenta i Pravitel'stva Rossiyskoy Federatsii*
SU	*Sobranie uzakonenii RSFSR*
SZ	*Sobranie zakonodatel'stva Rossiiskoi Federatsii*
US	United States of America
USSR	Union of Soviet Socialist Republics
Ved. RF	*Vedomosti S'ezda narodnykh deputatov i Verkhovnogo Soveta Rossiyskoy Federatsii*
Ved. RSFSR	*Vedomosti S'ezda narodnykh deputatov i Verkhovnogo Soveta RSFSR*
VKS	*Vestnik Konstitutsionnogo Suda*

List of Abbreviations

Glossary

T. Vassilieva

A. Institutions

Administration of the President *Administratsia Prezidenta*
All-Russian Congress of Soviets *Vserossiiskii S'ezd Sovetov*
All-Russian Central Executive Committee
Vserossiiskii Tsentral'nyi Ispolnitel'nyi Komitet
Audit Chamber *Schetnaia palata*
Committee of Constitutional Review
Komitet konstitutsionnogo nadzora
Congress of People's Deputies *S'ezd narodnykh deputatov*
Constituent Assembly *Uchreditel'noe Sobranie*
Constitutional Assembly *Konstitutsionnoe Sobranie*
Constitutional Conference *Konstitutsionnoe Sovesh'anie*
Council of People's Commissars *Sovet narodnykh komissarov*
Federal Assembly *Federal'noe Sobranie*
– Council of the Federation *Sovet Federatsii*
– State Duma *Gosudarstvennaia Duma*
Human Rights Commissioner *Upolnomochennyi po pravam cheloveka*
Procurator's Office *Prokuratura*
Procurator General *General'nyi prokuror*
State Council *Gosudarstvennyi Sovet*
Supreme Soviet *Verkhovnyi Sovet*
– Council of the Nationalities *Sovet Natsional'nostei*
– Council of the Republic *Sovet Respubliki*

Temporary Government *Vremennoe Pravitel'stvo*

B. Legislation

Codes
– Budgetary Code *Biudzhetnyi kodeks*
– Code of the Russian Empire *Svod zakonov Rossiiskoi Imperii*
– Tax Code *Nalogovyi kodeks*
– Criminal Code *Ugolovnyi kodeks*
Foundations of Legislation *Osnovy zakonodatel'stva*

C. Other Expressions

charter *ustav*
decision *opredelenie Konstitutsionnogo Suda*
decree *postanovlenie Pravitel'stva*
edict *ukaz*
guiding explanations *raz'asnenia*
numerically small peoples *malochislennie narody*
opinion *zakliuchenie*
order *rasporiazhenie*
prescription *predpisanie*
resolution *postanovlenie Palaty*
ruling *postanovlenie Konstitutsionnogo Suda*
standing orders *reglament*
treaties
– Federation Treaty *Federativnii dogovor*
– Union Treaty *Dogovor ob obrazovanii SSSR*

General Introduction

I. Bogdanovskaia, S.Yu. Danilov & T. Vassilieva

§1. Concise Description of Constitutional History

1. Russia has come a long way to the Constitutional State. Its constitutional development began later than in other European countries – only at the beginning of the twentieth century – and continued under different political regimes and forms of government. The history of constitutional law in Russia may be divided into several periods. The first period marked the birth of the Constitutional State (it lasted from 1905 until 1917), the second demonstrated the specificity of the Soviet constitutional model (1917 to the end of the 1980s) and the third is the transitional period to the Constitutional State (from the end of the 1980s up to the present).

I. General Retrospective of Russian Constitutional Development

A. Before 1917: The First Steps to the Constitutional State

2. Russia was formed as a State in the ninth century. From the fourteenth until the sixteenth centuries the separate principalities were united into Moscow principality.[1] As a result of the process of centralization, Russia became an autocratic monarchy in the fifteenth century. All undertaken reforms of this system (as a rule suggested from 'above', that is initiated by the Government) brought partial improvements but no overall success. Constitutional drafts began to appear as from the eighteenth century but none of them was realized.

The first real steps towards the restriction of the autocratic monarchy were taken at the beginning of the twentieth century. Acts of Tzar Nicholas II (the Manifest of 1905 and Edicts of 1906) declared the formation of a representative body. This was also reflected in the Basic Laws – the first part of the Codes of the Russian Empire (*Svod zakonov Rossiiskoi Imperii*, t. 1). Russia was on its way from autocratic to constitutional monarchy. The important steps were made towards a State under the

1. *See* N. Korkunov, *Russkoe gosudarstvennoe pravo*, t. 2 (St. Petersburg: Stasiulevich, 1905); A.D. Gradovskii, *Nachala russkogo gosudarstvennogo prava*, t. 2 (Moskva: Jurist, 2010; reprint).

rule of law. People were given political rights and freedoms – freedom of speech, freedom of association, personal immunity.

3. At that time Russia was a dualistic monarchy. The Tzar as the Head of State had many real powers. His person was sacred and inviolable and everybody had to obey him as appointed by God. He was able to convene and dissolve the State Duma (the first State Duma convened in March 1906 and was dissolved in June 1906, the second one convened in April 1907 and was dissolved in June 1907). He had the right of legislative initiative and the exclusive right to introduce the basic laws, and the power to sign laws. He was able to control the activity of the State Duma by appointing the Vice-Chairman. The Tzar adopted his own acts nominally countersigned by the Prime Minister or a minister who was responsible for that act. The Government was under the control of the Tzar since he appointed and dismissed ministers and other officials. The Head of State also declared war and peace, maintained relations with foreign countries and was Commander-in-Chief of the armed forces.

In fact, the bicameral representative body limited the autocratic monarchy. The lower chamber, the State Duma, was elected for five years. Part of the upper chamber, members of the State Council, was nominated by the Tzar and the other part was elected for nine years. Elections were held every three years for one-third of the elected members. The members of the State Council were not younger than 40 years old and had secondary education. The representative body had lawmaking powers, decided financial issues and controlled expenses.

The executive power was vested in the Council of Ministers. It was subordinated to the Tzar and at the same time was controlled by the State Duma and the State Council. A deputy had the right to interpellate a minister who was able to refuse to answer. If two-thirds of the State Duma considered the answer unsatisfactory, the Chairman of the State Council informed the Tzar.

The Russian Government was given limited legislative powers very early. When the State Duma was not in session the Council of Ministers was able to apply to the Tzar for legislative needs. Later, provisions adopted by the Government needed the approval of the State Duma.

4. Representative democracy in Russia developed in difficult and tumultuous times. The government system did not satisfy some social groups and there were several uprisings. The political situation became more complicated because of the First World War. It became necessary to take quick and serious steps to reform the system of government. In February 1917, the State Duma organized the Temporary Committee for the establishment of social order that concentrated strong powers. It formed the Temporary Government as the previous one retired. The Temporary Government consisted of the representatives of political parties. In March 1917, Nicholas II abdicated in favour of his brother Mikhail, who in turn abdicated on the advice of the Temporary Government. Russia became the Russian Republic, as was officially declared in the Manifest of the Temporary Government of 1 September 1917. However, the transformation of the monarchy into a republic and further attempts to reform the government and state organs was not a coherent constitutional reform. Nevertheless, the State tried to develop a democratic character and involved various social and political forces in the process of resolving the crisis. The Temporary Government, looking for social compromise, organized two conferences of representatives of the clergy, army, trade unions, ex-deputies of the State Duma, peasants, merchants, academic circles: the State Conference of August 1917 and the Democratic Conference of September 1917. The Democratic Conference organized the *Pre-parliament* – the Temporary Council of the Republic. It consisted of 555 members who represented various social and political groups. The State Duma continued to exist until the Chairman of the Temporary Government Kerenski dissolved it on 6 October 1917.

The governmental reform expanded not only to the central organs but also to the other elements of the system, including the local government. The development of the representative organs at different levels of the State created the possibility to involve more people in the administration of state affairs. At the same time the reform did not bring deep changes in the state mechanism. A new constitutional government was to be established by the Constituent Assembly. But it was held only in January 1918 when the Bolsheviks already had taken power.

The Bolsheviks received only 175 out of 715 mandates, and the Assembly did not approve the first acts of the Soviet power. Striving for dictatorship, Bolsheviks dissolved the Constituent Assembly after one day of debates. The constitutional law of Russia began to develop in accordance with the socialist model.

B. Soviet Constitutional Law

5. The Soviet constitutional model was opposed to that of the Western democracies.[2] The world was divided into the 'bourgeois' and the 'socialist' blocs. The greater part of the twentieth century has been coloured by the struggle of these models.

The constitutional law of Soviet Russia developed independently during a short period of time. In 1922, Russia became a Member State of the Soviet Union (USSR), and from that time on until the end of 1991 it depended upon the constitutional development of USSR. After the adoption of the Constitution of the Soviet Union of 1924, the Russian Constitution of 1918 was revised. Later, all the constitutions of Soviet Russia were adopted after the coming into force of the new Constitutions of the USSR and in correspondence with them. In fact, the Russian Constitutions of 1937 and 1978 repeated the basic provisions of the USSR Constitutions of 1936 and 1977.

The Soviet Constitutions traditionally were not a result of social compromise. They were considered more as ideological documents than as legal acts. The Constitutions had to demonstrate 'the development of the socialist achievements' and for that purpose, the Communist Party organized their amendment. Thus, the USSR Constitution of 1936 and the Russian Constitution of 1937 reflected the final construction of socialism, whereas the USSR Constitution of 1977 and the Russian

2. *See* H. Berman, *Justice in the USSR. An Interpretation of Soviet Laws* (Cambridge: Harvard University Press, 1963); Z. Unger, *Ideas and Forces in the Soviet Legal History* (A reader on the Soviet State and law, New York: Oxford, 1992).

Constitution of 1978 demonstrated in accordance with the ideas of their authors the model of 'developed socialism'. The Soviet Constitutions did not have direct operation, and courts rarely took decisions based on them. All of them were flexible and could be amended by ordinary laws. Under the dictatorship this meant that the governmental system could be easily changed in the interest of the ruling political group.

6. The established constitutional model was principally contrary to the Western ones. The Russian Constitution of 1918 declared the break with bourgeois civilization and the aim of building socialism all over the world. The Soviet Constitutions reflected the socialist theoretical conceptions. The socialist State was announced as the most developed form of government, as the next stage of social development – communism – would be without any state government. Thus, the Soviet State was considered as a transitional stage to a society without a state.

One of the main aims of the socialist State was establishing social justice interpreted as real equality of people. The aim of social justice justified different methods for its achievement (from the political oppression created by the dictatorship to the methods of economic policy, such as equal salaries for different kinds of work, labour as an obligation, low taxes because of the state redistribution of income). They varied between the period of the dictatorship and of the limited democracy. From the beginning, democracy was interpreted as the realization of the 'interests of the working people'. Correspondingly, the conception of the people's sovereignty was revised. In contrast with the previous governments which had searched for social compromise, the new power reflected the interests of one political group – Bolshevik-Communist – which were presented as the interests of the working people. Thus, decisions taken by the minority became legally binding for the majority. In the Constitution of 1918, the Russian Republic was declared a free society but in the form of a dictatorship. Such policy led to the Civil War and social confrontation during the whole Soviet period. Even at present, at the beginning of the twenty-first century, social compromise has not been achieved. Only the Constitution of 1978 reflected some liberal tendencies and, with the intent of erasing the differences between classes and social groups, recognized the whole people as a source of the state power. This implied the termination of the class struggle and the constitutional recognition of the end of the dictatorship.

7. The Soviet political regime determined the conception and policy in the sphere of human rights. Formally, the Constitutions proclaimed them. While the Constitution of 1918 contained several articles regulating the freedoms of conscience, expression, opinion, meetings, associations, press and free education, the Constitutions adopted later enlarged this list. The Constitutions of 1937 contained a special chapter on human rights in which social rights (right to work, to rest, to social security, to education), political rights (freedom of speech, press, meetings, demonstrations) and individual rights were proclaimed. These provisions were progressive for that time and to some extent influenced by the constitutional-making process in other countries. The Constitution of 1978 contained a special part regarding the relations between the State and individuals that included several chapters.

The Soviet Constitutions provided for obligations, and the first and the main one was the obligation to work. The criminal responsibility for those who did not work was established by the Criminal Code.

The interests of the State prevailed over the rights and freedoms of individuals. As the latter rights were considered given by the State, the State was able to establish any limits to them. Though the principle of equality was included in all the Constitutions, the volume of rights depended upon the social status. After the Revolution, electoral rights were not given to those who exploited other people or lived off bank savings, to clergymen and to former policemen. The workers had additional privileges. One deputy of the All-Russian Congress of Soviets represented 25,000 electors of towns or 125,000 residents of *gubernii*, rural regions. In contrast with the western democracies, the Soviet State supported the idea that a poor citizen was a 'good citizen'. The Soviet system divided the society, and a part of the people was considered 'enemies' of the others as well as of the Soviet power.[3] They were repressed and limited in rights. Some people who did not agree with the state policy had to leave the country.

8. The Revolution led to the principal changes in the state mechanism. The principles of the western Constitutional States – the separation of powers and the 'rule of law' – were rejected as they concealed the 'class sense' of the State. New principles were declared instead: revolutionary (later socialist)' legality, unity of the governmental system, including the unity of the legislative and executive powers. These principles and the principle of 'democratic centralism' limited the responsibility of the State, governmental organs and officials, and justified decisions and actions that violated human rights in the name of social interests. The previous state mechanism was scrapped entirely. The legislative, executive and judicial bodies were substituted by new ones. At the same time, it was impossible to reject all elements of the Constitutional State and to build a State on the principally new basis. The development of the socialist State demonstrated the existence of such elements, though sometimes they had other content. For example, representative democracy was developed under the domination of one political party; elections were held, but citizens did not have a real choice since there was only one candidate in every constituency; the status of a deputy was established, but he was considered the representative of the electors of his constituency and not of the whole people.

The government system had evolved from Lenin's idea of vast democracy, in which a majority of people governed society, towards a highly centralized state in which the standing executive organs had a more important role than the representative ones. All state powers were vested in the Soviets. Lenin rejected the conception of the representative body as a professional permanently working body. He intended to establish a governmental system in which the greater part of the working people could take part in the exercising of state power and elaborated the new concept of the Republic of Soviets The system of the state organs established after the October Revolution consisted of Congresses of Soviets of different territorial levels with the All-Russian Congress of Soviets at the top. It was elected by indirect elections. The All-Russian Congress of Soviets formed the All-Russian Central

3. *See* R. Conquest, *The Great Terror. Stalin's Purge of the Thirties* (London: Macmillan, 1968).

Executive Committee, which was the supreme controlling body of the state Russian Federation between the Congresses. The All-Russian Central Executive Committee, in turn, elected the Presidium. With time the role of the Congresses diminished (since 1922 they were convened once a year) while the role of the All-Russian Central Executive Committee and later of the Presidium was increased. The All-Russian Central Executive Committee looked more like a traditional Parliament. It had all powers belonging to the jurisdiction of the All-Russian Congress of Soviets except the exclusive powers to revise the Constitution and to ratify treaties. The Presidium was considered a working body of the All-Russian Central Executive Committee with controlling functions. It might confirm the acts of the government – called Council of People's Commissars – or repeal them, appoint the People's Commissars between the meetings of the All-Russian Central Executive Committee upon the proposal of the Council of People's Commissars, or convene the All-Russian Central Executive Committee.

The Council of People's Commissars exercised the executive power under the control of the representative bodies. Soon after the adoption of the Constitution of 1918, the Small Council of People's Commissars was established. The executive committees of the local Soviets were local executive bodies. Already in 1919 they were considered the supreme organs of the state power on their territory between the Congresses of Soviets. The executive committees had double subordination – to the Soviet of the corresponding level and to a higher executive committee – and formed a strong 'vertical' pole that became a typical feature of the Soviet centralized State. Being standing bodies, the executive committees concentrated real powers, whereas the representative bodies were convened in sessions for several days in order to approve formally and as a rule unanimously decisions prepared by the executive bodies.

After Russia became a member entity of the USSR, the system of the state organs was mainly preserved. The main changes were connected with the distribution of powers between the USSR and Russia as its member entity. Some People's Commissariats were abolished since their functions were transferred to the federal authorities (Foreign Affairs, Military Affairs, Foreign Trade), some became subordinated to the federal state organs as well as to the Russian ones.

The system of Congresses was cumbrous. The ruling party looked for a system which would be formally democratic but easier for control. It was established by the Constitutions of the USSR of 1936 and Russia of 1937 and existed with some modifications until the end of the Soviet period. The Congresses were substituted by the permanently working system of Soviets. The All-Russian Central Executive Committee was reorganized into the Supreme Soviet elected by people. The Presidium remained a narrow body empowered to adopt important political decisions. It directed the activity of the Supreme Soviet, convened its sessions and interpreted laws. With time the Presidium began to play a more important role. While there was no formal Head of State, the Presidium of the Supreme Soviet was considered by some scholars to be the collective Head of State. The Chairman of the Presidium had a strong political position.

The executive power was vested in the Council of People's Commissars. It was formed by the Supreme Soviet and worked under its control and under that of the Presidium, which had the power to annul its acts. Nominally, the Council laid down its powers and got them back at every session of the Supreme Soviet. The system nominally had similarities with parliamentary republics, but, in contrast with the Western parliamentary countries, the principle of responsible government was not recognized: the government could not be dismissed and the Supreme Soviet could not be dissolved.

9. The most serious experiments were made in the sphere of the judicial power. The consequences may be felt even at present since they gave birth to legal nihilism and a negative attitude towards the judicial power as the guarantor of human rights. The Bolsheviks did not estimate the judicial power as an important element of the state system, and the Constitution of 1918 even did not include any provision in this field. However, the Constitutions of 1937 and 1978 contained special chapters on the judicial power.

The judicial power was not an independent branch. The courts as repressive bodies performed the political tasks determined by the ruling political party. According to the Regulation on the Court System adopted by the All-Russian Central Executive Committee in 1926 (SU, 1926 No. 85), the courts defended the achievements of the socialist revolution, the interests of the working class and revolutionary legality, and even took care of legal education. First of all, the courts defended the interests of the State. The emergency courts – the revolutionary tribunals – had jurisdiction concerning crimes against the Soviet Republic (SU, 1919 No. 13). The judges had to be loyal to the existing power and have working experience in the new governmental bodies or trade unions. Under the provisions of the Regulation on the Court System of 1918 (SU, 1918 No. 85) the court was able to take decisions in accordance with the 'socialist legal conscience' in the case of gaps in law.

From 1917 until 1922, the judicial power was exercised by different judicial and non-judicial organs – courts, revolutionary and military tribunals, All-Russian Extraordinary Commission (Cheka)[4] – which performed their functions in various state bodies, both legislative and executive. The principle of the unity of justice was rejected from the beginning. The emergency courts (tribunals) established during the Civil War began to administer emergency justice under which some categories of cases were decided according to special procedures. That practice was also used later. From the beginning, the ordinary courts had limited jurisdiction and decided cases which were beyond the jurisdiction of the revolutionary tribunals and the All-Russian Extraordinary Commission. After 1922, the ordinary courts once more became the main bodies of the judicial power. The organization of courts and appointment of judges were under the control of the Soviets which elected judges, and of course of the Party structures at different levels. From the beginning, a system of assessors was adopted instead of a jury system. In each judicial district, the Council of People's Judges worked as the court of cassation. The members of the Council were elected by the Congress of judges of that judicial district and approved by the corresponding Soviets. At the end of the 1920s the court system stabilized. It consisted of three levels and was centralized. This system, with some modifications, existed until the end of the Soviet period.

---

4. *See* G. Leggett, *The Cheka. Lenin's Political Police* (Oxford: Oxford University Press, 1981).

The judicial reform included the reform of the professions of lawyer and prosecutor. In 1922, the Procurator's Office was established (SU, 1922 No. 36). Procurators worked within the system of the People's Commissariat of Justice and exercised control over the realization of the socialist legality and preliminary investigation. During the first years of the Soviet power, the investigation committees (later investigators) conducted the preliminary investigations at the courts. In the Soviet period, the Procurator's Office was strengthened and became fully independent of the courts.

10. The established constitutional system did not reflect the real governmental system. The gap between the texts of the Constitutions and reality was wide. The main decisions were taken by the Communist Party.[5] Russia did not have its own Communist Party. Within the territory of Russia itself, there were structures of the Communist Party of the USSR with the Communist Party of the Soviet Union (CPSU) Central Committee at the head The Communist Party of Russia was organized only in 1990 as an integral part of the Communist Party of the USSR. With time, the bodies of the Communist Party – committees at different levels – formed a system parallel to that of the State. They controlled the state organs, appointment of officials, and elections of deputies and judges. For the Communist Party, constitutional law was a democratic cover.

C. The Constitutional Law of the Transitional Period

11. Towards the end of the twentieth century, Russia again faced the necessity of governmental reform. The Soviet power was incapable to secure the social and economic development of the country. The reform began at the end of the 1980s, traditionally from 'above'. As before, the constitutional reform was a lasting one. It may be divided into two periods: from the end of the 1980s until 1993 when the results of *perestroika* were reflected in the amendments to the Constitution of 1978, and from 1993 until the present when the new governmental system was established. The transitional period meant the return to universal standards (the Rule of Law, the separation of powers, political plurality), and the alteration of the political regime and the form of government. The constitutional changes of the 1990s took place in accordance to provisions of the Edict of the President of the Russian Federation 'On Step-by-Step Constitutional Reform' of 21 September 1993.

During *perestroika,* Russia became an independent State and received an opportunity to develop its own constitutional model. On 12 June 1990, the Congress of People's Deputies adopted the Declaration on the State Sovereignty of the Russian Soviet Federative Socialist Republic (RSFSR) (Ved. RSFSR, 1990 No. 2). But this Declaration was not included in the text of the Constitution, nor was the latter revised in accordance with it.

Russia became a sovereign State in December 1991 when the Presidents of the RSFSR and Ukraine and the Chairman of the Supreme Soviet of Byelorussia signed

5. K. Ryavec, *Soviet Society and the Communist Party* (Amherst: University of Massachusetts Press, 1979).

an agreement regarding the denunciation of the Treaty of 1922 on the creation of the Soviet Union. This agreement was approved by the legislative organs of those States (Ved. RSFSR, 1991 No. 51). Russia has become a subject of the international law and the legal heir of the USSR. In accordance with the RSFSR Law of 25 December 1991 (Ved. RSFSR, 1992 No. 2) the country was given a contemporary official name – the Russian Federation (Russia), both names mentioned are equivalent by Article 1.2 of the Constitution.

12. *Perestroika* began with the alteration of the political regime and the development of democracy. The Constitution declared political plurality and a multiparty system as general principles. The famous Article 6 establishing the Communist Party as the keystone of the political system was abolished in accordance with the RSFSR Law of 16 June 1990 (Ved. RSFSR 1990, No. 3). The ideological terms were excluded from the text of the Constitution. The democratization of social life also concerned the sphere of human rights. The conception of human rights was revised. On 22 November 1991, the Supreme Soviet of the RSFSR adopted the Declaration of the Rights and Freedoms of Man and Citizen (Ved. RSFSR 1991, No. 52), which was included in the text of the Constitution in 1992. Human rights were declared effective as of birth. International law was given priority over domestic law in the sphere of human rights for the first time in the Russian history. The list of human rights was enlarged sufficiently, and the wording of articles was changed.

13. Like other post-totalitarian countries, Russia has easily accepted the idea of constitutional control. The supremacy of the Constitution was considered an important factor for the development of the State under the rule of law. The constitutional revision of 1989 provided for the establishment of a Committee of Constitutional Review, substituted by the Constitutional Court in 1990. The Constitutional Court was elected by the Congress of People's Deputies and consisted of fifteen judges. It examined the constitutionality of federal laws and other acts of the Congress of People's Deputies, the Supreme Soviet and its Presidium; of acts of the President, Council of Ministers and federal organs of executive power; of Constitutions, Charters and acts of the representative and executive organs of the Federal Entities; of internal treaties between the organs of state power of Russia and the Federal Entities and of international treaties of the Russian Federation. The Constitutional Court was as well competent to check the compliance with the Constitution of political parties, associations and law-enforcement agencies. It might settle conflicts of competence between the federal state organs or between federal state organs and state organs of the Federal Entities. It was empowered to give opinions regarding the incapacity of federal officials to perform their functions for reasons of health. The Constitutional Court played an active role not only in the legal but also in the political life of the country and went through a period of judicial activism.

14. The reform of the system of the state organs was an important part of the constitutional reform. After the Soviet period, Russia was able to make a choice between a presidential and parliamentary republic. However, the Soviet traditions were still rather deep, and Russia preferred to combine an American model of a presidency with the restoration of the system of Congresses of People Deputies known from the first years of the Soviet power.

From 1991, the President was the Head of the Russian Federation. This decision was adopted by the referendum of 24 April 1991, when 69.85% of the electors taking part in it supported the proposal to introduce the institution of a presidency. The President was the highest official of the RSFSR and the head of executive power. He was elected together with the Vice-President by popular vote for a term of five years and could not serve more than two consecutive terms.

The President had the right of legislative initiative and veto powers. He was competent to convene extraordinary meetings of the Congress of People's Deputies or of the Supreme Soviet but was not able to dissolve them. In fact, the President was not a strong political figure. His powers were balanced by the powers of the Supreme Soviet. The President appointed and removed from office the Chairman of the Council of Ministers upon the consent of the Supreme Soviet, appointed and removed from office ministers upon the proposal of the Chairman of the Council of Ministers. It is necessary to mention that the Ministers of Foreign Affairs, of Defence and of Security could be appointed only with the consent of the Supreme Soviet. The President directed the activity of the Council of Ministers and could submit to the Supreme Soviet proposals regarding the creation, reorganization or abolishment of ministries and departments. The Congress of People's Deputies controlled the activity of the President. It might demand to present a report, apply the procedure of impeachment or abolish an act of the President.

15. The representative organs, first of all the Congress of People's Deputies, then played a more important role. These bodies had a complex structure. The Congress of People's Deputies of the Russian Federation elected the Supreme Soviet of Russia, while the Congresses of the republics within the Russian Federation elected its own Supreme Soviets. The Congress of People's Deputies to some extent played the role of the constituent body in the transitional period. The representatives of the people were able to discuss the problems of the development of the country and to take important decisions. The Congress consisted of 1,068 deputies: 900 deputies were elected in the territorial constituencies, whereas 168 deputies in national-territorial ones (4 deputies from each republic, 2 deputies from autonomous *oblasts*, 1 deputy from autonomous *okrug* and 84 deputies from *krays*, *oblasts* and the cities of Moscow and St. Petersburg).

The Supreme Soviet was a standing legislative, administrative and control body of the Congress. The relations of the Congress and the Supreme Soviet in the early 1990s were quite similar to the relations of the All-Russian Congress of Soviets and the All-Russian Central Executive Committee in 1918–1936. Both Congresses were held once per year. The Supreme Soviet, in contrast with the All-Russian Central Executive Committee, consisted of two Chambers: the Council of the Republic and the Council of the Nationalities. Both Chambers were equal in its rights and functions. The Council of the Republic was formed from the deputies elected in territorial constituencies, and the Council of the Nationalities from the deputies elected in national-territorial ones. The Congress of People's Deputies elected the Chairman of the Supreme Soviet. The Presidium of the Supreme Soviet consisted of the Chairman of the Supreme Soviet, his first deputies and chairmen of the Chambers, committees and commissions.

16. The established governmental system was too complex. It was evident that this form was a transitional one. It gave a chance to renovate the political elite and make the political process more open to the public. But the position of the President was strengthened and that demanded the redistribution of powers.

As a result of *perestroika*, the Constitution of 1978 was amended more than 200 times. The first Congress of People's Deputies of the RSFSR formed the Constitutional Commission whose aim was to draft a new Constitution. Several alternative projects were elaborated by the initiative groups of Shahrai, Sobchak and Alekseev. The deputies of the Communist Party and of the Russian movement of democratic reform as well submitted their own drafts. At last, in May 1993 the President published his version.

Those drafts proposed models of the governmental system with different roles for the President and the Parliament. The main struggle was between the draft of the Constitutional Commission supported by the deputies and the Presidential one. For resolution of the conflict the President called a Constitutional Conference on 5 June 1993. It consisted of 250 representatives of the state bodies of the Russian Federation and its entities, local self-government, political parties, trade unions, social associations, mass movements and religious confessions, and businessmen divided into five groups. The draft of the Constitutional Conference was approved by the President on 12 July 1993. But the struggle for the choice of the form of government continued.

17. In September, the conflict between the branches of state power intensified. The President and the Supreme Soviet adopted a number of acts nullifying each other's powers. On 21 September 1993, the President issued an Edict No. 1400 (RG, 23 September 1993) that suspended the powers of the representative organs of the Russian Federation and proposed to the Constitutional Court not to hold its meeting before the election of a new Parliament – the Federal Assembly. On that very day, the justices of the Constitutional Court formulated their opinion that this edict was not in compliance with the Constitution. The deputies did not recognize the binding force of Edict No. 1400. On 22 September 1993, the Supreme Soviet adopted several resolutions according to which the powers of the President were annulled and his actions were considered a *coup d'état* (RG, 23 September 1993). In October, the conflict reached its peak and took the form of armed resistance in which the President had won. As a result of that he received additional powers, suspended the activity of the Constitutional Court, changed its Chairman and several representative organs of the Federal Entities.

On 15 October 1993, the President issued the Edict No. 1633 (SAPP, 1993 No. 42) regulating the proceeding of the popular vote on the draft of the Constitution. The referendum was called on the same day as the parliamentary elections. The final text of the constitutional draft was finalized early in November and was ready for official publication on 10 November 1993. The referendum took place on 12

December 1993. 54.8% of voters took part. The adoption of the new Constitution was approved by 58.4% of participants (Bul. CEC, 1994 No. 10). On 20 December 1993, the Central Electoral Committee approved the results of the referendum, and the Constitution came into force after their official publication on 25 December 1993. The constitutional law of Russia began another period of its development.

II. A Federalization Process

18. Although Russia was proclaimed a Federation in 1918, for a long time it did not possess all the features characteristic of a federation. It could be classified as a quasi-federation, or a unitary State with autonomous units. Only in 1992 were federal relations extended over the entire territory of Russia. At the same time the particularities of the modern model of federation may be understood only in the context of the historical development of the country.

A. Russia Before 1917

19. Russia was characterized by the multi-ethnic composition of its population (since the fifteenth century), socio-economic heterogeneity of regions and its enormous land mass. The central Russian-inhabited territories were surrounded by the ethnically diverse peripheral regions which were annexed or joined to Russia. The Russian Empire was a unitary centralized State. Though the autonomous status was granted only to Finland, the particularities of the local self-government and specific sources of law were admissible in other localities (e.g., the Realm of Poland, Baltic region, Bessarabia, Georgia, Chukotka).[6] The specific connections of certain ethnic groups with their traditional settlement territories were recognized by the central authorities in other cases. Up to the 1920s Russians could not settle on land allotted to nomadic and migratory non-Russians of the North, Siberia and Far East and certain territories might be leased only upon the consent of an ethnic community.

B. Independent Federal State

20. The development of Russia as an independent State continued between 1917 and 1922, but in the sphere of state structure and national relations, serious alterations took place. The priorities of the national policy of the Soviet authorities were formulated in the Declaration of the Rights of the Peoples of Russia of 2 November 1917 (SU, 1917 No. 2). According to this document, the equality and sovereignty of the peoples of Russia, their right to self-determination including secession and

---

6. *See* L.E. Lapteva, *Regional'noe i mestnoe upravlenie v Rossii (vtoraia polovina XIX veka)* (Moskva: Institut gosudarstva i prava, 1998); N. Topornin (eds), *Preemstvennost' i novizna v gosudarstvenno–pravovom razvitii Rossii* (Moskva: Institut gosudarstva i prava, 1996), 30–36.

formation of an independent State, abrogation of any national[7] or national-religious privileges or restrictions, and free development of national minorities or ethnic groups should be general principles in this field. It is necessary to note that during the Soviet power, the gap between those principles and the existing practice was large.

The creation of a federal State in Russia began from above. The decision regarding the transformation of the state structure into a federal one was adopted by the Constituent Assembly (Resolution of 6 January of 1918) and by the Bolsheviks (the Declaration of the Rights of the Working and Exploited People of 25 January 1918). According to the Constitution of 1918 the RSFSR was constituted as a Federation of national republics (Article 2). The typical characteristics of the Russian state structure – plurality of types of Federal Entities and ethnic factors as the basis for their formation – were laid down in that period. Unlike the Constitutions adopted later, the first Constitution of the Soviet Russia admitted the right to secession (Article 49(d)). Practically none of the Federal Entities formed at that time exist now. As a result of the Civil War most of them were abolished, while several territories of the former Russian Empire gained an independent status.

C. Russia as a Member State of the Soviet Union: 1922–1991

21. In 1922, Russia signed a Union Treaty and became an individual member entity of the Soviet Union. From that time on, its sovereignty was limited considerably and its constitutional status had become quite complicated. RSFSR was 'federation within federation'. As for the position of the autonomous entities within the Russian Federation, they had double subordination. The Constitutions and Regulations determining their status had to follow not only the general principles of the Constitutions of the USSR, but even their structure. The decisions regarding the formation of the constituent entities of the Russian Federation were subject to approval of the Soviet authorities.

During the existence of the USSR, the criterion of nationality was the basic one. The ethnic factor was taken into consideration both on the individual level (data regarding ethnic origin was given in the internal passports of citizens) and on the territorial one (the member entities were established as national-territorial units in the traditional settlement territories of the ethnic groups). Several times, the authorities of the Soviet Union gave the authorization for the creation of new member entities by secession from Russia (1924 – Turkmenistan and Uzbekistan, 1936 – Kazakhstan and Kyrgyzia). Though the Russian Constitution of 1937 included provisions regarding the prohibition of the alteration of its territory, sometimes changes to the administrative borders took place without the consent of Russia (e.g., the subordination the Crimea to Ukraine and several areas of Siberia to Kazakhstan, both in 1954). The reasons for subordination were called routine issues of economic (transport/supply) policy.

---

7. In the Russian language such terms as 'nation' and 'nationality' are used in their ethnic (not legal) meaning.

The most tragic decisions concerning the recognition of whole peoples as the enemies of the Soviet power and of the other population were also adopted by the authorities of the Soviet Union. In 1939–1945 Chechens, Karachais, Ingushs, Balkars, Kalmyks, Crimean Tatars, Germans, Finns and Koreans were deported to Central Asia and their national-territorial formations were abolished. According to the provisions of the Edict of the Presidium of the Supreme Soviet of the USSR No. 111 of 26 November 1948, the forced resettlement did not have time limits. Those persons could not return to the places of their traditional residence and were subject to hard labour. In the case of unauthorized exit, they were liable for twenty years of penal servitude. Only in 1957 were the surviving representatives of persecuted peoples allowed to return to the places of their traditional settlement in Russia.

Contemporary Russia has inherited the majority of problems in the sphere of ethnic relations and federal structure from the Soviet Union. After the break-up of the Soviet Union, the extensive territories with populations of mixed composition, as well as the lack of coincidence between the areas of settlements of the ethnic groups with the administrative boundaries, provoked a growing demand for the review of territorial division as well as conflicts with a clear ethnic dimension.

D. Soviet Model of the Russian Federation

22. Under the Soviet power the Constitution of the Russian Federation was oriented towards the concept of the federal State with unitary tendencies. The most important decisions of the autonomous entities were subject to federal approval, and the system of their governmental bodies was regulated rigidly. Among federal States, the territorial organization of Russia was unique. Component units were established in the areas inhabited by non-Russians on the basis of ethnic criteria, and covered only part of the state territory. The other part was comprised of territorial units – *krays* and *oblasts* – whose economic potential was higher than that of the republics and which were governed as if they were parts of a unitary centralized State. As a rule, the legal position of the constituent entities was transformed after every adoption of a new Constitution or constitutional revision.

Among the other specific features of the Russian Federation there were the following:

(a) It admitted the existence of different types of the constituent entities. According to the Constitution of 1918 in its original wording, national republics and unions of *oblasts* characterized by the particularities of the ethnic composition of population or a mode of life were considered Federal Entities, whereas under the provisions of that Constitution as amended in 1925 the unions of *oblasts* were substituted by the autonomous *oblasts*. The Constitution of 1978 additionally introduced a new type of constituent entities – autonomous *okrugs* established in the areas of traditional settlement of the numerically small peoples of the North and North-East. The process of their formation began in 1925 and they were mentioned in the Constitution of 1937 among the territorial units as national *okrugs* (Article 102). At different periods the constituent entities varied both in their number and denomination. The same types were represented by different individual entities. For instance, among twenty-one existing republics only Tatarstan, Bashkortostan, Daghestan and Yakutia were originally formed as republics.

(b) The Federal Entities had different legal status. Only the republics could adopt their Constitutions and laws. The status of the other Federal Entities was regulated either by the regulations adopted by the authorities of the constituent entities and subject to federal approval or by the RSFSR laws. The republics could establish their own high bodies of power, whereas the other constituent entities only the local ones. The most developed regulation regarding the particularities of the autonomous entities was contained in the Russian Constitution of 1978, according to which the republics were considered as States within Russia (Article 78.1) and their territory could not be changed without their consent (Article 80). The autonomous *oblasts* were classified as entities within the Russian Federation included into the territory of *krays* (Article 82.1), whereas the autonomous *okrugs* might belong to *krays* or *oblasts* (Article 84). The republics could participate in the decision-making process on issues within the jurisdiction of Russia and the USSR (Article 79.1), whereas the autonomous *oblasts* could only have contacts with the governmental and administrative bodies of the Russian Federation independently or through appropriate organs of *krays* (Article 83). The Constitution included no provisions regarding the powers of the autonomous *okrugs* in this field.

(c) The delimitation of powers between the Federation and its entities was not a constitutional issue until the adoption of the Constitution of 1978, but even that one specified that it applied only to the republics. The Basic Law enumerated the spheres of jurisdiction of the Russian Federation (Article 72), granting the residual powers to the republics which could take decisions independently outside the spheres of jurisdiction of the Soviet Union and Russia (Article 78.2). The list of powers of the Federation was made an open one, while the list of powers for its entities remained a closed one. At the same time, a right of self-determination for nations was preserved in the Constitution, and that produced the well-known political and legal consequences of 1990 and 1991.

(d) Constituent entities did not have special representation in the unicameral representative body of Russia, whereas from 1936 they were guaranteed a permanent quota of mandates in the Upper Chamber of the Parliament of the USSR. The republics had more mandates than the other entities who accordingly had different numbers of mandates.

(e) Since 1925, the legal acts of the entities of the Russian Federation were subject to the control of the federal authorities who could repeal them or suspend their activity. Under the provisions of the Constitution of 1978, the Presidium of the Supreme Soviet of the Russian Federation could repeal decrees and orders of the Council of Ministers of the autonomous republics, as well as decisions of the Soviet of the autonomous *oblasts* if they were not in compliance with the law (Article 115.10). The Council of Ministers of the RSFSR was empowered to suspend the operation of decrees and orders of the Council of Ministers of the autonomous republics or repeal decisions and orders of the executive committees of the Soviets of the autonomous *oblasts* (Article 128).

E. Transformation of the Soviet Federal Model

23. The process of the transformation of the RSFSR into a Federation of traditional type[8] began with the adoption of the Declaration of the State Sovereignty of 12 June 1990 that was oriented towards the broadening of powers of the autonomous entities. According to the constitutional revision of 15 December 1990, the rules regarding the territorial subordination of the autonomous *oblasts* and *okrugs* were changed in the Russian Federation. The autonomous *oblasts* became directly subordinated to the Federation, whereas the autonomous *okrugs* could decide whether they continued to be a part of the territory of *krays* (or *oblasts*) or became directly subordinated to Russia. The governmental and administrative bodies of the autonomous *oblasts* and *okrugs* were entitled to establish direct contacts with the appropriate bodies of the Russian Federation.

The development of the country after the break-up of the USSR was characterized by the changes in the priorities of the legal regulation of the interethnic relations. The most important ones were the following: the recognition of the multi-ethnic composition of the Russian Federation at the constitutional level; consideration that the violent measures taken against the persecuted peoples were unlawful and criminal and admission of the obligation to reinstate their rights; granting the right of cultural national autonomy that was admissible only during the first years of the Soviet power to all ethnic communities.

In 1991, several autonomous *oblasts* (Adygeia, Gornii Altai, Karachaevo-Cherkessia and Khakassia) were reorganized into republics. In 1992 Chukotka, which was an autonomous *okrug* within the Magadan *oblast*, became directly subordinated to the Russian Federation. On 30 March 1992, the Federation Treaty regulating the new system of distribution of powers was concluded. Among the participants, there were *krays*, *oblasts* and cities of republican significance which became new Federal Entities. The conclusion of that Treaty revealed the conflict potential of the Russian Federation. The representatives of Tatarstan and the Chechen-Ingush Republics did not sign the Federation Treaty, whereas Bashkortostan put forward special conditions for signing. In the Protocol to the Treaty, the republics-participants considered it necessary to guarantee at least 50% of mandates in one of the Chambers of the legislative body to representatives of republics, autonomous *oblasts* and *okrugs*. At the same time *krays, oblasts*, Moscow and St. Petersburg in their Protocol to the Treaty claimed to equalize the legal status of all Federal Entities and put forward their suggestions in this field.

The lack of the reaction of the federal authorities provoked various regional initiatives. In 1993, the Vologda *oblast* held a regional referendum regarding the equalization of its status with that of republics, the Sverdlovsk *oblast* proclaimed itself the Ural Republic, and several constituent entities (the Tambov, Vologda, Kirov and Sverdlovsk *oblasts*) elaborated drafts of their Constitutions. The federal authorities reacted properly. The Constitution of 1993 substantially mitigated the 'asymmetry' of the state structure and equalized the status of the Federal Entities.

---

8. *See* P. Azrael & P.P Zubarevich (eds), *Evolutsia vzaimootnoshenii tsentra i regionov Rossii: ot konfliktov k poisku soglasia* (Moskva: Kompleks – Progress, 1997).

§2. Profile of the Form of Government

24. In accordance with the Constitution, Russia is a democratic, law-based federative State with a republican form of government (Article 1). The established system of government is based upon principles that contrast with the priorities of the previous Constitutions. Those basic principles belong to the foundations of the constitutional order and enjoy special protection. At the same time, the constitutional rules may be deemed the model of the system of government and of the relations between the State and the individual, that does not exist in practice yet.

I. The State Governed by the Rule of Law

25. In the Soviet Union, the concept of the Rule of Law never was recognized.[9] According to Soviet legal doctrine and practice, the law had a position subordinate towards the state power and could not restrict it. The return to the idea of the State governed by the rule of law began in the period of *perestroika.* The present Constitution reflects all the basic elements of this concept. The process of forming a 'rule of law'-based State is in a starting phase. Legal nihilism and ignorance are the distinct features of Russian legal and spiritual culture. At the same time the constitutional provisions detailed and concretized by the doctrine and decisions of the Constitutional Court ensure the possibility of the transformation in the future of the country into a State under the rule of law.

26. The Constitution of 1993, inspired by the ideas of natural law, provides for the subordination of the state power to the law. It establishes the precise spheres of competence of the governmental bodies and appropriate procedures for resolving conflicts with the participation of the Constitutional Court and the President. According to the Constitution, the seizure of power or usurpation of state authority is prosecutable under federal law (Article 3.4).

The recognition of the supremacy of the Constitution and its direct operation should prevent the arbitrariness in governmental bodies or officials. In the event of their illegal actions, inactions or abuse of power, access to justice and the right to state compensation for damage caused by those illegal actions are guaranteed to everyone (Articles 52, 53 of the Constitution).

27. The Constitution has the highest legal force; no other source of law may contravene it (Article 15.1 of the Constitution). When it is not clear whether laws or normative acts, or internal or international treaties, are in compliance with the Constitution, they may be subject to constitutional review. Besides that, the Constitution determines the guidelines for the development of the whole legal system. The

9. *See* V.A. Chetvernin, 'Osnovy konstitutsionnogo stroia Rossii: doctrina i praktika', in *Stanovlenie konstitutsionnogo gosudarstva v posttotalitarnoi Rossii* (Moskva: Institut gosudarstva i prava, 1998), 13–24; E.V. Novikova (ed.), *Verhovenstvo prava kak factor ekonomiki* (Moskva: Mysl, 2017), 9–20.

text of the Basic Law currently in force contains fifteen references to the necessity of the adoption of a federal constitutional law and more than fifty regarding a federal law.

The distinct feature of a State governed by the rule of law is the supremacy of laws. At present the number of laws is increasing in Russia, for a law-based State needs developed legislation. The legal reform presupposes as well the improvement of the legislative technique, and the revision of old and outdated laws. In fact, a due lawmaking process securing a high level of legal culture is an inherent part of the State under the rule of law, but currently Russia does not correspond to that high standard. The rapidly developing relations need more effective lawmaking mechanisms, ensuring the internal integrity and coordination of the legislation.

28. The priority of international law is an axiom for the State governed by the rule of law. According to this concept, generally recognized principles and norms of international law are considered an integral part of the Russian legal system (Article 15.4 of the Constitution). Currently, federal legislation is brought in compliance with international law, especially in the sphere of human rights. It is necessary to note that the banning of capital punishment was taken in accordance with the international obligations of the country, although public opinion was against this measure.

The law-based State presupposes a new type of relations between the State and its citizens, as far as the recognition, observance and protection of the rights and freedoms are the obligations of the State. In the Russian constitutional system, human rights are the supreme value; their catalogue and system of guarantees are enlarged, and the role of the courts in this field is strengthened. The Constitution establishes certain limits of legislative activity in the sphere of human rights. The adoption of laws that abolish or diminish rights and freedoms is prohibited (Article 55.2) and the possibilities of the statutory restrictions are limited as well (Article 55.3, 56).

II. The Separation of Powers

29. As a result of the reform of the governmental system at the end of the 1980s, the separation of powers has been recognized as a constitutional principle. It was included in the revised text of the Constitution of 1978, although the other provisions based upon the concept of concentration of powers by Soviets were not in compliance with it. In accordance with the Constitution of 1993, the state power is exercised on the basis of separation of the legislative, executive and judicial powers, the bodies of which are independent (Article 10). As far as there are two levels of power – the state power being exercised in the Russian Federation and in its entities (Article 11.1, 11.2) – this rule is applied to the governmental bodies of the component units as well as to the federal authorities.

The Constitutional Court of Russia considers this principle the basic one for the organization of the system of government. According to the legal position formulated in the Judgment of 18 January 1996 (VKS, 1996 No. 1), the separation of powers presupposes the establishment of a system of legal guarantees and checks and balances that excludes the possibility of concentration of power by one of them and ensures the independent functioning of all the branches of power as well as their cooperation.

30. The principle of the separation of powers determines the organization of the federal governmental bodies. The Federal Assembly is vested with the legislative power; the government, with the executive power, and the courts of the Russian Federation, with the judicial power. The President as the Head of State ensures the coordinate functioning and collaboration of the bodies of the state power.

There are various forms of coordination of activity of the federal governmental bodies provided for by the Constitution. The State Duma and the President participate in the procedure of nomination of the Chairman of the Government. The Council of the Federation appoints the judges of the high judicial instances and the Procurator General upon the proposal of the President. The adoption of the federal budget is impossible without the coordinated activity of the government and the Federal Assembly. At present the federal governmental bodies are seeking a compromise within the constitutional framework in order to ensure the realization of their powers and normal functioning of the system of government.

31. The separation of powers presupposes a system of checks and balances of powers (mostly unknown to Soviet constitutional doctrine and practice). That means that certain decisions must be approved by the other governmental bodies and there is a possibility of suspension or cession of the activity by those bodies of state power which act beyond the sphere of their competence. The edicts of the President on the introduction of a state of emergency or martial law must be confirmed by the Council of the Federation. The activity of the Federal Assembly in the sphere of legislation is balanced by the vetoing powers of the President and by constitutional review. The powers of the President are restricted by the possibility of impeachment proceedings by the Chambers of the Federal Assembly. The Constitutional Court in its Judgment of 18 January 1996 emphasized that powers connected with a cession of activity by a governmental body are valid if they are balanced and based upon law (VKS, 1996 No. 1). In some cases, the Constitution of 1993 sets certain limits in this field. According to the provisions of Article 109 the President may dissolve the State Duma in most situations (*see* paragraph 94), but he cannot use this power from the moment the Chamber files an accusation against him and in several more cases indicated by Article 109.

III. A Federative Republic

32. The integrity of the State is one of the general principles guiding federal relations (Articles 5.3, 4.3 of the Constitution).[10] A unilateral decision to change the status of a Federal Entity and secede from the Russian Federation is considered inadmissible. The status of a constituent entity may be changed only by mutual agreement between the Federation and that entity in accordance with the federal

10. *See* I.A. Umnova, *Konstitutsionnye osnovy Rossiiskogo federalisma* (Moskva: Delo, 1998), 99–177.

constitutional law (Article 66.5 of the Constitution). Goods, services and financial resources can move freely within the territory of the country, as the Constitution prohibits the establishment of custom borders, duties, levies or any other obstacles (Article 74.1).

The unity of the system of the state power that has as its sole source the multinational people of the Russian Federation, does not exclude the existence of different levels of power. Like every federal or regional State, Russia is based upon the delimitation of areas of jurisdiction and powers between the governmental bodies of the Russian Federation and the governmental bodies of its entities. The present model is flexible: the delimitation may be regulated by common constitutional rules and special agreements between the federal authorities and a constituent entity or entities of the same type.

The principles of the ethnonational policy are significant for Russia as a multiethnic society. The Constitution recognizes the principles of equality under law and self-determination of all the peoples of the country. According to the provisions of the Declaration on the State Sovereignty of 1990, one of the aims of the state sovereignty is to guarantee the enjoyment of the right to self-determination in political and cultural sphere to the peoples inhabiting the country.

33. Though the Federal Entities have various designations and belong to different types, they are legally equal. All of them enjoy equal rights in their relations with the federal governmental bodies (Article 5.1, 5.4 of the Constitution). In particular this takes expression in the uniformity of the constitutional approach towards the delimitation of spheres of jurisdiction and powers between the Russian Federation and its constituent entities, and in the common rules of interrelations established by the federal legislative bodies.

Under the legal position of the Constitutional Court formulated in the Judgment of 15 July 1996 (VKS, 1996 No. 4), the legal equality of constituent entities does not mean equality of their potential and levels of socio-economic development which in many respects depend upon their territory, geographic position, population or economic structure. Those regional particularities must be taken into account in order to ensure the balance of interests of the Federation and its component units and to combine them with the common standards determined by the federal governmental bodies in the spheres of jurisdiction of the constituent entities.

The application of the principle of equality to an autonomous *okrug* which is part of a territory of a *kray* or *oblast* has special features. It presupposes a particular relation between those entities and an extension of the jurisdiction of the *kray* (*oblast*) over the territory of the autonomous *okrug* in certain cases. The Constitutional Court of the Russian Federation held in its Decision of 17 July 1996 that *krays* (*oblasts*) and autonomous *okrugs* are obliged to maintain the existing political, social, ethnic and other relations through various forms of collaboration, including the redistribution of spheres of jurisdiction and powers, their delegation or common utilization, in order to ensure the interests of the population. Unilateral actions in the sphere of common interests are not admissible.

IV. A Democratic Republic

34. The Soviet system of power was based upon the one-party system, monolithic state ideology, and the special status of certain classes and groups. The present Constitution is oriented towards basic democratic values and traditions. It considers the people of Russia as the bearer and the unique source of sovereignty (Article 3.1) and provides for the right of citizens to take part in the administration of state affairs directly or through their representatives (Article 32.1). The constitutional model presupposes various forms of people's participation and expression of their opinion.

In contrast with the previous practice, the compulsory ideology is banned, the political plurality[11] and ideological diversity, and the multiparty system are all recognized among the foundations of the constitutional order (Article 13). That means an end to the practice of the persecution of citizens on the basis of their opinions or convictions as was common in the Soviet State. The Constitutional Court of the Russian Federation in its Judgment of 12 February 1993 (VKS, 1994 No. 1) stresses that any attempt by the bodies of executive power to repress initiatives to create social associations may be classified as an infringement of a constitutional right.

V. A Social State

35. According to the Constitution, modern Russia is a social State whose policy aims to create conditions ensuring a dignified life and the free development of an individual (Article 7.1).[12] The Russian concept of the social State differs from such concepts in the Western democracies and presupposes the protection of labour and health of people, a guaranteed minimum wage, state support for the family, motherhood, fatherhood and childhood, disabled and elderly citizens, a system of social services, state pensions, allowances and other guarantees of social protection. The general principles of the social State are developed in the other constitutional provisions (Articles 37–44). At the same time those rights are not institutionally protected in the transitional period, since the State does not have enough resources to perform its functions and cannot ensure the same level of social services and social guarantees that existed under the Socialist State.

VI. A Secular State

36. The Russian Federation, like USSR, is a secular State (Article 14.1 of the Constitution). There is no compulsory religion in the country. Religious organizations are separated from the State and cannot perform governmental functions. The governmental bodies and the bodies of local self-government do not use religious

11. *See* S.A. Avak'ian, *Politicheskii pluralism i obsh'estvennye ob'edinenia v Rossiiskoi Federatsii: konstitutsionno–pravovye osnovy* (Moskva: Rossiiskii juridicheskii izdatel'skii dom, 1996).
12. *See* N.V. Varlamova, 'Sotsial'noe gosudarstvo v postsovetskoi Rossii: rozovaia mechta ili zhestokaia real'nost'?', in *Stanovlenie konstitutsionnogo gosudarstva v posttotalitarnoi Rossii*, *supra*, 67–94.

ceremonies in their activity. The affiliation to a specific religion is not compatible with fulfilling any civil service duties and is not considered a qualification for access to the state civil service: according to the Federal Law of 27 July 2004 'On the State Civil Service in the Russian Federation' (SZ, 2004 No. 31), in the wording of the Federal Law of 30 December 2015, state servants may not use their official position in the interests of religious associations.

§3. State Territory

37. The land mass of the Russian Federation is 17.075 million square kilometres. The country spans 11 time zones. 73% of its territory belongs to Asia and the rest to Europe. Russia is a northern country as 62% of its territory belongs to the northern regions.

With the denunciation of the Union Treaty of 1922 and the disintegration of the USSR, the geopolitical situation of Russia has changed substantially. Now it borders on thirteen states, Azerbaijan, Belarus, China, Estonia, Finland, Georgia, Kazakhstan, Latvia, Lithuania, Mongolia, Norway, North Korea and Ukraine. It has a maritime border with the United States of America (US), Canada and Japan. The maritime border of the Russian Federation (38,000 kilometres) is longer than the land one (20,000 kilometres).

Under the provisions of the Russian Federation Law of 1 April 1993 'On the State Border of the Russian Federation' (Ved. Russian Federation, 1993 No. 17), as amended by the Federal Law of 3 July 2016, the borders of the Russian Federation are determined by the international treaties currently in force and the legislative acts of the former Soviet Union. If the border of Russia with a contiguous State is not internationally legalized, a border treaty must be concluded. The process of the delimitation and the demarcation of the state border is not finished yet. During the last years the Russian Federation concluded the border treaties with Lithuania in 2003, Ukraine in 2004, Kazakhstan in 2005, Latvia in 2007 and the additional Agreement regarding the Eastern part of the state border with China in 2005. There are boundary disputes with Japan, Ukraine (since 2014) and Georgia.

38. According to the Constitution, the territory of Russia includes the territories of its entities, the internal stretches of waters and the territorial sea, as well as the air space over these (Article 67.1). The determination of the status and protection of the border, territorial sea, air space, exclusive economic zone and continental shelf of the Russian Federation belongs to the federal jurisdiction (Article 71(m)). Though the exclusive economic zone and the continental shelf are not an integral part of the State territory, the Russian Federation possesses sovereign rights and exercises jurisdiction over them (Article 67.2). The status of the continental shelf and the exclusive economic zone extending to 200 miles is regulated by the Federal Law of 30 November 1995 'On the Continental Shelf of the Russian Federation' (SZ, 1995 No. 49), as amended on 2 May 2015, and by the Federal Law of 17 December 1998 'On the Exclusive Economic Zone of the Russian Federation' (SZ, 1998 No. 51), as amended on 2 May 2015, in accordance with the generally recognized norms of international law.

39. The Russian Federation currently (April 2018) consists of eighty-five Federal Entities (there were eighty-nine after the adoption of the Constitution of 1993). Entities are divided into six categories: republics, *krays*, *oblasts*, cities of federal significance, an autonomous *oblast* and autonomous *okrugs*. There are large differences between the constituent entities as regards their territory, geographic position, population and economic structure. For instance, according to data of the Federal Service of State Statistics of 1 January 2010, the population of Federal Entities varies from 32,000 persons in the Chukotka autonomous *okrug* to more than 12.5 million in Moscow City. These differences also exist between entities belonging to the same category. In the Altai Republic there are less than 211,000 residents whereas the population of Tatarstan exceeds 3.778 million.

The territory of Russia is divided into divisions which had not existed previously: the federal districts of Central, North-West, South, North Caucasus, Volga, Ural, Siberian and Far East. Each of them includes several Federal Entities: in particular, the Central Federal District – seventeen *oblasts* and the city of federal significance, the North Caucasus District– six Republics and *kray*. The list of the federal districts is approved by the Edict of the President No. 849 of 13 May 2000 (SZ, 2000 No. 20), in force and as amended by the Edict of 19 January 2010.

Interregional cooperation is currently proceeding through the formation of regional associations for economic cooperation and the conclusion of agreements among individual component units. There are the following associations for economic cooperation in the Russian Federation: the Far East and Transbaikal Association, the Siberian Accord Association, the Ural Region Association, the North-West Association, the Association for the Cooperation of Republics, Krays and Oblasts of the Northern Caucasus, the Central Black Earth Association, the Greater Volga Association and the Central Russian Association.

§4. Population

40. According to data of the Federal Service of State Statistics of 1 January 2018, the total population of Russia is 146.2 million. The overwhelming majority of citizens and permanent residents live in the European part of the country (79%). The urban population accounts for 74% of the total. By 2017, annual marriage rate is 8.5 per 1,000 persons and rate of divorce is 4.5. The last national population census was taken in 2010, and the official data was published in June 2011.

Russia is a multi-ethnic State, but it is dominated by a single ethnic group. The majority of its citizens identify themselves as Russians (79% according to data of the census of 2010). They constitute between 85% and 98% of the population in 49 Federal Entities, and two-thirds of the population in 25 constituent entities. According to the data of micro census of 1994, which covered 5% of the population in all Federal Entities except the Chechen Republic, there were 172 ethnic groups in Russia, that is 45 more in comparison with census of 1989. In spite of the substantial cultural distance between the ethnic groups, Russia is a traditional place of settlement for most of them. According to data of the census of 2002 among the most numerous groups there are Tatars (3.8%, in 1989 – 3.7%), Ukrainians (2.0%, in 1989 – 2.9%), Bashkirs (1.1%, in 1989 – 0.9%), Chuvashs (1.1%, in 1989 – 1.2%),

Chechens (0.9%, in 1989 – 0.6%), Armenians (0.7%, in 1989 – 0.3%) and Mordovians (0.58%, in 1989 – 0.73%). The Federal Entities are polyethnic, the titular ethnic groups constitute the majority on the territory of seven of twenty-one republics. There are forty-five ethnic groups counting not more than 50,000 persons which are recognized and registered as 'numerically small indigenous peoples'. Most of them live in the northern regions.

41. The escalation of interethnic and regional conflicts after the break-up of the USSR and the political instability in some new independent States resulted in the exodus of forced migrants in the post-USSR. In 1992–1996 more than 2.6 million immigrants from the Commonwealth of Independent States (CIS) and Baltic countries moved to the Russian Federation. By 1 January 2010, 57,999 persons had received the status of refugee or forced migrant (779 refugees and 57,220 forced migrant).

Part I. Sources of Constitutional Law

I. Bogdanovskaia & T. Vassilieva

Chapter 1. Treaties

§1. International Treaties of the Russian Federation

42. The Constitution of the Russian Federation, like many of the Supreme/Basic Laws/constitutions adopted recently across the world, regulates the relations between international and internal law on the basis of the primacy of the international norms and rules.[13] Generally recognized principles and norms of international law and the international treaties of the Russian Federation are a constituent part of its legal system and in the case of the conflict between a domestic law and an international treaty of the Russian Federation, the international obligations have a priority (Article 15.4). The adherence to the principles and norms of international law is specifically emphasized in the field of human rights and freedoms and regarding the rights of the numerically small indigenous peoples (Articles 17.1, 69).

Those approaches were not typical beforehand. In accordance with the legal traditions of the Soviet school of international law, a treaty was considered the main source of international law. The Constitution of 1978, as amended on 1992, lists a number of principles that determine the relations with other States (Article 28), but the primacy of the generally recognized principles of international law was admitted only in the sphere of human rights (Article 32).

43. The Federal Law of 15 July 1995 'On International Treaties of the Russian Federation' (SZ, 1995 No. 29), as amended on 12 March 2014, in compliance with the 1969 Vienna Convention, defines international treaties of the Russian Federation as agreements concluded between the Russian Federation and another State (States), international organization or other formation authorized to conclude international treaties, in written form and regulated by international law, whether embodied in a single instrument or in two or more related instruments and whatever its particular designation. These treaties may have an interstate, intergovernmental or

13. *See* I.A. Koniuhova, *Mezhdunarodnoe i konstitutsionnoe pravo: teoria i praktika vzaimodeistvia* (Moskva: Formula prava, 2006); M.A Mitiukov, et al. (ed.), *Obshepriznanye printsipi i normi mezhdunarodnogo prava, mezhdunarodnye dogovori v praktike konstitutsionnogo pravosudia* (Moskva: Mezhdunarodnye otnoshenia, 2004).

interdepartmental character. The provisions of this federal law extend to the treaties of the former USSR insofar as Russia is a signatory as the legal heir of the Soviet Union.

44. In accordance with the constitutional provisions, treaty-making powers belong to the competence of the Russian Federation (Article 71(j)), whereas fulfilment of the international treaties of the Russian Federation is listed among the matters of joint jurisdiction (Article 72.1(n)). The President and the Federal Government are vested with the treaty-making powers. A vast number of interstate agreements must be approved by the Chambers of the Federal Assembly – the State Duma and the Council of the Federation.

The constitutional and statutory provisions establish certain limits for the autonomy of the federal governmental bodies in this field. International treaties may not include rules in contravention of the Constitution of the Russian Federation. Those agreements that have not yet come into force may be subject to preliminary review by the Constitutional Court (Article 125.2). Treaties, which are not in conformity with the Constitution, do not come into force and are not implemented (Article 125.6). If a treaty contains rules requiring the adoption of a constitutional amendment, ratification may take place only after the amendment of the Constitution. When the subject matter of a treaty regards a participation in an interstate association or the transfer of power to it, an agreement may not authorize restrictions on human rights and freedoms or contravene the foundations of the constitutional order of the Russian Federation (Article 79).

Though federal governmental bodies practically have the monopoly of power in this field, the Federal Entities have possibilities to take part in a treaty-making process. If a matter is within areas of jurisdiction of a constituent entity, a treaty is concluded with the consent of its governmental bodies. When a treaty affects a matter of joint jurisdiction, a draft or its basic provisions are submitted to the bodies of state power of the Federal Entity, which may put forward their suggestions. (The federal bodies, however, are not bound by these suggestions). The authorized federal governmental body decides upon the necessity of the participation of the representatives of the constituent entity in the preparation of the draft or in the process of negotiations with the consent of the governmental bodies of that entity.

45. The entities of the Russian Federation have limited powers in the sphere of international cooperation. Under the provisions of the Federal Law of 4 January 1999 'On the Coordination of the International and External Economic Contacts of the Entities of the Russian Federation' (SZ, 1999 No. 2), as amended on 13 July 2015, they may conclude agreements with Member States or territorial units of other countries and international organizations, and establish contacts with the governmental bodies of a foreign State upon the consent of the Federal Government. These agreements of course are not qualified as international treaties, and the federal governmental bodies accept no responsibility regarding obligations of the Federal Entities except in cases when the Federal Government guarantees an agreement or consents to it.

Agreements concerning international and external economical contacts cannot include provisions that are not in conformity with the Federal Constitution, universally recognized principles and norms of international law, federal legislation, international treaties of the Russian Federation, and treaties on the delimitation of areas of jurisdiction and powers between the bodies of state power of the Russian Federation and those of the constituent entities. Besides that they may not violate the legitimate interests of the other constituent entities.

§2. Internal Agreements

46. The Constitution of the Russian Federation, unlike the majority of federal constitutions across the world, allows the possibility of using a treaty-making process for regulating the relations between the federal authorities and the Federal Entities in the field of the delimitation of powers. It is possible to distinguish several classes of those treaties.[14]

A Federation Treaty (Article 11.3) may be defined as an agreement having internal validity, concluded between the federal authorities and the authorities of all constituent entities or the constituent entities of the same type. On 31 March 1992, Federal Government bodies signed several agreements on the delimitation of areas of jurisdiction and powers: the first with the republics; the second with *krays*, *oblasts*, the cities of Moscow and St. Petersburg; the third with the autonomous *oblast* and autonomous *okrugs*. These agreements, having an identical structure and objects of regulation but establishing different areas of jurisdiction, bear the collective title of the Federation Treaty of 1992.

Before the adoption of the Constitution of 1993 it was considered a constituent part of the Basic Law and was published as an appendix to it. The framers of the new Constitution recognized the independent character of that document but proclaimed the priority of the constitutional provisions in the case of a conflict between them (Article 1 of Concluding and Transitional Provisions of the Constitution). In fact, the most significant provisions of the Federation Treaty were incorporated into the text of the Basic Law directly. For that reason it clearly possesses an auxiliary character at present. At the same time it is necessary to note that the Federation Treaty was mentioned among the basic sources of law determining the relations between the contracting parties in several bilateral treaties (e.g., with Bashkortostan, Kabardino-Balkaria, Udmurtia, Buriatia and Yakutia).

47. The treaties on delimitation of areas of jurisdiction and powers concluded between the federal authorities and the authorities of a Federal Entity (Article 11.3 of the Constitution) provoked discussions among the leading politicians and lawyers specialized in constitutional law. The treaty-making process initiated by republics was very intensive in 1996–1997. As a rule, those treaties were bilateral, but in

14. *Federativnii dogovor. Dokumenty, kommentarii* (Moskva: Respublika, 1992); I.A. Umnova, *Konstitutsionnye osnovy sovremennogo rossiiskogo federalisma* (Moskva: Delo, 1998), 53–75; K. Postovoi & Yu.A. Tikhomirov (eds), *Federativnoe ustroistvo: realizatsia Konstitutsii Rossiiskoi Federatsii* (Moskva: Institut zakonodatel'stva i sravnitel'nogo pravovedenia, 1995), 55–64.

several cases the contracting parties were the governmental bodies of a *kray* (*oblast*) and an autonomous *okrug* within it. Up to 2001, the Russian Federation has concluded forty-six treaties of this kind.

The treaties on delimitation of areas of jurisdiction and powers were concluded for an indeterminate period, the only exception being the agreement with Moscow that has a ten-year term. On behalf of the Russian Federation, they were signed by either the President alone or together with the Chairman or a first Deputy Chairman of the Government. On behalf of a Federal Entity they were signed by the senior officials of comparable rank. Sometimes the heads of the representative bodies of the Federal Entities signed treaties alongside with the heads of executive power. The bilateral treaties with republics were drafted in the official languages of Russia and the appropriate constituent entity.

As a rule, the signing of a basic treaty was accompanied by the conclusion of a whole range of intergovernmental agreements (e.g., twelve with Tatarstan, eight with Bashkortostan, fifteen with Yakutia) that are considered constituent parts of the treaty. These agreements on delimitation of powers with regard to specific areas of jurisdiction were usually concluded for a five-year term and signed by the heads of executive power. In most cases those agreements were put into force by the conclusion of the basic treaty.

At the end of the century, the federal bodies of state power decided that these treaties have exhausted their political and juridical potential and the federal law was recognized as the basic source of law for regulation of federal relations. According to the provisions of the Federal Law of 24 June 1999 'On the Principles and the Procedure of the Delimitation of Areas of Jurisdiction between the Bodies of State Power of the Russian Federation and the Bodies of State Power of Entities of the Russian Federation' (SZ, 1999 No. 26, this law is not in force since 2003), the concluded treaties ought to be brought to conformity with the constitutional provisions. At that time several Federal Entities (Kirov, Arkhangelsk, Ulyanovsk, Chelyabinsk oblasts) have initiated the process of denunciation of those treaties. At present only two treaties on delimitation of areas of jurisdiction and powers – with Yakutia of 1995 and with Tatarstan of 2007 – are in force.

48. The particularities of the state structure determine the necessity of delimitation of areas of jurisdiction between a *kray* (*oblast*) and an autonomous *okrug* within its territory. According to the Constitution, relations between *okrugs* and *krays* or *oblasts* may be regulated by a federal law or an internal treaty (Article 66.4). In spite of the fact that the Constitution indicates only that kind of interregional treaties, component units conclude different types of agreements regarding friendship and cooperation, socio-economic relations, and coordination of activity of the legislative bodies.

Chapter 2. The Constitution

§1. Typification

49. Russia traditionally has had written constitutions.[15] The present Constitution adopted by popular vote on 12 December 1993 is also a written one. It consists of a preamble, the main text and concluding and transitional provisions. The preamble to the Constitution is not considered a part thereof. It indicates the aims and several basic principles. The main text consists of nine chapters regarding the foundations of the constitutional order (Chapter 1), human rights and freedoms (Chapter 2), federalism (Chapter 3), the system of the federal governmental bodies (the President of the Russian Federation, the Federal Assembly, the government and the judicial power) (Chapters 4–7), the local self-government (Chapter 8) and the constitutional amendments and the revision of the Constitution (Chapter 9).

The Constitution of 1993 differs from all the previous Soviet Constitutions, since it does not contain ideological provisions and recognizes universal constitutional principles: democracy, the separation of powers, the rule of law and political plurality. The Constitution aims to introduce Russia into the world community. The Constitution entrenches the results of the governmental reform: it establishes a new system of government and federal relations. It contains a new conception of human rights and freedoms based on natural law.

The time that has passed since the adoption of the present Constitution shows that gradually it is becoming a real Basic Law as the legal system is developed in accordance with it, in particular because of the activity of the Constitutional Court.

50. The Constitution has supreme legal force and priority over any other sources of law. Laws and legal enactments may not contravene it (Article 15.1 of the Constitution). In case of conflict between the Constitution and an internal treaty, the Constitution has priority (the first Concluding and Transitional Provision). Laws must not contradict the Constitution, otherwise they may be declared unconstitutional by the Constitutional Court. Constitutional review is considered an immanent element of the supremacy of the Constitution. Any act issued by a State body is deemed constitutional until it is otherwise established. In those cases when it is not clear whether a law or act is in compliance with the Constitution, a court should apply to the Constitutional Court to resolve the issue. If the latter considers that act or some of its provisions unconstitutional, the whole act or some provisions lose their force (Article 125.6 of the Constitution). The Constitution determines the hierarchy of the sources of law. Under the provisions of the Federal Constitutional Law of 31 December 1996 'On the Judicial System of the Russian Federation' (SZ, 1997 No. 1), as amended on 5 February of 2014, a court, having established that an act of a governmental or other body is incompatible with the Constitution of the Russian Federation, federal constitutional law, federal law, generally recognized principles and norms of international law, the international treaty of the Russian

15. S.A. Avak'ian, *Konstitutsia Rossii, priroda, evolutsia, sovremennost* (Moskva: Rossiiskii juridicheskii izdatel'skii dom, 1997).

Federation, or the Constitution (Charter) or law of a subject of the Russian Federation, delivers its judgment in accordance with those provisions having higher legal force. The amendment to the Law made in 2014 was necessary to regulate issues connected with abolishing the High Arbitration Court of the Russian Federation during judicial reforms.

51. The Constitution has direct effect and is applicable in the whole territory of the Russian Federation. Organs of state power and local self-government, officials, citizens and their associations must abide by the Constitution of the Russian Federation and the federal laws (Article 15 of the Constitution).

The articles of the previous Constitutions were realized through numerous acts; in fact they were 'dead letters' if they were not detailed by ordinary laws. In accordance with the Guiding Explanation of the Plenum of the Supreme Court of 31 October 1995 (RG, 25 December 1995), in the process of the administration of justice the ordinary courts examining an individual case are obliged to evaluate the content of a law or an act that is applied or is subject to application in the case and, when it is necessary, apply the Constitution as the direct operative act. There are already examples of the courts taking decisions based on the Constitution.

52. In the Russian Federation (like in the United States or Germany), the Federal Entities have their own constituent acts: constitutions (republics), or charters (all others). The Constitution of Russia of 1993, being federal, established new principles of interaction between the Basic Laws of the Federation and its entities. Under the Soviet power, the Constitutions of the republics were adopted in accordance with the Constitution of Russia, which in turn was based upon the Constitution of the USSR. At present the Federal Entities having the status of republics may adopt constitutions while the others may adopt charters (Article 66.1, 66.2 of the Constitution). The constitutions and the charters have equal legal force, since the Federal Entities have equal status (Article 5.1 of the Constitution). The constituent acts of the Federal Entities have more differences with the federal Constitution than previously. Since the federal Constitution has supremacy throughout the territory of the country (Article 4.2), the Constitutional Court may examine the compliance of those constitutions and charters with the federal Constitution (Article 125.2(b)). The constituent acts of the Federal Entities must be based on the same principles as the federal Constitution.

§2. Procedure for Amending the Constitution

53. The Constitution of the Russian Federation is a rigid one since it may only be changed, amended or revised by a special procedure. In the Russian doctrine, that is considered an important element of constitutional stability. Although no serious amendments have yet been adopted, the idea of constitutional reform is discussed in Russia from time to time, especially regarding the separation of powers between the executive and legislative branches. The revision of the Constitution is regulated by Chapter 9 of the Constitution and the Federal Law of 4 March 1998 'On the Procedure of the Adoption and Coming into Force of the Amendments to the Constitution of the Russian Federation' (SZ, 1998 No. 10), as amended on 8 March 2015.

The Constitution of the Russian Federation does not contain provisions that may not be amended or revised. Four different procedures for its revision are established: the first for the revision and amendment of Chapters 1, 2 and 9; the second for the revision of Chapters 3–8; and two others for changing Article 65.

I. Initiative for the Revision of the Constitution

54. Any revision of the Constitution may be initiated by the President of the Russian Federation, the Council of the Federation as a whole, the State Duma as a whole, the Government of the Russian Federation, not less than one-fifth of the members of the Council of the Federation or the deputies of the State Duma. The Federal Entities may initiate this procedure through their legislative (representative) bodies.

II. Procedure for Revision of Chapters 1, 2 and 9

55. The most complex procedure is established for the changing of Chapters 1, 2 and 9 (the foundations of the constitutional order, human rights, the constitutional amendments and the revision of the Constitution). These chapters cannot be revised by the Federal Assembly, but the latter gives the authorization for implementation of the procedure. The submitted proposal must be supported by three-fifths of the total number of the members of the Council of the Federation and deputies of the State Duma (Article 135.2). The next step is the convocation of the Constitutional Assembly. The organization and the powers of this body, mentioned in Article 135 of the Constitution, should be regulated in detail by a federal constitutional law, which has as yet not been adopted. According to the Constitution, the Constitutional Assembly decides whether there are grounds for and a necessity to change the Constitution. It either rejects the proposal or elaborates a draft of a new Constitution, which must be adopted by two-thirds of the total number of its members or subjected to a referendum. The Constitution is considered adopted on the referendum if more than one-half of the electors taking part in the nation-wide referendum have voted for it, on condition that more than one-half of the electorate participates (Article 135.3). Thus, in fact, Chapters 1, 2 and 9 may be revised only by adoption of a new Constitution.

III. Procedure for Amendment of Chapters 3–8

56. Chapters 3–8 of the Constitution may be revised according to the procedure prescribed for the adoption of the federal constitutional laws but in the form of a law of the Russian Federation on the amendment of the Constitution (Judgment of the Constitutional Court of 31 October 1995 (SZ, 1995 No. 45), Federal Law of 4

March 1998 'On the Procedure of the Adoption and Coming into Force of the Amendments to the Constitution of the Russian Federation', as amended on 8 March 2015). The draft has to pass three readings and is subject to compulsory examination in the Council of the Federation. The amendment must be adopted by not less than two-thirds of the deputies of the State Duma and then by not less than three-fourths of the members of the Council of the Federation. Any disagreements between the Chambers may be resolved by a conciliatory commission. The President of the Russian Federation must sign the approved act within fourteen days.

The amendments come into the force after their approval by the legislative bodies of not less than two-thirds of the Federal Entities whose legislative (representative) bodies must examine the amendment within a year after it was adopted by the Chambers of the Federal Assembly, and then inform the Council of the Federation. The Council of the Federation on the next day after the end of the term given for the examination of the amendments by the legislative bodies of the Federal Entities determines the results. The resolution of the Chamber may be appealed to the Supreme Court by the President of the Russian Federation or the legislative bodies of the Federal Entities within seven days after its adoption.

The President must sign the law of the Russian Federation on the amendment of the Constitution within seven days. The law comes into force on the day of its publication. Within one month the President must subject to publication the text of the Russian Constitution with the amendments. In the event of failure an amendment may be introduced into the State Duma for a second time, but not earlier than a year after the determination of the results.

IV. Changing of the Provisions of Article 65

57. A special procedure is established for the changing of Article 65 of the Constitution (Article 137 of the Constitution) in which the entities of the Russian Federation are enumerated. If changes take place as a result of the admission of a new member into the Russian Federation or its formation within the country, as well as in connection with the alteration of the constitutional status of a constituent entity, an amendment is inserted in the constitutional text on the basis of the appropriate federal constitutional law that regulates the issue.

This procedure was applied several times in 2004–2014 mostly due to the process of unification of several constituent entities: Ust-Ordyn Buryat autonomous *okrug* became the part of Irkutsk *oblast* and lost its status as the constituent entity since 1 January 2005; Perm *oblast* and Komi-Permyak autonomous *okrug* formed Perm *kray* since 1 December 2005; Taimyr (Dolgano-Nenets) and Evenk autonomous *okrugs* became the part of Krasnoyarsk *kray* and lost their status of constituent entities since 1 January 2007; Kamchatka *oblast* and Koryak autonomous *okrug* formed Kamchatka *kray* since 1 July 2007; Chita *oblast* and Aginsk Buryat autonomous *okrug* formed Zabaikalskyi *kray* since 1 March 2008. The Crimean Republic and City of Sevastopol were admitted to the Russian Federation as its new Federal Entities, according to provisions of Article 65 of the Constitution and on the basis of a Treaty of the Russian Federation of 18 March 2014.

58. Changes of the names of constituent entities are incorporated in the text of the Constitution by edict of the President based on the decision of the interested constituent entity adopted in accordance with the procedure established by it. The Constitutional Court has put forward certain limits in this field in its Judgment of 28 November 1995 (VKS, 1995 No. 6). The relevant procedure cannot be applied to a change of name which affects the foundations of the constitutional order, human rights and freedoms, or the interests of the other constituent entities, the Federation or other States. It cannot require a change in the composition of the Federation or in the constitutional legal status of its constituent entities. Furthermore, a new name cannot indicate a form of State not provided for by the federal Constitution, affect the integrity or the secular character of the State, imply territorial claims, include ideological or socio-political characteristics that are not in compliance with the Constitution of the Russian Federation, or ignore historical and ethnic traditions.

This procedure was applied several times when North Ossetia (1996), Ingushetia (1996), Kalmykia (1996), Chuvash Republic (2001) and Khanty-Mansi autonomous *okrug* (2003) changed their names. The renaming of the capital cities of the Federal Entities needs regulation on the level of ordinary federal laws. For instance, the capital of Ingushetia has got a new name on the basis of Federal Law of 26 December 2000 'On Renaming of the Republic Ingushetia Capital'.

Chapter 3. Legislation and Equivalent Legislative Rules

59. Laws (statutes adopted either by the representative bodies or by popular vote) have become an important source of the modern Russian legal system.[16] The number of laws has increased. The Supreme Soviet annually adopted about ten acts (1937–1946 – 38 laws; 1946–1950 – 14, 1974–1979 – 48), while the Federal Assembly currently adopts more than 150–200 acts per session (e.g., in 2009 the picture was the following: spring session – 220 laws, autumn session – 174, spring session of 2010 – 249). In contrast with the Soviet period, the modern Russian legal system is based on the principle of the supremacy of the law as a factor in building a State ruled by law. The majority of countries of Western Europe recognized this principle in the nineteenth century in the process of codification and adoption of their constitutions. Russia does so on the threshold of the next century. This is the result of a totalitarian regime and weak traditions of the representative bodies. In the present legal system, the principle of the 'supremacy of the law' is strengthening mainly because of the activity of the European Court of Human Rights (the European Convention was ratified by Russia on 5 May 1998) and the Constitutional Court of the Russian Federation. The 'supremacy of the law' means a democratic procedure for the adoption of laws, and appropriate content and place of laws in the system of the sources of law. In the laws themselves, the will of the people is transformed into the will of the State. In its Judgment of 18 January 1996 (VKS, 1996 No. 2) the Constitutional Court concluded that it also means that all state authorities agree with their content. The laws must correspond to the Constitution, the new concept of human rights and international law (Articles 15, 18 of the Constitution). Only such laws may have superiority over the other sources of law.

60. Laws may be divided into several categories:

(1) *Laws for amendment of the Constitution.* According to the Federal Law 'On the Procedure of the Adoption and Coming into Force of the Amendments to the Constitution of the Russian Federation', as amended on 8 March 2015, these laws differ from others since they change the text of the Constitution and become an integral part of it. The laws for amendment of the Constitution are adopted according to the procedure similar to the procedure established for federal constitutional laws, but must also be ratified by the majority of the Federal Entities. On 30 December 2008, two laws of this kind have been adopted – 'On the Changing of the Terms of Mandate of the President of the Russian Federation and of the State Duma', which had extended the mandate of the Head of State to six years and of the Chamber to five years (Article 81 of the Constitution), and 'On the Control Powers of the State Duma towards the Government of the Russian Federation Provided for the Annual Report of the Government on its Activity to the Chamber'. The latter one has widened the

16. *See* V.A. Kazimirchuk (ed.), *Drama rossiiskogo zakona* (Moskva: Juridicheskaia kniga, 1996); Yu.A. Tikhomirov (ed.), *Konstitutsia, zakon, podzakonnyi akt* (Moskva: Juridicheskaia literatura, 1994).

sphere of competence of the lower chamber of the Federal Assembly in the area of Chamber relations with executive bodies of State power (Article 114 of the Constitution).

(2) In 2014, more amendments to the Constitution were adopted. Two of them are dated 5 February 2014: 'On Additional Power of the President of the Russian Federation over Dismissing Deputy of the Procurator General of the Russian Federation and other Officers of the Procurator Office' (Articles 71, 83 and 102 of the Constitution) and 'On Transfer of Powers of the High Arbitration Court of the Russian Federation to the Economic Disputes Department of the Supreme Court of the Russian Federation'. These concern firstly a redistribution of powers between superior courts in Russia and secondly a decrease in their number from three to two (Articles 125, 126 and 128 of the Constitution). The Amendment of 21 July 2014 'On Forming Composition of the Council of Federation of the Federal Assembly of the Russian Federation' entrenches the right of the President to appoint from time to time Russian citizens as members of the Council, but under reservation that the number of such appointed persons may not be more than 10% of the main part of members of the Upper Chamber of the Federal Assembly (Article 95 of the Constitution). The latter amendment may be seen as one more attempt to strengthen checks and balances in the relations between the legislative branch and the President who occupies a place above of all branches of power within the constitutional mechanism of Russia.

(3) *Federal constitutional laws.* The Constitutional Court of the Russian Federation in its Judgment of 31 October 1995 (VKS, 1995 No. 6) pointed out that unlike the amendments a federal constitutional law is adopted to implement the Constitution; therefore, it may not change the constitutional provisions or become the integral part of it. It does not change constitutional provisions but develops them. Those laws regulate subjects determined by the Constitution: state of emergency (Article 56), admission of a new member entity into the Russian Federation or its creation within it, changes of the status of Federal Entities (Articles 65, 66, 137), the state flag, emblem, and anthem (Article 70), the referendum (Article 84), the regime of martial law (Article 87), the Human Rights Commissioner (Article 103), the government (Article 114), the judicial system (Article 118), the Constitutional Court, the Supreme Court (Article 128), and the Constitutional Assembly (Article 135). At present the majority of federal constitutional laws have been adopted with exception of acts prescribed by Articles 66 and 135.

(4) Federal constitutional laws are adopted according to the procedure established by the Constitution. It has some distinctive features: compulsory examination by the Council of the Federation, a qualified majority for approval – two-thirds of the deputies of the State Duma and three-fourths of the members of the Council of the Federation – and the lack of the Presidential veto power. Federal constitutional laws are adopted in accordance with the Constitution and have a legal force lower than the Constitution but higher than ordinary laws, which themselves may not contravene federal constitutional laws (Article 76.3 of the Constitution).

(5) *Ordinary federal laws.* These laws are adopted by the Federal Assembly of Russia or by referendum. They regulate the issues belonging to the jurisdiction of the Federation or to the joint jurisdiction of the Federation and its entities. At present they are the basis for the development of the Russian legal system. These ordinary federal laws are adopted according to the procedure established by the Constitution and the standing orders of the Chambers of the Federal Assembly. Federal laws must be adopted in accordance with the Constitution and federal constitutional laws, but they have a higher legal force than other sources of law listed below. By way of example, for instance, are the Federal Laws of 27 July 2010 'On Organization of Providing State and Municipal Services in the Russian Federation' (SZ, 2010 No. 31) and of 28 December 2013 'On Providing Social Services for Citizens of the Russian Federation' (SZ, 2013 No. 48) recognizing and entrenching the modern principle of a 'service state', instead of the practice of a dominating (ruling) state.
(6) *Laws of the Federal Entities.* The Federal Entities are empowered to adopt laws operating throughout their territory (Article 76 of the Constitution). They regulate issues belonging to the jurisdiction of the Federal Entities or to joint jurisdiction. The analysis of the existing legislation shows that the total amount of laws varies substantially in different constituent entities; that the percentage of regional laws on issues belonging to spheres of joint jurisdiction is increasing; and, that attempts to regulate issues of the jurisdiction of the Russian Federation are not rare.[17] The laws of the Federal Entities cannot contravene federal laws adopted within the federal jurisdiction or the joint jurisdiction. In the event of conflict between a federal law and a law of a Federal Entity, the federal law is applied.
(7) *Laws of the USSR and RSFSR.* In the transitional period, some acts adopted previously by the Supreme Soviets of the USSR or the RSFSR may keep their legal force. According to the resolution of the Supreme Soviet of the RSFSR of 12 December 1991 (Ved. RSFSR, 1991 No. 51), the laws of the former Soviet Union may be applied until the adoption of new legislation insofar as they do not contradict the Constitution and current legislation. The second Concluding and Transitional Provision of the Constitution establishes that laws and other legal acts in effect in the territory of the Russian Federation before the Constitution came into force are applied insofar as they do not contravene the Constitution of the Russian Federation.

61. Though the acts of the President of the Russian Federation must be adopted in accordance with the Constitution and laws, some of these acts have a legal status similar to that of laws. Since the Constitution of 1993 does not list the issues belonging to the competence of the Federal Assembly, the normative powers of the President may be interpreted very loosely. According to the Constitutional Court of the Russian Federation, as formulated in its Judgment of 30 April 1996 (VKS, 1996 No. 3), the issuing of Presidential edicts on matters subject to statutory regulation is

17. *See* Yu.A. Tikhomirov, 'Sootnoshenie federal'nogo zakonodatel'stva i zakonodatel'stva oblasti kak sub'ekta Rossiiskoi Federatsii', in *Zakon oblasti kak sub'ekta Rossiiskoi Federatsii*, ed. Tikhomirov (Voronezh: Izdatel'stvo Voronezhskogo universiteta, 1996), 14–20.

admissible if such edicts fill a gap in the legal regulation and are in compliance with the Constitution and federal laws. However, these acts are in force only until the adoption of an appropriate law. At the same time, it is necessary to mention that the number of such acts has substantially diminished in recent years (2010s).

Chapter 4. Jurisprudence

62. Following the traditions of the Roman-German legal family, the courts of the Russian Federation are considered law-enforcement bodies. Their main task is to resolve social conflicts. Case law, for a long time, was not considered a source of law. That logically corresponds to the principle of the 'supremacy of law'. A court decision had binding force only for the parties to the conflict (res judicata). At present, the role of the courts has expanded. In the transitional period when norms have to be correlated to the rapid changes in social relations, the courts play an important role in the development of the legal system. Recognition of case law as a source of law is currently discussed in the legal literature. The main issue is whether a judicial practice as a whole, acts of the plenum of the High Courts,[18] or even a decision in a concrete case, may be considered a source of law. The guiding explanations of the High Courts issued in the form of acts of the Plenums of the Supreme Court (Articles 126, 127 of the Constitution) are of high authority. Sometimes they contain in fact a new norm that may be later included in a law.[19] The decisions of the Constitutional Court as the 'negative legislator' have a special role. Their legal nature is also discussed. According to one position, those decisions are prejudices, for they establish the legal facts which are binding on the other courts.[20] Another view is that the decisions of the Constitutional Court have the character of judicial precedent.[21]

It is necessary to note that the Constitutional Court in the Judgment of 5 February 2007 (SZ, 2007 No. 7) ruled that by the ratification of the European Convention on Human Rights the Russian Federation recognized the jurisdiction of the European Court of Human Rights as compulsory in the field of interpretation and implementation of the Convention and the Protocols to it in the case of the supposed violation of their provisions by Russia. Therefore, according to the position of the Constitutional Court, the rulings of the European Court – as far as they interpret on the basis of 'the commonly recognized principles and norms of international law', the substance of the rights and freedoms provided for by the Convention, including the right to fair trial – are a component part of the Russian legal system, and for that reason they must be taken into account by the federal legislator in the process of the regulation of social relations and by the law-enforcement bodies – in the process of implementation of these norms. The judges of the Constitutional Court have called for a study and generalizing the experience of the European Court in the sphere of

18. *See* R.Z. Livshits, 'Sudebnaia praktika kak istochnik prava', in *Sudebnaia praktika kak istochnik prava*, ed. Topornin (Moskva: Institut gosudarstva i prava, 1997), 3–15.
19. *See* V.M. Zhuikov, 'Princip verhovenstva prava I pravovye standarty osushestvlenia pravosudia; problem realizatcii v Rossii' in: *Vernovenstvo prava kak factor ekonomiki*, ed. Novikova (Moskva: Mysl, 2017), 532–551; *idem*. 'K voprosu o sudebnoi praktike kak istochnike prava', in *Sudebnaia praktika kak istochnik prava*, ed. Topornin: 16–23.
20. T.G. Morsh'akova, 'Razgranichenie kompetentsii mezhdu Konstitutsionnym Sudom i drugimi sudami', *Vestnik Konstitutsionnogo Suda*, no. 6 (1996): 22–31.
21. V.A. Tumanov, 'Piat' let Konstitutsionnoi justitsii v Rossii: uroki, problemy, perspektivy', *Vestnik Konstitutsionnogo Suda*, no. 6 (1996): 10–15.

overturning the decisions of courts in national jurisdictions. The approach of the Supreme Court of Russian Federation since the mid-1990s until the mid-2010s was a similar one (*see* paragraph 65).

However, in the past two years, the Constitutional Court of Russia has revised its former approach. In the Judgment of 19 April 2016 and in Decision of 10 November 2016 in the case '*Anchugov and Gladunov v. Russia*' (SZ, 2016 No. 12 and No. 39) and especially in the Judgments of 19 January 2017 and of 20 April 2017 in the case '*YUKOS Co. v. Russia*' (SZ, 2017 No. 2 and No. 11) the Court has ruled that, because of the supreme legal force of the Russian Constitution, it is impossible for the Russian Federation to fulfil every decision of the European Court on Human Rights. (Yet, on the other hand, the Judgment told courts to continue 'to note and take into account' decisions of the latter). It means that bodies of State power in Russia hold a right to follow verdicts of the European Court on Human Rights, but are not obliged to do it. The Supreme Court of Russia had taken the same position. These important and in some respect unexpected judgments may slow down a process of modernization of the Russian Federation legal system as a whole and judicial practice in particular.

Also the Constitutional Court in its Judgment of 21 January 2010 (SZ, 2010 No. 6) recognized the precedential character of the legal positions formulated in the rulings of the Plenum of the High Arbitration Court of the Russian Federation (now no longer existing). The Constitutional Court pointed out that in the Russian judicial system the interpretation of a law by the High Courts has 'a serious influence upon the case law and de facto is obligatory for the inferior courts'.

63. In contrast with the countries of Western and Southern Europe, the Russian universities were established late (the first one only in the mid-eighteenth century), and academic jurisprudence did not play the same role in the development of the Russian legal system. (But some legal scholars, for example, Count Michail Speranskii, Joseph Petrazhitskii and Evgeny Pashukanis, are well-known internationally). Legal doctrine is presently not considered a source of constitutional law[22] because of the strong domination of the positivistic approach. Nevertheless, doctrine has an indirect influence on the lawmaking process and sometimes on law enforcement. It links such legal theory with laws and legal practice and plays an important role in the elaboration of new regulations. The Constitution of 1993 and the Declaration of the Rights and Freedoms of Man and Citizen were elaborated with the participation of legal scholars. The concept of constitutional control was also first initiated and elaborated by legal scholars and then implemented into the law.

22. M.V. Baglai, *Konstitutsionnoe pravo Rossiiskoi Federatsii* (Moskva: Norma, 1997): 29.

Chapter 5. Unwritten Law

64. Unwritten law is of no importance in Russian constitutional law, which in general is based on the supremacy of the positive law. Another reason is that legal customs are formed over time, whereas the period of development of the present constitutional model has been a short one. Meanwhile, norms are created on the border of the constitutional law and political space in which they are realized. They are a kind of convention. With time they may be included in the law, or else remain a constitutional-political custom. For example, the President of Russian Federation consults periodically (no less than three times a year) with the Chairmen of the Chambers of the Federal Assembly and of the Government. This State Council, often called 'the council of four', is the result of political practice, and therefore its activity is more a political convention than a legal one. The Government of Russia meets weekly and in the 2010s sometimes held its meetings outside the federal capital (*see* below paragraph 213) probably also on the basis of convention (constitutional custom).

Another convention was disallowed by the Constitutional Court. Deputies of the Lower Chamber of the Federal Assembly in the 1990s had established the practice to delegate their vote to colleagues. Voting in the Chamber is secret, as a result a deputy can vote for several others using an electronic system. The Constitutional Court found such practice unconstitutional (but not retroactively so, as not to question the constitutionality of already existing laws).

65. General principles are recognized in the Russian legal system. They may have independent character or be included in laws. For example, the legal system follows the principle *ignorantio non excusa*, and criminal law is based on the principle *nulla crimen sine lege*. These general principles are used in case of a gap in the law. The decision may then be taken by analogy. Such practice is permitted in civil law but forbidden in criminal law. As a rule, the general principles of law are contained in the text of the legal acts. Some are recognized by the ratification of the international document containing them. The universally recognized principles of international law in the sphere of human rights and freedoms had direct operation in Russia until 2017 (*see* above paragraph 62).

According to the Guiding Explanations of the Plenum of the Supreme Court of 31 October 1995, the principles and norms of international law may be enforced directly. The Constitution includes general principles (norms-principles). Their general character is filled with concrete content, as a rule, by the Constitutional Court. In its Judgment of 27 January 1993 (VKS, 1993 Nos 2–3), the Court held that the principles of justice, legal equality and other have a high degree of generalization, a universal character and the priority over any other provisions. The Constitutional Court in examining individual cases refers to those principles and sometimes interprets them more broadly.

Chapter 6. Administrative Regulations and Orders

§1. At the National Level

66. According to the Russian doctrine, acts are divided into normative and individual ones. Normative acts are binding for all persons and may be applied many times. Individual acts concern specific persons and are applied only once. In fact, only normative acts are considered sources of law. The Constitutional Court exercises control only over normative acts. The Constitution and laws are normative acts.

The executive bodies are law-enforcement bodies but also have lawmaking powers. They may adopt normative and individual acts – acts of law enforcement. The President issues edicts and orders (Article 90.1 of the Constitution), but only edicts may have normative character (Article 115.1 of the Constitution) and be subject to constitutional review (Article 125.2(a) of the Constitution). The Government issues decrees and orders (Article 115.1 of the Constitution), but only decrees may have normative character and be subject to constitutional review (Article 125.1(a) of the Constitution).

Administrative regulations and orders, as normative acts, are adopted by different bodies – the President, the Chambers of the Federal Assembly, the Government and federal bodies with executive power. These numerous acts have a different legal force and designation (instructions, orders, decrees, edicts, letters, etc.). But all of them have the status of 'subordinate legislation'. This means that they must be adopted in accordance with the Constitution and laws.

The above-mentioned bodies may adopt acts within their competence. Insofar as in the Russian legal system the lawmaking sphere is not determined, the borderline between legislation and 'subordinate legislation' may vary in different situations, and acts of the same body may have different validity. For example, normative edicts of the President may have the force of law as well the force of 'subordinate legislation'. The resolutions adopted within the competence of the Chambers of the Federal Assembly (Articles 102, 103 of the Constitution) may have internal validity (e.g., standing orders of the Chamber, committees and commissions) or general validity (e.g., decrees of the State Duma on amnesty, decrees of the Council of the Federation confirming the border changes between the constituent entities or approving edicts of the President of the Russian Federation on the introduction of a state of emergency or martial law).

In fact, the acts of the federal bodies of executive power have their own hierarchy and the place of an act is determined by the status of the body that issued it. At the top are the acts of the Government, then of the federal ministries, services and agencies which may be binding for a more narrow circle of subjects. For the implementation of the principles of the rule of law and of the supremacy of law, it is necessary to establish frameworks for the lawmaking powers of the federal bodies of executive power and a system of control. The 'subordinate' legislation is controlled by the courts, procurators or by a higher standing executive body. Acts of the Government may be repealed by the President if they contradict the Constitution, laws or edicts of the President. Acts of the federal bodies of executive power may be repealed or abolished by the Government.

There is no parliamentary control over the subordinate legislation. All existing forms of control are *ex post facto*. The only form of preliminary control is the registration by the Ministry of Justice of acts of the federal bodies of executive power affecting the rights, freedoms and obligations of man and the citizen, having interdepartmental character or establishing the legal status of an organization.

§2. At the Level of the Constituent Entities

67. The constituent entities may issue legal acts (Article 76 of the Constitution), the categories of which are determined by their constitutions and charters. The bodies empowered to issue them, as well as the designations of those acts, depend upon the type of constituent entity or established form of government. Legal enactment issued on the matters belonging to the jurisdiction of the Russian Federation or joint jurisdiction is subject to constitutional review (Article 125.2(b) of the Constitution). The President of the Russian Federation may suspend the operation of acts of the bodies of executive power of a constituent entity in the event that they contravene the Constitution, federal laws or international obligations of the Russian Federation, or if they violate human rights and freedoms, pending the decision of the matter by the appropriate court (Article 85.2 of the Constitution).

§3. At the Level of the Local Authorities

68. Though the local government is not considered in modern Russia as a part of the state power, the bodies of local self-government may adopt acts which are considered sources of constitutional law. The municipalities have their charters that are subject to state registration. Non-compliance with the Constitution, laws of the Russian Federation or of the constituent entities are the only grounds for rejection of the registration. The categories of other acts of the bodies of local self-government, their designation and the procedure of their adoption are regulated by the charters of those individual municipalities. In several constituent entities, normative acts of the bodies of local self-government are subject to constitutional review by the Constitutional (Charter) Courts (e.g., Karelia, Daghestan, Sverdlovsk and Voronezh *oblasts*).

Chapter 7. Codification, Interpretation and Publication

§1. Codification

69. Following the traditions of the Roman-German model, Russia is a country of codified law. The process of codification began in the 1920s when the main European codes were adopted. In contrast with other countries, the codification in Russia occurred three times: in the 1920s, in the 1950s and 1960s, and in the 1990s/2000s. All codifications were large-scale: within a rather short period, codes were adopted in the different spheres of law. A number of specialized codes were adopted in the 1990s and 2000s: 1995 – the Criminal Code, as amended on 22 November 2016, 2000 – the second Part of the Tax Code, 2001 – the third Part of the Civil Code, as amended on 9 March 2016, the Labour Code, as amended on 30 December 2015, the Criminal Procedure Code, the Administrative Code, as amended on 26 April 2016; 2002 – the Civil Procedure Code, the Arbitration Procedure Code, as amended on 19 December 2016; 2006 – the fourth Part of the Civil Code, as amended on 9 March 2016, the Water Code, as amended on 28 November 2015, and the Forestry Code, as amended on 1 May 2016. The present legal reform has features distinct from all the previous reforms undertaken under Soviet power. The Codes now do not contain ideological provisions, are oriented towards human rights and freedoms protection and are developed in accordance with international law and foreign practice. The Codes adopted in the transitional period do not exclude the adoption of laws in the same field; moreover, the provisions of the Civil Code are developed by the current legislation.

Codes are not the only kind of the codified acts in the Russian Federation. The Foundations of Legislation were implemented extensively in the USSR law as the basis for the unified development of the legal system of the Federation and its entities. At present, the Constitution does not provide for such sources of law but some Foundations adopted previously are still in force (e.g., the Foundations of Culture Legislation of 1992, the Foundations of Health Care Legislation of 1993). In some fields such codified acts as charters are adopted (e.g., the Charter of the railways or water transport).

§2. Interpretation

70. An interpretation may be official or unofficial. Official interpretation is given by a competent body and is binding for those who apply the acts in question. The Constitutional Court is the single federal governmental body empowered to give an official interpretation of the Constitution which is compulsory for all legal subjects. A ruling on the interpretation of the Constitution is adopted at the plenary meeting of the Court and must be approved by a majority of not less than two-thirds of the total number of justices.

An official interpretation of an act may be given by a body that issued it. According to the Constitutional Court as formulated in its Judgment of 17 November 1997 (VKS, 1997 No. 6), an act of interpretation must be adopted in compliance with the same procedure and have the same form as the act that is interpreted. Thus, the

President, the Government and the Federal Assembly may interpret their acts (authentic interpretation). As a rule, the body issuing the act is empowered to interpret it, but in rare cases this power may be delegated. A Guiding Explanation may be given by the Supreme Court or the High Arbitration Court in the form of an act adopted by the Plenum.

Professional, or doctrinal, interpretation as a form of unofficial interpretation is undertaken by legal scholars. As a rule it is important for the uniformity of the law-enforcement legislation. For example, different legal schools have published their Commentaries to the Constitution since the 1980s to the present.

§3. Publication

71. According to the Constitution (Article 15.3), laws are subject to official publication; otherwise they are not applied.[23] As for legal acts, this rule is interpreted narrowly: only enactments affecting rights, freedoms and obligations of man and citizens cannot be applied unless they have been officially published.

Under the provisions of the Federal Law of 14 June 1994 'On the Procedure for Publication and Coming into Force of Federal Constitutional Laws, Federal Laws, Acts of the Chambers of the Federal Assembly' (SZ, 1994 No. 8), as amended by Federal Law of 25 December 2012, federal constitutional and ordinary laws are subject to official publication within seven days after their signing by the President. Acts of the Chambers must be published not later than ten days after their adoption. International treaties of the Russian Federation that need statutory approval are published simultaneously with the federal laws on their ratification. Their first publication in the official newspaper, *Rossiiskaia Gazeta,* or in the periodical 'Collection of legislation of the Russian Federation' (*Sobranie zakonodatel'stva Rossiiskoi Federatsii*) is deemed official publication. Those acts come into force ten days after their official publication, if it is not established otherwise in their text.

72. In accordance with the Edict No. 763 of 26 May 1996 (SZ, 1996 No. 22), as amended by the Edict No. 736 of 28 June 2005, edicts and orders of the President as well as decrees and orders of the Government are subject to official publication. This rule does not apply to those acts and provisions that contain state secrets or confidential information. The normative acts of the President, as well as acts of the Government, affecting rights, freedoms and obligations of man and the citizen, or establishing the legal status of federal bodies of executive power and organizations, come into force seven days after their official publication; the other acts, on the day of their issuing, if it is not established otherwise in their text. Their first publication in the newspaper *Rossiiskaia Gazeta* or in the periodical 'Collection of legislation of the Russian Federation' (*Sobranie zakonodatel'stva Rossiiskoi Federatsii*) is deemed official publication.

---

23. V.A. Pigolkin (ed.), *Opublikovanie normativnykh aktov* (Moskva: Juridicheskaia literatura, 1978).

73. Normative acts of the federal bodies of executive power affecting the rights, freedoms and obligations of man and the citizen, having interdepartmental character or establishing the legal status of an organization registered at the Ministry of Justice, are subject to official publication. This rule does not apply to those acts and provisions that contain state secrets or confidential information. Normative acts are published in the *Rossiiskaia Gazeta* newspaper and in the Bulletin of the Normative Acts of the Federal Bodies of Executive Power.

Part II. Form of Government

I. Bogdanovskaia & T. Vassilieva

Chapter 1. General

§1. Introduction

74. The Constitution of 1993 declares the multinational people of Russia the bearer of sovereignty (Article 3.1). People may exercise it through referenda and free elections that are considered the supreme direct manifestation of their power or through the organs of state power and local self-government (Article 3.2, 3.3). The present Constitution for the first time establishes a ban on the usurpation of the state power (Article 3.4).

In a federal State, the concept of sovereignty may have additional aspects because of the existence of different levels of power. As a rule, federal authorities do not recognize the sovereignty of their entities, but Soviet legal doctrine admitted it. Though the RSFSR was characterized as a sovereign soviet socialist State (Article 68 of the Constitution of 1978) the provisions about its sovereignty were a dead letter. In the period of democratization of the political regime and transformation of the governmental system, Russia adopted a Declaration of State Sovereignty on 12 June 1990 (Ved. RSFSR, 1990 No. 21), the main aim of which was to determine the framework of its sovereignty within the USSR and to establish economic, political and legal guarantees thereof. Declarations were also adopted by the republics within Russia that claimed recognition of their sovereign status. Those declarations contained provisions regarding the right to secession, supremacy of the laws of the republics in their territory, and the right to conclude treaties with other republics, independent States or supranational organizations. Under those conditions the federal authorities had to find an adequate solution. In the Federation Treaty and in the revised text of the Constitution of 1978, the republics were recognized as sovereign.

The Constitution of 1993 is oriented towards a different concept of sovereignty. It proclaimed the extension of the sovereignty of Russia over its entire territory, the supremacy of the Federal Constitution and laws, and the integrity and inviolability of the territory of the country (Article 4). At the same time the constitutional provisions represent a compromise. The sovereignty of the republics is not mentioned, but they are recognized as States (Article 5.2). That has opened the possibility of differing interpretations. As noted in the contemporary Russian legal literature, there existed a conflict between the recognition by the Constitution of the unitary and indivisible sovereignty of the Russian Federation, and the practice of its denial by the constitutions, charters and legislation of the Federal Entities, as well as by the several bilateral treaties concluded by the Russian Federation and its entities.[24]

These contradictions were mitigated by the Constitutional Court of the Russian Federation, which in its Judgment of 7 June 2000 (SZ, 2000 No. 25) ruled that the Constitution of the Russian Federation does not provide for any other bearer of sovereignty and the source of power than the multinational people of Russia, and therefore does not suppose any other state sovereignty besides the sovereignty of the Russian Federation. The Court pointed out that in accordance with the constitutional provisions the sovereignty of the Russian Federation precludes the possibility of existence of two levels of sovereign powers having supremacy and independence, that is it does not regard the sovereignty of the republics, as well as other constituent entities.

75. According to the Constitution, the state power is exercised in the Russian Federation and in the entities of the Russian Federation (Article 11.1, 11.2). Among the federal bodies of state power there are enumerated the President as the Head of State (Articles 11.1, 80.4), the Federal Assembly as the legislative body (Articles 11.1, 94), the Government exercising the executive power (Articles 11.1, 110.1), and the courts of the Russian Federation administrating justice (Articles 11.1, 118.1). Each Chamber of the Federal Assembly – the State Duma and the Council of the Federation – is considered organs of state power.

76. The existing form of government of the Russian Federation has the following distinctive features:

(a) The President and the State Duma, the Lower Chamber of the Federal Assembly, are elected by popular vote. The Government does not lose its powers after the parliamentary elections but must resign upon the election of the new President.
(b) Though the State Duma is entitled to give its consent to the appointment of the Chairman (Head) of the Government, the President plays the main role in the process of forming the Government. The Government does not present its programme to the Chamber and the latter does not designate its members. The post of member of the Government since the 2000s is incompatible with the status of deputy of the State Duma.
(c) The President is not considered the Head of the executive power, but he determines the main guidelines for the domestic and foreign policy of state; adopts normative edicts mandatory for the Government and may repeal its acts. Several federal ministers are subordinated directly to the President.
(d) The President has the right of legislative initiative and vetoing powers. His acts as a rule do not need countersigning by a minister. The Administration of the President is considered a state body. Its organization and functions are defined

24. I.A. Umnova, *Konstitutsionnye osnovy sovremennogo rossiiskogo federalizma* (Moskva: Delo, 1998), 113–114.

by the Presidential Edicts of 2 May 2003 and of 6 April 2004 'On the Administration of the President of Russian Federation'.

(e) The State Duma is empowered to adopt a motion of non-confidence in the Government, but this power is restricted. The President may take a decision on the resignation of the Government at any time and on the basis of any reasons, but his possibilities to dissolve the State Duma are limited too.

77. Among Russian legal scholars there is still no consensus regarding the form of government of the Russian Federation. It is characterized as a semi-presidential republic of the French type with certain particularities,[25] a presidential republic[26] and an unusual form of government that does not belong to the classical types of presidential and semi-presidential republic.[27] The existing hybrid system, established in a period of crisis and the transformation of the regime, may evolve towards various forms of government, and the political practice constantly demonstrates attempts to change its configuration.[28]

§2. Political Parties, Lobbies and Interest Groups

78. In Russia, political parties began to form at the end of the nineteenth century and were legalized in 1905.[29] Soon after the October Revolution of 1917, the multiparty system was transformed into a one-party system. Though officially they were not abolished, their publications were prohibited, offices closed, municipal and parliamentary mandates annulled, so between the early 1920s and late 1980s no conditions existed for any political party activity except that of the Communist Party. According to the Constitutional Court, as formulated in its Judgment of 30 November 1992 (VKS, 1993 Nos 4–5), for a long period, a regime based upon violence and of unlimited power held by a small group of communist functionaries with the General Secretary of the CPSU at its head existed in the Soviet Union. As the Constitutional Court stressed in its Ruling, the Communist Party of the RSFSR did not have independent status, but was an integral part of the CPSU. The President of Russia considered the CPSU not a political party by nature. In the Edict of 6 November 1991 (Ved. RSFSR, 1991 No. 45) the Communist Party was classified as a specific mechanism of formation and realization of political power by means of interlocking the State and Party bodies and by direct subordination of the state structures to the Communist Party. On 20 July 1991, the President issued an Edict, often

25. *See* M.V. Baglai, *Konstitutsionnoe pravo Rossiiskoi Federatsii* (Moskva: Norma, 1997), 122; B.N. Topornin, 'Vstupitel'naia stat'a', in *Konstitutsia Rossiiskoi Federatsii. Nauchno prakticheskii kommentarii*, ed. Topornin (Moskva: Jurist, 1997), 71.
26. A.N. Medushevskii, *Demokratia i avtoritarism: rossiiskii konstitutsionalism v sravnitel'noi perspektive* (Moskva: ROSSPEN, 1997), 591.
27. V.A. Chetvernin (ed.), *Konstitutsia Rossiiskoi Federatsii: Problemnyi kommentarii* (Moskva: Tsentr konstitutsionnykh issledovanii Moskovskogo Obsh'estvennogo Nauchnogo Fonda, 1997), 352–353.
28. *See* N.V. Varlamova, *Konstitutsionnyi protsess v Rossii (1990–1993)* (Moskva: Tsentr konstitutsionnykh issledovanii Moskovskogo Obsh'estvennogo Nauchnogo Fonda, 1998), 136–138.
29. *See* S.A. Zaslavskii, *Politicheskie partii Rossii. Problemi pravovoi institutsionalizatsii* (Moskva: Institut prava i publichnoi politiki, 2003); S.V. Vasil'eva, *Konstitutsionno-pravovoi status politicheskoi oppozitsii* (Moskva: Institut prava i publichnoi politiki), 2010.

called 'Edict on Depolitization', that put an end to the activity of the structures of the political parties and mass social movements, except for trade unions, within state organs, institutions and organizations of the RSFSR and further banned their creation in future (Ved. RSFSR, 1991 No. 31).

At the end of the twentieth century began a revival of the multiparty system. The registration of the charters of the political parties at the Ministry of Justice and their territorial structures was authorized by the Resolution of the Presidium of the Supreme Soviet of 15 January 1991 (Ved. RSFSR, 1991 No. 2). At that time, the majority of political associations might be classified as protoparties – transitional ones forming into real ones.[30] In spite of the visible diversity of parties and political movements, a number of which were represented in the Federal Assembly and in the organs of state power of the Federal Entities, such parties did not play an important role in the political life of the country. The forming of Russian democracy was not based upon the party system. The President of Russia did not belong to any political party. The members of Government acted in a personal capacity. It is necessary to note that at the parliamentary elections of December 1995 the Central Electoral Commission registered forty-three electoral associations that appeared on the ballot; among them, eleven had the designation of a party and seven of a political movement.[31] As a result of the election, only the Communists and the Liberal Democrats could form independent factions in the State Duma. On 1 January 1999, the Ministry of Justice of the Russian Federation registered 141 All-Russian political associations (RG, 16 January 1999). On 1 January 2010, according to data of the Ministry there were seven registered All-Russian political parties, four of which had their factions in the State Duma.

79. Political parties are mentioned in the Constitution indirectly by means of establishing guarantees for political diversity and a multiparty system (Article 13.3). At the same time, the general constitutional rules regarding public associations are applied to political parties. They are equal before the law (Article 13.4) and enjoy the freedom of activity (Article 30.1). Prohibited are the creation and activity of parties whose aims and actions are directed towards the forcible alteration of the foundations of the constitutional order and violation of the integrity of the country, undermining the state security, the creation of armed groups or the stirring up of social, racial, national or religious dissent (Article 13.5). A legal position of those public associations is regulated by the Federal Law of 11 July 2001 'On Political Parties' (SZ, 2001 No. 29), as amended on 9 March 2016. According to the provisions of the Federal Law, a party ought to meet several requirements as the following: (1) have regional branches in more than half of the constituent entities; (2) comprise not less than 45,000 members, have regional branches with not less than 450 members in more than half of the constituent entities and other regional branches with not less than 200 members until 1 January 2012 and since than comprise not less than 40,000 members, have regional branches with not less than 400 members in more than half of the constituent entities and other regional branches

30. Yu.A. Yudin, *Politicheskie partii i pravo v sovremennom gosudarstve* (Moskva: Infra-M, 1998), 41.
31. Yu.K. Abramov & T.K. Golovina, *Politicheskie partii i dvuzhenia Rossii. 1996. Ezhegodnik* (Moskva: Press Ltd., 1996): 551–552.

with not less than 150 members; (3) locate the governing bodies of a party, its regional branches and other structural subdivisions in Russian territory exclusively.

It is necessary to note that in Russia only federal political parties may be established: the Federal Law does not provide for regional parties. Every party must have an internal constitution and a party programme, but the main objectives of any party are formulated by the above-mentioned Federal Law of 11 July 2001: shaping of public opinion, political education and training of citizens, expression of opinion on any issue of public life and informing of it the public and the bodies of state power, nomination of candidates at the federal, regional and local elections, participation in those elections and in the activity of the elected bodies. Structural subdivisions of a party are formed on a territorial basis, they may not be created within public authorities' bodies, Armed Forces, law enforcement and other state bodies, governmental and non-governmental organizations. The creation of parties aimed at the performance of the extremist activity or based on the professional, racial, national and religious affiliation is prohibited. A party may not comprise only the representatives of a certain profession as its members.

Those associations are created freely at their constituent congress or through the transformation of an All-Russia public association into political parties. In order to receive the status of legal entity or take part in elections, political parties must be registered by the authorized federal body of state registration and the territorial agencies thereof. That federal body of state regulation, the Russian Commission on Review upon Communications (Roskomnadzor) under the Government of the Russian Federation, publishes annually a list of political parties and its regional branches indicating the dates of registration in official periodicals and makes public the constitutions, programmes, financial reports of political parties and the contact information regarding the governing bodies of those parties on its official site. By the mid-2010s more than forty political parties have been registered in Russia. Of those, four are federal parliamentary parties having caucuses in the lower Chamber of the Federal Assembly, the State Duma.

80. The above-mentioned Federal Law provides for an individual membership in the party. Legal persons, aliens and stateless persons may not be members of the Russian political parties. A citizen may be a member of only one political party. The restrictions regarding the membership in the parties may be provided for by the federal legislation. For instance, policemen may not be members of political parties (Federal Law of 7 February 2011 'On Police', SZ, 2011 No. 7, as amended on 3 July 2016), military personnel, public prosecutors and judges may not be members of any public associations, pursuing political aims (Federal Law of 27 May 1998 'On the Status of the Military', SZ, 1998 No. 22, in the wording of 28 December 2010; Federal Law of 17 January 1992 'On the Procurator's Office of the Russia Federation', SZ, 1992 No. 8, in the wording of 3 July 2016; Russian Federation Law of 26 June 1992 'On the Status of Judges in the Russian Federation', Ved. Russian Federation, 1992 No. 30, in the wording of 14 December 2015). A member of the Public Chamber must suspend his membership in the political party during his term of office according to the Federal Law of 4 April 2005 'On the Public Chamber of the Russian Federation', SZ, 2005 No. 15, as amended on 28 November 2015. The designation of these prohibitions/limitations aims at overcoming a heritage of well-rooted politization and ideologization of public bodies and all public life as existed in the USSR between 1917 and 1991.

81. The Federal Law provides for the state financial support of the political parties in accordance with their electoral results and the restrictions regarding the donations. The total amount of annual donations of a party and its regional branches may not exceed RUB 4.33 billion; the amount of donations from the same legal entity, RUB 43.3 million; and from the same individual, RUB 4.33 million.

A political party may be liquidated by decision of the Supreme Court of Russia on the basis of following grounds: non-observance of the restrictions regarding the creation of a party; non-elimination of violations which served as grounds for the suspension of its activity during a time term set by a court decision; non-participation in elections; non-existence of necessary amount of regional branches with established amount of members, the lack of necessary number of members, systematic non-submission data necessary for updating of the information of the State register of legal entities.

§3. Referendum

82. According to the Constitution of the RSFSR of 1978, 'the most important issues of state life' might be subject to popular discussion or put to a direct popular vote (referendum) (Article 5).[32] It was not defined, however, who decides and how, whether an issue is 'the most important' or not. During the period of the 'socialist democracy', this Article was never applied and the nation-wide discussions regarding draft laws of general importance were held and led by the authorities of the Soviet Union. It is necessary to note that in the period of the democratization of the political regime, the RSFSR Law of 16 October 1990 'On the Referendum of the RSFSR' (Ved. RSFSR, 1990 No. 21) was adopted two months earlier than the appropriate law of the Soviet Union. Referenda were called several times in 1991–1993. The result of the referendum of 17 March 1991 was the introduction of the post of the President of the Russian Federation. Several issues regarding the functioning of the system of the governmental bodies were put to referendum on 25 April 1993 (confidence in the President, approval of the social and economic policy of the President and the Government, the need to hold early elections for the offices of President and People's Deputies of the Russian Federation). The Constitution of 12 December 1993 was adopted by popular vote. Since that time no nation-wide referendum has been held in Russia.

83. According to the Federal Constitutional Law of 28 June 2004 'On the Referendum of the Russian Federation' (SZ, 1995 No. 42), in the wording of 6 April

32. *See* Yu.A. Dmitriev & V.V. Komarova, *Referendum v sisteme narodovlastia* (Moskva: Manuscript, 1995); S.Yu. Danilov. *Referendum v sovremennom mire: sravnitelnyi analiz predmetov i posledstvyi. Sovremennoye pravo, no 8 (2012)*: 25–34; no. 9: 29–32.

2015, draft laws, laws and other issues of state importance may be put to a nation-wide vote. The right of initiative belongs to the Constitutional Assembly in the case of the drafting of a new Constitution, to the citizens of Russia and to the federal bodies of state power in the case of holding a referendum obligatory on the basis of the international treaty of the Russian Federation or a federal constitutional law. Citizens may form an initiative group consisting of regional divisions, at least 100 citizens each, which represent more than half of the Federal Entities. A regional division must be registered with an electoral commission of a Federal Entity and collect totally not less than 2 million signatures of citizens. According to the Federal Constitutional Law mentioned above, the number of signatures collected in any Federal Entity cannot exceed 50,000. The collected signatures are submitted to the Central Electoral Commission which, after their examination, sends all the materials to the President and informs the Chambers of the Federal Assembly.

In order to call a referendum, the President must have an opinion of the Constitutional Court confirming the observance of the procedure established for the initiative. The referendum may be held upon the issues belonging to the jurisdiction of the Russian Federation and to the joint jurisdiction. Certain issues cannot be put to referendum: changing of the status of the Federal Entities, provided for by the Constitution of the Russian Federation; preliminary termination of powers or prolongation of a term of office of the President or of the State Duma, as well as the holding of early elections or changing a term of these elections; election, appointment, preliminary termination of powers, suspension or prolongation of a term of office of the state officials of the Russian Federation; personal composition of the federal bodies of state power and other federal state bodies; election, preliminary termination of powers, suspension or prolongation of a term of office of the bodies established and officials elected in accordance with the international treaty of the Russian Federation; adoption of emergency or urgent measures for the protection of the health or security of the population; and other issues recognized by the Constitution or a federal constitutional law as belonging to the exclusive jurisdiction of the federal bodies of the state power. A referendum cannot be held during a state of emergency or martial law, or within three months after the termination of those regimes. It may not take place during the last year of the President or the State Duma mandate or in the period of the nation-wide electoral campaign. It cannot be held within two years after the official publication of the results of a previous referendum with the same content or meaning.

The President is empowered to call a referendum. It may be held on any Sunday between 60 and 100 days after the issuing of the edict by the President, but its date cannot coincide with an official holiday, a day before or after it, as well as any Sunday which is announced as a working day. A decision is considered adopted by nation-wide referendum if more than one-half of the voters taking part in it voted for that decision and more than one-half of all eligible voters took part in it. The results of a referendum are subject to publication by the Central Electoral

Commission within three days after their determination. In every Federal Entity, the results of voting in that constituent entity must also be published. The decision comes into force on the day of the official publication and does not need additional confirmation. It may be changed by a new referendum in the Russian Federation, if the decision adopted by the referendum does not provide otherwise.

84. According to the legislation currently in force, referenda are used at different territorial levels. The organization of a local referendum and a referendum in a Federal Entity is regulated respectively by the charter of a municipality or the law of a Federal Entity. The Federal Law of 12 June 2002 'On the Fundamental Guarantees of the Electoral Rights and the Right to Participate in the Referendum of the Citizens of the Russian Federation', (SZ, 2002 No. 24), as amended on 3 December 2015, in force since 9 February 2016, establishes the basic requirements and restrictions in this field. Within Federal Entities, a referendum may be held upon the issues belonging to their jurisdiction and to joint jurisdiction, if there is no constitutional provision or a federal law regulating that matter. The topic of a local referendum may not go beyond the jurisdiction of a municipality. In both cases, the issues of a referendum may not restrict or abolish the commonly recognized human rights and the constitutional guarantees of their implementation as well as contravene the federal legislation (and the regional legislation in the case of a local referendum).

Like in many European states, in the Russian Federation certain issues may not be put to a referendum: a preliminary termination of powers or prolongation of a term of office of the bodies of state power and local self-government; the formation of the bodies of state power and local self-government and their personal composition; election, approval, appointment or consent for appointment to, or removal from, office of deputies or officials; adoption or modification of the appropriate budget; implementation and alteration of the financial obligations of a municipality or of a Federal Entity; and adoption of emergency or urgent measures for the protection of the health or security of the population. According to federal law, the establishment of other restrictions on issues that may be subjected to a referendum is prohibited.

The group submitting an initiative for popular vote must consist of at least twenty persons for a regional referendum and ten persons for a municipal one.

Summarizing, it may be said that after 1991 in the constitutional mechanism of Russia two fundamental trends are combined. One is reflected in strengthening the checks-and-balance machinery among the branches of power, and between them and of Head of State, in weakening police powers and of the office of Procurator General, and in a true equality of religious believers and non-believers. That trend, while being a product of erasing long-term autocratic rule, has opened the door for a rising share of average citizens extensively invoking the institution of human rights and freedoms. The first trend was already prevalent in the 1990s and the first half of the 2000s. The second trend, which came to be a predominant one since the mid-2000s, is reforming executive power positions, including police forces and the office of Procurator General, widening the spheres of competence of the Head of State at the expense of all branches of power, of moving towards a one-party situation for the legislative bodies of State power at a federal and regional levels, while nonetheless preserving the non-party status of the President at the same time. Also the second trend is directed towards a restricted interpretation of the secular state principle and a rise in the activities and influence of the Russian Eastern Orthodox church. For more details, *see* Chapters 2, passim.

Chapter 2. Head of State

T. Vassilieva

85. In Russia, the Head of State is the President (Article 80.1 of the Constitution).[33] He is one of the federal organs of state power but does not belong to any specific branch of power (Article 11.1 of the Constitution). As the Head of State, the President represents the country within its territory and in international relations (Article 80.4 of the Constitution) and determines the basic guidelines of the domestic or foreign policy of Russia (Article 80.3 of the Constitution) that are formulated in his annual Messages to the Chambers. Being responsible for the coordinate functioning and collaboration of all the organs of state power (Article 80.2 of the Constitution), the President meets with the party leaders or state officials (federal and regional), establishes special commissions consisting of the representatives of different organs of state power; and, uses conciliatory procedures.

As the guarantor of the Constitution and of human rights and freedoms (Article 80.2 of the Constitution) the President may initiate a proceeding in the Constitutional Court or request an interpretation of the Constitution (Article 125.2 and 125.5 of the Constitution); reject an adopted federal law submitted for promulgation (Article 107.3 of the Constitution); repeal decrees and orders of the Government (Article 115 of the Constitution); and, suspend the operation of an act of a body of executive power of a Federal Entity (Article 85.2 of the Constitution). He adopts measures to safeguard the sovereignty of the Russian Federation, its independence and state integrity (Article 80.2 of the Constitution). In its Judgment of 31 July 1995 (SZ, 1995 No. 33), the Constitutional Court of the Russian Federation underlined that state integrity is one of the foundations of the constitutional system of the Russian Federation, an important condition for the equal legal status of all citizens irrespective of their place of residence, and a guarantee of their constitutional rights and freedoms. It thus follows from the Constitution that the President is obliged to take measures in this field and ensure the implementation of the powers of the Federal Government through the territory of the Russian Federation, including such spheres of federal jurisdiction as defence or security.

§1. Election

86. Unlike the USSR, Germany or Italy, the President of the Russian Federation is elected by direct popular vote. Two laws, in particular, govern presidential elections: the Federal Law of 10 January 2003 'On the Election of the President of the Russian Federation' (SZ, 2003 No. 2), as amended on 5 December 2017, and the

33. *See* M.V. Baglai. *President Rossiiskoi Federatsii I Soedinennych Shtatov Ameriki* (Moskva: Norma, 2008); L.A. Okun'kov, *Prezident Rossiiskoi Federatsii: Konstitutsia i politicheskaia praktika* (Moskva: Infra-M 1996); Yu.I. Skuratov, 'Konstitutsionnie osnovy i praktika funktsionirovania prezidentskoi vlasti', in *Konstitutsionnyi stroi Rossii* 1, ed. Glushko, et al., (Moskva: Institut gosudarstva i prava, 1992), 72–83; Yu. I. Skuratov, 'Parlament i Prezident v Rossiiskoi Federatsii', in *Konstitutsionnyi stroi Rossii*. ed. Glushko & Stepanov (Moskva: Institut gosudarstva i prava, 1995), 68–77.

Federal Law of 12 June 2002 'On the Fundamental Guarantees of the Electoral Rights and the Right to Participate in Referendum of the Citizens of the Russian Federation' (SZ, 2002 No. 24) as amended on 3 November 2015, in force since 9 February 2016, and as further amended on 5 February 2018. The date of the Presidential election is determined and published by the Council of the Federation. The decision is adopted not earlier than 100 days before and not later than 60 days before that date. As a rule, voting takes place on the second Sunday of that month, in which the previous presidential elections took place (Article 5 of the Federal Law 'On the Election of the President of the Russian Federation'). Two tours (rounds) of popular voting are foreseen by law.

Any citizen at least 35 years old and permanently living in Russia for ten years may be elected President (Article 81.2 of the Constitution). This rule does not apply to persons declared incapacitated by a court or deprived of their freedom by a court sentence (Article 32.3 of the Constitution), as well as to persons having a citizenship or a residence permit of the foreign state, a conviction for a grave and special grave crime or for a crime that has an extremist nature. The candidates are nominated by the political parties or by way of self-nomination. In the latter case a candidate must be supported by a group of at least 500 electors. A party may nominate only one candidate, who is not a member of the other party. Each candidate must be supported by at least 2,000,000 electors, but the number of signatures collected in a Federal Entity cannot exceed 500,000. The candidates nominated by those parties which are represented in the State Duma or in the legislative bodies of state power of at least one-third of the constituent entities do not need to collect signatures of electors.

The candidate who holds state or elected municipal office, is a civil or municipal servant, a member of any administrative bodies of any associations except political parties, may not use the privileges of their office or position. Those nominees who are state or municipal functionaries or engaged in the mass media must suspend their professional activity after the registration. This rule does not apply to the incumbent President or the Chairman of the Government acting as a Head of State and to the deputies. These persons continue to perform their functions, but they may not use the privileges of their office during the election process. Only the Chairman of the Investigation Committee may initiate a criminal proceeding against those persons who take part in the presidential elections. The candidates may not be arrested or submitted to administrative sanctions by a court without the consent of the Chairman of the Investigation Committee in the first case and the Procurator General in the second case.

The Federal Law 'On Election of the President of Russian Federation', as amended on 5 December 2017, contains a number of recently adopted additional demands on candidates for the Presidency. In particular, any candidate for President of Russia now is obliged not to have any deposits in foreign banks abroad and has to report scrupulously about his/her property: real estate, transport facilities, sources of income and expenditures for the three years prior to the date of election. The data is accessible to the public. These provisions appear to be consequences of increasing popular demand for closing more channels of f political and economic conflict of interest and other forms of corruption.

It is possible to withdraw from the election but not later than five days before polling day or a day before – in the case of emergency A candidate needs 50% plus one of the valid votes cast to win in the first round. It is necessary to note that before 2007 a minimum voter turnout of 50% was required. For example, during the presidential election of 2008 the Central Election Commission registered four candidates, the most successful were Dmitrii Medvedev (70.3% of total votes cast) and the Chairman of the Communist Party, Gennadii Ziuganov (17.7%). For the elections of 2012, the outcome was the following: Vladimir Putin, 63.6% and Gennadii Ziuganov, 17.2% of total votes cast respectively. In the recent presidential election of 18 March 2018, seven candidates were registered. Incumbent President Vladimir Putin received 76.7% of total votes cast, while Pavel Grudinin, a new Communist candidate, finished a distant second with 11.8% of votes cast. All the other candidates won 11.5% votes combined.

§2. Legal Status

I. Mandate

87. Under the provisions of the Constitution in its original wording, the President is elected for four years and can serve a maximum of two consecutive terms (Article 81.1, 81.3). Boris Yeltsin having been elected for his first presidency in 1991, when the term of office was a year longer, continued to perform his functions until the expiry of the term for which he was elected (Articles Concluding and Transitional Provision of the Constitution). The Constitutional Court confirms in its Decision of 5 November 1998 that in the case of Boris Yeltsin, the term of office was not interrupted by the adoption of the new Constitution of 1993, and his re-election for a second term took place in June/July 1996 (SZ, 1999 No. 1). After the amendment of the Constitution on 30 December 2008, the President is elected for six years. The President enters into office following an official announcement of the voting results by the Central Electoral Commission. The Chairman of the Constitutional Court takes the oath of the elected President on a special copy of the Constitution of the Russian Federation in the presence of the members of the Council of the Federation, deputies of the State Duma and justices of the Constitutional Court in the Kremlin.

88. As a rule, the President performs his functions until the expiry of his term of office, when the newly elected President takes his oath. He may cease to exercise his powers temporarily or prematurely in some special cases. According to the Judgment of the Constitutional Court of 6 July 1999 (SZ, 1999 No. 29), the President may take a decision to vest temporarily the performance of his duties in the Chairman of the Government. In extraordinary situations, when the President is unable to do so, the Chairman of the Government carries them out, with some limits. As acting President, the Chairman is not able to dissolve the State Duma, to call a referendum or submit proposals for constitutional amendment or revision (Article 92.3 of the Constitution). In the 1990s in spite of the worsening health condition of Boris Yeltsin (also rendered in the Western press as 'Yeltsin'), temporarily cessation of his powers was not frequent. Only once did the Chairman of the Government perform the presidential functions, from 7 a.m. on 5 November until 6 a.m. on 6 November 1996, when Yeltsin had a heart operation. In the event of resignation, persistent inability to perform his functions for health reasons or removal from office, the President may terminate his office prematurely (Article 92.2 of the Constitution). In that case, an extraordinary election is held not later than three months after the President had ceased to exercise his powers. It is necessary to note that the first President of Russia Yeltsin terminated preliminary his powers in December 1999, empowered the Chairman of the Government to perform his functions in accordance with the Edict of 31 December 1999 No. 1761 (SZ, 2000 No. 1. P.2). The only extra presidential elections in the constitutional practice of Russia were held on 26 March 2000.

The Constitution of 1993 establishes two grounds for the removal of the President from office: high treason or grave crime (Article 93.1). Previously that procedure could be initiated on the basis of the violation of the Constitution, a law or the presidential oath. The Criminal Code currently in force classifies as treason any actions consisting of espionage, disclosure of state secrets to a foreign State or organization or their representatives, as well as assistance in their activity aimed at damaging the national security of the Russian Federation (Article 275). A crime punishable by deprivation of freedom from five to ten years may be classified as grave (Article 15.4).

A proposal to file an accusation may be put forward by at least one-third of the deputies of the Lower Chamber of the Federal Assembly (State Duma) (Article 93.2 of the Constitution). In that case a special commission is formed to check the reasons of the accusation and ensure compliance with the established procedure. On the basis of the conclusion of the commission, the Chamber makes a final decision that must be approved by two-thirds of deputies by secret ballot or by nominal ballot papers. Within five days a resolution of the State Duma is passed to the Upper Chamber of the Federal Assembly – Council of the Federation. To begin the hearing the Upper Chamber must have the opinion of the Supreme Court confirming that the actions of the President contain the elements of a crime, and of the Constitutional Court regarding the compliance with the procedure established for filing an accusation. The President of the Russian Federation, the Chairman of the Government, members of the special commission of the State Duma, and the Chairmen of the Supreme and the Constitutional Courts of the Russian Federation are invited to participate in the meeting of the Council of the Federation. The decision, regarding the removal of the President from office, must be adopted by the Upper Chamber within three months after the accusation was first filed. The President's term ends prematurely if two-thirds of the members of the Council of the Federation approve the accusation.

89. In 1998, a proposal to file an accusation against Boris Yeltsin was put forward by the deputies of the State Duma. The initiators of the proposal accused the President of committing several crimes:

(1) break-up of the Soviet Union caused by the conclusion of the Belovezh Agreement of December 1991 (Article 64 of the Criminal Code of the RSFSR);[34]
(2) seizure of power resulting in the use of violence against the Supreme Soviet of the RSFSR that led to the infringement of the rights of the deputies and caused the death of peaceful citizens during the fire at the White House (Articles 64, 70, 102, 171 of the Criminal Code of the RSFSR, Articles 195, 188, 278, 280 of the Criminal Code of the Russian Federation);
(3) use of the armed forces in the Chechen Republic as a result of the order of the President, acting as the Supreme Commander-in-Chief, regarding measures to restore the constitutional legality and law and order in the territory of that republic (Article 171 of the Criminal Code of the RSFSR, Article 286 of the Criminal Code of the Russian Federation);
(4) undermining of the defence potential of Russia and the break-up of the armed forces (Article 275 of the Criminal Code of the Russian Federation);
(5) actions in the process of reforms leading to the genocide of the Russian people (Article 357 of the Criminal Code of the Russian Federation).

On 19 June 1998, a special commission was formed in which all the factions and groups were represented proportionally. On 15 May 1999, a vote by nominal ballot papers took place in the State Duma. The proposal did not gain the established number of votes. At the same time, it should be remembered that all the accusations were supported by the majority of the deputies of the State Duma: the issue regarding the use of the armed forces in the Chechen Republic received the most votes (284), whereas the accusation of the genocide of the Russian people had the lowest number of votes (238).

II. Incompatibility, Immunity and Unaccountability

90. The Constitution of 1993, unlike that one of 1978, does not give special attention to the issue of incompatibility of the presidential office. We may conclude that in such a case, the general rules regarding the separation of powers and admissibility of teaching, scientific or other creative activities may be applied. The previous legislation regulated this issue rigidly. The President had to be politically neutral and suspend his party membership during his mandate. The office was incompatible with the status as a people's deputy, any other state office, appointment in commercial or social bodies and associations, as well as with business undertakings.

The Constitution applies the principle of immunity to the President without any limits (Article 91) and no other federal law regulates this aspect of his status. The President cannot be subjected to criminal proceedings or administrative measures. He is not responsible to Parliament for his actions and does not need to enjoy the support of the Chambers, except in the impeachment proceeding. Russian law does not give special protection to the President and the general provisions concerning the commitment of crimes against public officials may be applied to the Head of

34. The Criminal Code of the RSFSR was in force until 1 Jan. 1997.

State. The Criminal Code currently in force penalizes encroachments on the life of a state official which aim to stop his governmental or political activity or which are out of revenge (Article 277), or insults connected with official duties (Article 319).

III. Personal Powers

91. All the powers of the President are personal. In accordance with the Constitution he has the right to act on his own in many cases. Russian law does not know the concept of divided powers or require a countersigning of his acts, although sometimes a federal law may provide for it. For instance, an instrument of ratification of an international treaty is signed by the President and countersigned by the Minister of Foreign Affairs. The division of powers under the current system of government presupposes that the principal decisions of the President are not subject to parliamentary control. The President of Russia has vast personal powers, and there is no formal machinery to curb them except in the case of an impeachment proceeding. It is necessary to take into account that the person, occupying the post of the Russian Federation President since 1991, is not a party member and thus does not depend upon a party programme or party solidarity. (Putin, while being the head of political movement 'Popular Front', created in the 2000s, is nominally not a member of that movement). Probably it may be seen as some sort of constitutional convention or custom. It is necessary to note also that, on the other hand, the Federal Law as it now stands does not ban a nomination of a party member to run as a candidate in the Presidential elections.

§3. Competence

I. The Powers of the President Are Broader than Enumerated Ones

92. In comparison with previous legislation, the Constitution of 1993 substantially broadens the powers of the President and limits the possibilities of parliamentary control of his basic decisions. Besides that, it establishes no restrictions upon his powers, whereas earlier, the President could not use them to transform the state structure or to dissolve or suspend an activity of any legitimately elected organ of state power. The interpretation of the constitutional provisions by the Constitutional Court authorized a further expansion of the presidential powers. According to the Judgment of 31 July 1995 (SZ, 1995 No. 33), the President must act in accordance with a procedure established by the Constitution. When this procedure is not stated in detail and concerns powers not listed in the Articles 83–89 of the Constitution, their common framework is determined by the principle of the separation of powers (Article 10 of the Constitution) and the requirement of Article 90.3 according to which edicts and orders of the President should not contradict the Constitution and the federal laws. The Russian constitutionalists point out the tendency of the broadening of the presidential powers by means of the adoption of federal laws: the legislators granted to the first President, B. Yeltsin (1991–1999), 168 new powers, to the second President, V. Putin (first term, 2000–2004, second term, 2004–2008), 234 powers, to the third President, D. Medvedev (2008–2012), 32 powers.[35] The powers granted to the current President, Putin, within his second term of 2012–2018, are detailed in the Amendments to the Constitution of 5 February 2014 and 21 July 2014.

II. Powers Regarding the Federal Assembly

93. The President calls elections of the State Duma. His powers in this field are limited, for he acts within a framework rigidly determined by a federal law. And even in the case when the President for some reason does not use his powers, the election will take place after the expiry of the mandate of the State Duma under the guidance of the Central Electoral Commission. The President plays an important role in the legislative process. He has his plenipotentiary representatives in the State Duma and in the Council of the Federation who inform the Chamber about the position of the President and advocate it in the process of the parliamentary discussions. Unlike his colleagues in the US and France, the President has the right of legislative initiative and uses it quite frequently (e.g., forty-eight draft laws arising from presidential initiative in 1997 and thirty-eight in 1998). As a rule, the President submits drafts of general importance (e.g., Civil and Criminal Codes). Joint initiatives are not so common. One of the rare examples was the Federal Constitutional Law of 31 December 1996 'On the Judicial System of the Russian Federation' (SZ, 1996 No. 49), as amended on 5 February 2014, initiated by the President and the deputies of the State Duma altogether.

If the Council of the State Duma takes a decision to include a draft law in the calendar of the Chamber, a draft is sent to all persons enjoying the right of legislative initiative. The common practice is that the President submits his opinion upon every draft law after its adoption in first reading. If the President considers that a part of this draft law is not in compliance with the Constitution or, on the contrary, that it is a law of general importance (e.g., constitutional amendments or electoral issues) he may submit his opinion before the first reading. When many amendments are included in the text of a draft law after the first reading, the State Duma may ask the President to present his opinion upon the revised text before second reading. This tactic is applied when the Chamber is interested in resolving all disagreements in advance in order to speed up the legislative proceeding and escape the application of the presidential veto. For instance, this method was applied in the process of adoption of the Federal Law of 24 June 1999 'On the Election of the Deputies of the State Duma of the Federal Assembly of the Russian Federation', as amended on 29 February 2014, in force since 5 April 2016.

The President signs and promulgates federal constitutional and ordinary laws, and submits them for official publication. According to the Constitution, he has the power of veto regarding federal laws and cannot suspend the coming into force of federal constitutional laws. A suspending veto may be used with regard to an entire law. Sometimes the President may return a federal law to the Chamber on the basis

35. M.A. Krasnov, 'Polnomochia Presidenta Russian Federation, delegirovannye zakonodatel'stvom', in *Gosudarstvo i pravo: Vyzovy XXI veka* (Moskva: Elit, 2010), 59.

of non-observance of the rules of the legislative proceeding established by the Constitution. The most common reason is the lack of an opinion of the Government regarding the expenditures funded out of the state budget. The Constitutional Court in its Judgment of 22 April 1996 (VKS, 1996 No. 3) considered this practice admissible. In 1998, the President of the Russian Federation signed 193, rejected 67 and returned 9 federal laws, whereas in 1997 the number of rejected and returned laws was respectively 74 and 11.

There were several serious controversies between the President and the Chambers in this area. For half a year the President refused to sign the Federal Constitutional Law 'On the Government of the Russian Federation' adopted by the State Duma on 11 April 1997 and approved by the Council of the Federation on 14 May 1997 (SZ, 1997 No. 19), in force since 17 December 1997, as amended on 3 July 2016. According to the President, some provisions were in conflict with the Constitution. At last the conflict was solved by a compromise: the signing of this federal constitutional law was conditioned on the requirement to approve amendments submitted by the President. The conflict of competence regarding the signing of the Federal Law 'On the Cultural Values Transferred to the Soviet Union as a Result of the Second World War and Located on the Territory of the Russian Federation' was resolved by the Constitutional Court in its Ruling of 6 April 1998 (RG, 21 April 1998). The President returned the law adopted by the State Duma and approved by the Council of the Federation twice (in May and June 1997) arguing that the constitutional provisions concerning the legislative process had not been observed. The President put forward several reasons: the members of the Council of the Federation voted through questionnaires (one of the methods of voting provided for by the standing orders of that Chamber), and the Deputies of the State Duma had not observed the rule of personal vote, for a quorum of deputies had not been present. The Constitutional Court held that the President was not competent to ensure compliance of the standing orders with the constitutional provisions and obliged the President to sign the law. The Court stressed that nothing prevented the President from applying to the Court to control the constitutionality of that law, but that preliminary control was not within Presidential sphere of competence.

Every year the President informs the Federal Assembly about the basic guidelines for foreign and domestic policy. The full version of the Message is submitted in written form to the members of the Council of the Federation and the deputies of the State Duma. The abridged version is presented by the President personally at a joint meeting of both Chambers in the Kremlin. Unlike the Italian practice, no discussion takes place. The Federal Assembly does not formulate an answer.

94. The early dissolution of the State Duma is a Presidential prerogative, although it has not yet been used once. This procedure may take place only in connection with the process of forming a government, when the State Duma rejects three times the candidates submitted for the post of the Chairman, or with a motion of non-confidence. Taking into account the constitutional provisions, the right of dissolution may be classified as a personal choice of the President, who is not obliged to motivate his decision or have preliminary consultations with the higher state officials.

At the same time, the Constitution restricts this power in relations to the Lower Chamber (Article 109.3–109.5). Its dissolution should not be used during: first, a state of emergency or martial law, second, within the last six months of a presidency, and third, after the filing of accusations against the President by the State Duma. Fourth, the dissolution based on the non-confidence motion is not valid within a year following the election of the Chamber.

III. Powers Regarding the Judiciary

95. The President appoints directly the judges of all the federal courts, except for those of the highest ones (Article 128.2 of the Constitution). An average number of appointments is about 1,000 judges per year. As for the justices of the superior instances (the Constitutional Court (including its Chairman since 2009) and of the Supreme Court) the President, however, shares de facto his powers with the Upper Chamber. These judges are appointed by the Council of the Federation, but only upon the proposal of the President (Article 83(f)). It is necessary to emphasize at the same time that the President has no right to dismiss judges. It is one of the balances within the system of the division of powers. The procedure of appointment of the Procurator General is similar, but in his case the President may also submit a proposal to the Upper Chamber to remove the latter from office.

Under President Boris Yeltsin there were several serious disagreements between the President and the Upper Chamber of the Federal Assembly dealing with the appointment or removal from office of the Procurator General. In April 1994, the President appointed an acting Procurator General and submitted his candidacy to the Council of the Federation, which rejected it several times. In 1999, the Council of the Federation refused three times to approve the discharge of the Procurator General. Since 2000, there were no examples of such sort in the Russian constitutional practice.

At present, the President, according to the Amendment to the Constitution of 5 February 2014, has also received the right to dismiss every procurator officer across Russia, except for those of a city and *raion* scale. There is however no analogous provision concerning President's power over dismissing judges.

96. The President grants pardons (Article 89(c) of the Constitution). It is necessary to note that the President issues edicts concerning individual cases upon application of interested persons, whereas the State Duma is empowered to declare a general amnesty (Article 103(f) of the Constitution) and grant pardons to convicted persons belonging to a certain category or having committed a certain type of crime. The President has established a Commission for the preliminary examination of the applications of convicted for pardon, in 2001 it was abolished and the appropriate commissions were established in the constituent entities. The Department on the ensuring of the constitutional rights of citizens, a subdivision of the Administration of the President, supervises the enforcement of the presidential edicts in this field, generalizes the practice and statistics and completes archives.

IV. Powers Regarding the Government

97. Although the President is not the head of the executive power, he has vast opportunities to guide, influence and control the activity of the Government of the Russian Federation. Besides the fact that he has discretionary powers in its creation, he may give direct instructions dealing with matters within his power to any federal minister over the Head of Government. The considerable number of bodies of federal executive power like the Federal Security Service, the Frontier Guard Service, the Federal Body of State Registration of Communications (*Roskomnadzor*), the Central Electoral Commission, the Federal Migration Service, the Federal (Public) Archives, the Economic Council, and so on, are directly subordinated to him. The President is entitled to chair the meetings of the Government (Article 83(b) of the Constitution). He may dismiss it, abrogate its acts or issue an edict dealing with matters within the competence of executive power.

V. Regulatory Powers

98. The President issues edicts and orders (Article 90.1 of the Constitution). Particularly, some guidelines important for the status and behaviour of civil service employees are contained in Presidential Edict No. 680 'On the Officials Reports Regarding Their Conflicts of Interests' of 22 December 2015. It regulates provisions and procedures of personal accountability regarding conflicts of economic and political interests within the State public service. As a rule, edicts may have normative and individual character, whereas orders may be applied only to individual persons or relations. For instance, by edict of individual character, the Head of State has dismissed in the 2010s several high officials of Federal Entities on the basis of 'loss of confidence' (*see* further paragraph 213). The President regulates the procedure for exercising his constitutional powers, and upon the proposal of the Government approves the regulations establishing the status of federal bodies of executive power subordinated to him by normative edicts. An individual act may be issued in the event of appointment, granting of an award or rank, citizenship or pardon.

VI. National Defence and Foreign Affairs

99. The President of the Russian Federation as the Supreme Commander-in-Chief of the Armed Forces of the Russian Federation determines the basic guidelines of military policy and approves the military doctrine of the Russian Federation (Article 83(h) of the Constitution). At present the basic guidelines of military doctrine are approved by Edict No. 146 of 5 February 2010 (SZ, 2010 No. 7). The provisions of the military doctrine may be concretized in the messages of the President to the Federal Assembly and corrected within the framework of the strategic military planning. He approves the nuclear weapons programme and other special tests and gives authorization to perform such tests. The President appoints and dismisses the High Command of the Armed Forces (Article 83(k) of the Constitution). He issues orders and directives whose enforcement is obligatory.

100. The President represents the Russian Federation in international relations, determines the basic guidelines of foreign policy and exercises guidance over it (Articles 80.3, 80.4, 86(a) of the Constitution). He conducts negotiations, signs the international treaties of the Russian Federation and instruments of ratification, accepts credentials and letters of recall of accredited diplomatic representatives, and appoints and recalls diplomatic representatives of the Russian Federation in other States and international organizations (Articles 86(b)–(d), 83(l) of the Constitution). The President establishes the proceedings for coordination of the international and external economic contacts of the Federal Entities upon a proposal of the Government.

101. The President heads the Security Council (Article 83(g) of the Constitution). Under the provisions of the Federal Law of 28 December 2010 'On the Security' (SZ, 2011 No. 1), as amended on 5 October 2015, and Edict No. 715 of 25 May 2012 'On the Security Council of the Russian Federation', as amended on 11 April 2016, the Council is a deliberative body which prepares the decisions of the President in the sphere of national security, defence, military building, defence industry, military and technical cooperation of the Russian Federation with the foreign countries and in the other spheres connected with the protection of the constitutional system, sovereignty, independence and territorial integrity of the Russian Federation, international cooperation in the field of national security. The members of the Security Council are appointed and dismissed by the President and take part in its meetings in person: they cannot delegate their powers to any other official. The members and the Secretary of the Security Council may not have a citizenship or a residence permit in the foreign country.

There are permanent and ordinary members of the Council, the latter have deliberative vote only. Among the permanent members of the Council, ex officio, are the Chairman of the Government, Chairman of the State Duma and the Council of the Federation, the federal Ministers of Defence, Internal and Foreign Affairs, the Director of the Federal Security Service, the Head of the Administration of the President. The Procurator General, Mayor of Moscow, President of the Russian Academy of Sciences, the Directors of the Frontier Guard Service and the Federal Control Service on the drugs circulation, several representatives of the President in the federal districts, as well as federal Ministers of Finance, Justice, Internal Affairs and Emergency Situations have the status of ordinary members. The Security Council develops and specifies the strategy of the national security of the Russian Federation, examines the draft laws and legal acts within the sphere of its jurisdiction, prepare the drafts of the legal acts of the President on national security.

The President is a Head of the Consultative Economic Council (Edict No. 818 of 31 October 2013 'On the Economic Council of the Russian Federation', as amended on 30 April 2016). Also the President is the Chairman of the State Council imposed according to the Presidential Edict No. 129 'On the State Council of the Russian Federation' of 1 September 2000, as amended on 9 April 2014. That body is unknown in most states. It includes, as members, the Speakers of the Lower and Upper Chambers of the Federal Assembly, parliamentary leaders of parties in the

State Duma and, if necessary and by invitation, high officials of the executive bodies of the Federal Entities (part of them at the same time are members of the Council of the Federation). The State Council meets at least three times annually. Politically, it is a mechanism of maintaining relations between the Head of State and (1) the legislative branch and (2) regional leaders.

VII. Other Powers

102. Unlike his French colleague, the President of Russia calls referenda (Article 84(c) of the Constitution), but cannot initiate them. In accordance with the Federal Constitutional Law 'On the Referendum of the Russian Federation' of 28 June 2004, as amended on 6 April 2015, a popular voting may take place on the basis of a popular initiative (not less than 2 million citizens) or upon an initiative of the Constitutional Assembly that may refer a draft of the new Constitution to the popular vote.

Before the adoption of the Constitution of 1993, the Congress of People's Deputies was empowered to call a referendum upon a popular initiative (not less than 1 million citizens) or the request of the one-third of the people's deputies (the RSFSR Law of 16 October 1990 'On the Referendum of the RSFSR'). In 1993, President Boris Yeltsin took the decision to hold a referendum on the draft of the new Constitution on his own initiative, without congressional authorization (Edict No. 1633 of 15 October 1993).

103. The President resolves citizenship matters (Article 89(a) of the Constitution). He gives Russian Federation citizenship and reverses such decisions; reinstates citizenship and gives permission for the withdrawal from it. All the petitions dealing with these matters are submitted to the President through the governmental bodies which exercise migration control or the diplomatic or consular institutions. Each petition is examined by the Commission on citizenship matters established by the President. The President examines the proposals of the Commission and takes decisions on the individual cases. The total amount of petitions was 15,000 in 1998 and 10,000 in 1997 (RG, 18 May 1999).

104. The President grants political asylum to foreign citizens and stateless persons in accordance with generally recognized norms of international law (Articles 89(a), 63.1 of the Constitution). The regulation on the procedure of the examination of petitions and granting asylum was approved by Edict No. 746 of 21 July 1997 (SZ, 1997 No. 30) in the wording of 27 July 2007.

Asylum is granted to persons seeking protection due to persecution or a real danger of being subjected to persecution in their national country or a country of their habitual residence for reasons of socio-political activity and convictions that are in compliance with democratic principles recognized by the international community and norms of international law.

A petition is submitted to the President through a territorial agency of the Federal Migration Service. The Service conducts a preliminary examination and asks the Ministries of Internal and Foreign Affairs and the Federal Security Service for their opinions, and then submits its proposals to the Commission on the citizenship matters. Taking into account the national interests of the Russian Federation and the proposals of the Commission, the President decides whether or not he will grant political asylum. Edicts on granting asylum are not so common among the presidential acts. The President may reverse his decision and deprive a foreign citizen or a stateless person of the status of political refugee for reasons of national security, because of his actions being contrary to the rules and principles of the United Nations, or because of his conviction for a crime.

105. The President has vast powers and needs a special apparatus for ensuring his activity. Those functions are performed by the Administration of the President, mentioned in the Constitution (Article 83(i)). It is classified as a state body and plays an important political role in the current system of government in Russia. It has a large staff (more than 1,000 persons). The Head of the Administration is the state official 'of highest influence' and a member of the Security Council ex officio.

It is a substantive feature of Russian Federation constitutional order after 1993 that the President has plenipotentiary representatives in both Chambers of the Federal Assembly, in the Constitutional Court, in the Supreme Court and in every federal district of the Russian Federation. These persons are classified as federal state servants belonging to the Administration of the President. Those persons are appointed to and removed from office by the President at pleasure (Article 83(j) of the Constitution) and discharged in the event that the President ends his term of office prematurely. Apart from that, the duration of their term of office is not defined by law.

Certainly within Russian constitutionalism there is a tangible trend since the mid-2000s and through the 2010s to extend the Presidential power sphere, first of all in relations between the Head of State and the Executive. At the same time, that power is far from being yet an absolute one. Still, there are balances to the power of the President concerning his relations with the legislative and judicial branches (for more, *see* below Chapters 3 and 4).

Chapter 3. The Legislature

I. Bogdanovskaia & T. Vassilieva

§1. The Organ of State

I. Bicameral System

A. Introduction

106. Russia has no strong tradition of representative democracy. A bicameral parliament (the State Duma and the State Council) with limited powers was organized in the Russian Empire at the beginning of the twentieth century but soon it was replaced by the Soviet model in three successive forms: the first – a two-level representative body, the Congress of Soviets and the All-Russian Central Executive Committee (ACEC, *see* above paragraph 8) elected by it; the second – the bicameral one-party Supreme Soviet; the third – the Congress of People's Deputies and the bicameral Supreme Soviet elected by it. The present bicameral Federal Assembly is the fifth type of representative body. In contrast with the Soviet models, the Federal Assembly is an independent body in the system of the separation of powers. It is based on the idea of people's representation and people's sovereignty. The Constitution of Russia of 1993, for the first time in Russian constitutional practice, had used the term 'parliament' concerning the federal representative body. As a representative body, the Federal Assembly represents the entire multinational people (Lower Chamber – State Duma) and Federal Entities (Upper Chamber – the Council of the Federation). The State Duma consists of 450 members elected by the popular vote (Article 95.3 of the Constitution). Any citizen aged 21 and older having the right to take part in elections may be elected to that Chamber. This rule does not apply to persons declared incapacitated by a court or deprived of their freedom by a court sentence (Article 32.3 of the Constitution), as well as to persons having a citizenship or a residence permit of the foreign state, a conviction for a grave and special grave crime or for a crime that has an extremist nature.

The Council of the Federation consists of two representatives from each Federal Entity: one from the representative body thereof and one from the executive body (Article 95.2 of the Constitution). The rules concerning the formation of this Chamber were not stable. The members of the first Council of the Federation were elected (Edict of the President of 11 October 1993 No. 1626 'On the Elections to the Council of the Federations of the Federal Assembly of the Russian Federation', Bul. CEC, 1993 No. 3). According to the Federal Law of 5 December 1995 'On the Procedure of Formation of the Council of the Federation' (SZ, 1995 No. 50), as amended on 3 December 2012, the members of the Council of the Federation were the heads of the executive and the legislative (representative) bodies of the Federal Entities. Since 2000, the representatives of the constituent entities work in the Chamber on the permanent and professional basis, one of them is elected by the legislative (representative) body and another is appointed by the high state official of the constituent entity (Federal Law of 5 August 2000 'On the Order of Formation of the Council of the Federation', SZ, 2000 No. 32), as amended on 3 July 2016. Under the amendments adopted by the Federal Law of 14 February 2009, a member of the Council of the Federation may be appointed a citizen of Russia aged 30 or older, who does not have another citizenship or a residence permit in any foreign country. In accordance with the Amendment to the Constitution of 21 July 2014, a share of the Council members, appointed by the President, may not exceed 10% of main corps of the Upper Chamber. (The Head of State has not used this power yet). Under that Amendment there is one guarantee for the members: an Upper Chamber member, who is not a Presidential appointee, may not in any case be dismissed by the President during the member's first term in office.

A representative of the legislative body of a constituent entity may be elected among the members of the regional parliament or the deputies of the municipal representative bodies of that entity and must resign after the election to the federal parliament. This amendment entered into force on 1 of January 2011, and on that very day ceased its force amendment adopted by the Federal Law of 21 July 2007, in accordance of which the member of the Council of the Federation might be a person who lived at least ten years totally on the territory of that constituent entity. Though the State Duma and the Council of the Federation are not equal in status and have different lists of powers, they in fact demonstrate more a 'division of labour', than a division and balance of powers. Together, as the Federal Assembly, they fulfil representative and legislative functions.

B. Reasons for the Bicameral System

107. Russia has a bicameral representative body because it is a federal State having a wide expanse. The State Duma expresses the interests of the whole people while the Council of the Federation represents the interests of the Federal Entities. This Chamber has powers concerning federal matters and relations within the Federation.

In a federation, the upper chamber may be elected and the Federal Entities are represented by an equal number of members (e.g., in the US each state elects two senators). In other federal States, the Federal Entities may elect the members of the upper chamber to a differing number of seats, according to their respective proportion of the population (as in Austria and Australia, for example); or members of the upper chambers may be appointed (as in Canada). In Russia, the Federal Entities have equal representation in the Council of the Federation. Unlike the German Bundesrat, the Council of the Federation, being a Chamber of the Federal Assembly, represents not only the governments of the Federal Entities but also their representative bodies. The Council of the Federation represents de facto the regional elite. The participation of the regional elite in decision-making on federal issues has to promote uniformity in the government of the Federation. Note that members of the Council of the Federation are officially *members* of that Chamber (the media and the general population often call them 'senators'), while members of the State Duma are officially *deputies*.

II. Classification of Members of Parliament

108. The members of the Council of the Federation do not organize political associations. During a long period, when a single-member plurality system was used at the parliamentary elections, deputies of the State Duma formed two kinds of associations: deputy caucuses and deputy groups, the latter consisted of independent deputies. Deputy groups consisted at least of thirty-five members, since 2003 – of fifty-five members. Caucuses and deputy groups had equal status and were registered by the Temporary Secretariat and later by the Committee on the Standing Orders. A deputy might be a member of only one association. Deputies were not strictly bound by the 'party' discipline. As the political party system was in the process of formation, the deputies were not afraid to leave associations because of their future political career; they had a possibility to organize new associations or become 'independent' deputies. Now the deputies are elected in accordance with the party-list system, and therefore there are no party groups in the State Duma. After the elections of September 2016 to the State Duma the picture of the political forces in the lower chamber is the following: the caucus of 'Unified Russia': 343 seats (313 in the previous election); KPRussian Federation (Communist Party): 42 seats (57 in the previous election); LDPR (Liberal Democratic Party): 39 seats (40 previously); 'Just Russia':– 23 seats (38 previously); others, 3 seats (3 previously). According to the Federal Law of 8 May 1994 'On the Status of the Member of the Council of the Federation and on the Status of the Deputy of the State Duma of the Federal Assembly of the Russian Federation' (SZ, 1994 No. 2), as amended on 3 May 2016, a State Duma deputy may change his caucus (party affiliation) without termination of his powers only in the case of a dissolution of the party providing he is not currently a member of it. It is necessary to note that under the provisions of the Federal Law of 11 July 2001 'On Political Parties' (SZ, 2001 No. 29), as amended on 9 March 2016, representatives of those political parties which do not have deputies in the State Duma may take part in its plenary meeting at least once a year.

III. Electoral System

109. The elections to the State Duma are regulated by the Federal Laws of 12 June 2002 'On the Fundamental Guarantees of the Electoral Rights and the Right to Participate in Referendum of Citizens of Russian Federation' (SZ, 2002 No. 24), in the wording of 9 March 2016, and of 18 May 2005 'On the Elections of the Deputies of the State Duma of the Federal Assembly of the Russian Federation' (SZ, 2005 No. 21), in the wording of 5 April 2016. In examining the Russian electoral system, it is necessary to note that Russian elections are held in the country with political parties in the process of formation. Before the adoption of the Federal Law of 18 May 2005 the State Duma was elected in accordance with the 'mixed' electoral system (225 deputies were elected according to the proportional party-list system in federal constituency with 5% 'threshold' and 225 according to the majority one in the single-member territorial constituencies). In 2008, the 'threshold' rose to 7%. And since 2005 only political parties, not movements or independent candidates, could take part in parliamentary elections. In 2009, the privileges were granted to the minority parties: those associations which achieved more than 5% but less than 6% of votes were guaranteed a mandate, two mandates were guaranteed to parties which had more than 6% and less than 7% of votes. Because of this, smaller parties held three seats in the Lower Chamber since 2011 election. In accordance with the Federal Law of 17 May 2016 'On Increasing of Financing Political Parties' every party represented in the Lower Chamber and receiving no less than 6% of votes during the most recent parliamentary elections gets a fixed subsidy paid out the federal budget: RUB 152 per vote (versus RUB 110 up to 2016). This has much in common with the current electoral system of Germany.

One-seat electoral constituencies are formed for a ten-year term. The most scarcely populated one is Altay (around 200,000 inhabitants); the most populated is Moscow City (around 12,500,000 inhabitants). In accordance with the Federal Law 'On Adopting Scheme of One-Seat Constituencies for Electing Members of the State Duma' of 30 November 2015, in force since 1 January 2016, the distribution of seats between eighty-five Federal Entities of Russia is the following:

One seat	Thirty-two entities
Two seats	Twenty-six entities
Three seats	Six entities
Four seats	Ten entities
Five seats	Three entities
Six seats	Two entities
Seven seats	Two entities
Eight seats	Two entities
Eleven seats	One entity
Fifteen seats	City of Moscow

As for presidential elections, all the Russian Federation territory is treated as a single electoral constituency (Article 4 of the Federal Law 'On the Election of the President of the Russian Federation').

110. The electoral process consists of several stages. The first stage begins with the calling of elections by an edict of the President and finishes with the registration of candidates; the second stage is the electoral campaign itself; the third one is voting day; and the fourth is the tallying up of the results. The elections are universal, equal, direct and by secret vote.

A. *Electoral Bodies*

111. The electoral administration of Russia at parliamentary elections consists of electoral commissions: central, regional, territorial (*raion*, city and others) and district which constitute a system. The decision of the inferior electoral body may be appealed to a higher standing body or to a court. The Central Electoral Commission is formed on an equal basis by the President, the State Duma, and the Council of the Federation (in total fifteen members) for a five-year term (Articles 20.1 and 21.3 of the Federal Law of 18 May 2005 'On the Election of the Deputies of the State Duma of the Federal Assembly of the Russian Federation', as amended on 5 April 2016. The electoral bodies of the Federal Entities are formed by the legislative and executive bodies of constituent entities. The territorial and district commissions are formed by the higher standing commissions. The polling stations are formed also for five years. If an electoral riding has no more than 1,000 electors, a polling station may have from 3 to 9 workers; between 1,001 and 2,000 electors, from 7 to 12 persons; and any number of electors above 2,000 persons within the riding demand up to 16 workers at the polling station.

The law foresees counter-corruption measures. At any level of the system, deputies, the heads of local administration (mayors), judges, prosecutors, spouses and close relatives of candidates and their spouses cannot be members of electoral commissions (Article 29 of Federal Law 'On the Fundamental Guarantees of the Electoral Rights of the Citizens of the Russian Federation … ').

B. Electoral Constituencies

112. For the election of deputies a federal electoral constituency including all the Russian territory is formed. Those electors who live outside the territory of the country are considered attached to that constituency, but they may vote in the embassies at the place of their residence.

C. Electoral Lists

113. All citizens not younger than 18 years old living in the territory of a constituency are registered by the local electoral bodies and included in electoral lists. The lists are checked twice a year. The electoral lists are presented for public viewing not later than twenty days before the elections. The local electoral commission must examine complaints regarding mistakes in the electoral lists. The decision of the commission may be appealed to a higher standing commission or to a court. If any citizen cannot be present in his constituency on voting day, they had the right to receive in advance from the local electoral polling station an 'otkrepitelnyi (detaching) talon', a certificate for voting outside the constituency, and thus to exercise their voting right in any other constituency across Russia. That control procedure, Soviet-born and regularly creating public discontent, was annulled in 2017 by the Federal Law of 1 June 2017 On Amendments to Federal Law 'On Election of the President of the Russian Federation' for Presidential elections, but it remains implemented in parliamentary and municipal elections. Simultaneously, a procedure of detaching was made more flexible (Article 27.4.1): it was entrenched that a citizen who cannot vote at his domicile address may, by submitting a relevant request, get permission not only to go to his local polling station (the old condition) but also to the local Centre of the newly created Multifunctional Service (a new condition).

D. Nomination of Candidates

114. After the declaration of the election day, candidates may be nominated, and they must submit their personal data to local electoral commissions. Lists of candidates may be submitted to the electoral commissions only by the registered political parties. The list must be accompanied by the party report on its income and expenditures before the campaign. Any party may have only one list of candidates, which must be approved by its congress or conference. Law provisions regulating the personal status of a candidate are rather minimal. Candidates must be Russian citizens not younger than 21 years old. Army officers and judges have a right to be candidates, but their functions as a judge are suspended during the electoral campaign. Up to 2005, candidates might be party members or persons not belonging to any party, but in any case a list of candidates may not consist of more than 50% of non-party members. A list of candidates in Russian parliamentary elections forms a single bloc or entirety: electors may not vote for individual candidates. But a list may be divided into federal and regional parts. The federal part may not include more than ten candidates. A regional part is divided into regional groups of candidates representing a constituent entity. A regional group may represent not more than 3 million and not less than 650,000 electors. A regional part must include all the constituent entities, and the total number of regional groups may not be less than 80. Any person having the right to be elected (passive electoral rights) may initiate his or her nomination through a regional branch of a political party. If his candidacy is supported by ten members of that party, it must be examined by a party conference.

115. The lists of candidates are submitted to the Central Electoral Commission together with the necessary documents within 30 days after the publication of the decision on calling elections. The parties submitted their lists, except the parliamentary ones, must collect 120,000 signatures of electors, among which only 5% may belong to the same constituent entity and the signatures of electors living abroad may not exceed 5,000. All data may be verified. The signatures recognized non-valid may not be more than 5% of all signatures otherwise registration is declined. The decision of the Central Electoral Commission on registration of the federal list of candidates may be appealed to the Supreme Court of Russia within five days. Before the last Presidential election of 2018 no less than ten such appeals were submitted from various places of Russia. Every appeal was rejected by the Supreme Court (*see*, e.g., the Appeals Definitions of the Supreme Court of Russian Federation of 24 January 2017, of 12 and 25 January 2018, of 5 and 22 February 2018).

E. Electoral Campaign

116. In accordance with the Federal Law 'On the Fundamental Guarantees of Russian Federation Citizens Rights for Participation in Electoral/Referendum Affairs of Russian Federation' of 12 June 2002, as amended on 5 February 2018, electoral campaign at the federal level in Russia may exceed at least forty days. (At the regional level, that figure is not less than thirty days, and the municipal level, not less than twenty days). Up to 2007, parties and other public associations enjoyed a right to form electoral blocs/coalitions at all levels of electoral process. The blocking of parties and other associations is cancelled since 2007 at the federal level.

The electoral campaign is the most important and the most visible part of the electoral process and takes place between the registration of candidates and voting day. At this stage, the candidates officially work with the electorate. It is forbidden by law to provide electors a free service, to present gifts or to pay money to electors. In such cases, the court may decide to revoke the registration of a list of candidates. The electoral bodies control the use of mass media and secure equal rights for all candidates. Each party participating in elections has to establish at the outset an electoral fund. An electoral fund may be established by a regional branch of a party, if it has a regional group in a federal list.

In period of the electoral campaign any party must submit two financial reports indicating its sources of income and reasons for expenditures, the first one simultaneously with the submission of a list of candidates; the second one, after voting day, within thirty days after publication of the results of elections. No one-party candidate is permitted to spend more than RUB 40 million in any constituency during the campaign period. Because of the scrupulous conditions in the legislation, cases of financial abuse during electoral campaigns since 2000s are rather rare.

F. Voting Day

117. According to the current federal legislation, voting day for regular election of State Duma deputies has to be announced by the President of Russia no earlier than 110 days before the expiry of the term of powers of the State Duma and no later than 90 days before. Voting days for election to bodies of constitutional entities and local self-government until 2010 were set by the appropriate bodies of State power on their own. Since 2011 procedures of voting at these elections are synchronized with voting days for the State Duma elections if elections at both levels take place in the same year. If not, elections of high officials have to take place on the second Sunday of September. Voting day in the Presidential election is set by the Upper Chamber of the Federal Assembly.

Of note are the current provisions of Article 102 of the Federal Law 'On the Elections of Deputies of the State Duma of the Federal Assembly of the Russian Federation'. Its version of 5 April 2014 claims that the 2016 elections to the Lower Chamber must take place on the third Sunday of September of that year. Nevertheless it is still not possible to conclude whether this must become the convention or guideline thereafter.

Other ways of expressing the electorate's will, such as voting by post or by proxy (as used in some Western states), are not foreseen by the Russian Constitution or federal legislation (like the Soviet one). However, in the 2010s that method of voting began to emerge for the first time in Russian constitutional history in regional and municipal elections. Currently at least seven Federal Entities, including the City of Saint Petersburg and Murmansk, allow and in fact use voting by post. The Constitutional Court of Russian Federation had recognized that such practice does not contradict the Constitution (Decision of the Constitutional Court of 15 April 2014; VKS, 2014, No. 3).

An elector may vote only in person. Disabled voters and those in hospital are served by polling station personnel who provide them access to ballots and polls. Like most states, participation in elections at any level is voluntary and not compulsory in Russia.

G. *Results of Election*

118. The Central Electoral Commission determines the results of the election in the federal electoral constituency. The lists of candidates that have received more than 7% of votes take part in the distribution of the mandates, if there are at least two parties which achieved that result and they represent more than 60% of electors who took part in this parliamentary elections. It is necessary to note that the Constitutional Court in its Judgment of 17 November 1998 (SZ, 1998 No. 48) pointed out that the 5% barrier could be unconstitutional if only one electoral association has passed it, as it would be contrary to political pluralism and democracy. At the same time, the Constitutional Court held that it was necessary to estimate this provision very carefully, because in different political situations it might have different results and to some extent limit proportional representation. The votes given for the lists of candidates are divided into 225 – the number of deputy mandates (electoral quota). The number of votes given for each list of candidates is divided by the electoral quota. Mandates are redistributed according to the method of the greatest remainder of the votes.

§2. Legal Status

I. Mandate of the Member of Parliament

A. *Representative Character of the Mandate*

119. The present Constitution fundamentally changes the status of the deputy.[36] All Soviet Constitutions supported the idea of the imperative mandate, of the electors' control over the deputies who worked in a non-professional capacity ('without resigning the main workplace'). They had the right to recall at any time a deputy who was not able to fulfil his obligations or who performed them in an unsuitable way. According to the current law, deputies have a free mandate while fulfilling their parliamentary duties on a professional basis.

36. M. Baglai considers that Russia is only on the way to the free mandate of the deputies because some features of the previous system have been kept (e.g., to make reports to the electors concerning the deputy's activity). *See*: M.V. Baglai, *Konstitutsionnoie pravo Rossiiskoi Federatsii* (Moskva: Norma, 1997), 536.

A member of the Council of the Federation represents the entities of the Russian Federation while a deputy of the State Duma is an elected representative of the people. A deputy of the State Duma works on a permanent basis. The members of the Council of the Federation represent legislative and executive bodies of the constituent entity.

B. The Term of the Mandate

120. Since 30 December 2008, the State Duma is elected for a five-year term (previously, a four-year term). That amendment to Article 81 of the Constitution is intended to strengthen the positions of the Lower Chamber of the Federal Assembly in the system of organs of State power. Yet, on the other hand, it has increased the distance between the Chamber and electorate. The powers of the State Duma expire from the day when the newly elected Chamber begins its work. In the case of the dissolution of the State Duma, the powers may cease before the end of term.

121. The mandate of a deputy of the State Duma begins from the day of the election and is terminated on the day of the beginning of the work of the newly elected State Duma. The term of a member of the Council of the Federation is determined by the term of the powers of the legislative or the executive body of a Federal Entity. His or her mandate begins from that very day when a decision on his or her appointment (election) is entered into force. A member of the Council of the Federation starts his or her work on the tenth day after entering it into force. A mandate is terminated on the day of entering into force a decision on appointment (election) of his or her successor. A deputy's mandate may be terminated earlier by his own written statement; if he forfeits the Russian citizenship or becomes a citizen of a foreign state; if he is elected into another representative body or to another elected post (outside the Federal Assembly), becomes a civil or municipal servant; if a court sentenced him for criminal actions or declares him dead; if he is declared incapacitated or if he dies. Of course, a mandate of the member of the Council of the Federation may be terminated preliminary by the legislative or executive body of the Federal Entity, and a deputy's mandate is discontinued in the case of dissolution of the State Duma. The latter is terminated as well if a deputy leaves his caucus in accordance with his written statement. A Chamber adopts a resolution regarding the discontinuance of a deputy's mandate in which the day when the power of a deputy terminated is indicated.

II. Incompatibilities, Immunities and Privileges

A. Incompatibilities

122. A deputy of the State Duma cannot be at the same time a member of the Council of the Federation, and *vice versa*. According to the principle of the separation of powers, a deputy of the State Duma or a member of the Council of the Federation cannot be a member of the Government (as is also the case under the

French and US constitutional models too). An exception has been made for the deputies of the first State Duma in the 1990s. A deputy of the State Duma cannot be a member of any other representative body of the state or local self-government. He may not work as a state civil servant or have another source of income except for teaching, research or another creative activity, as prescribed by the Federal Law 'On the Status of the Member of the Council of Federation and of the Deputy of the State Duma of the Federal Assembly of the Russian Federation'. That Law has no clear-cut provisions concerning conflicts of interest and remains therefore a subject of fierce debate. Still, the legislation does not specify who and what criteria defines, for example, whether the term 'creative activity' covers various sorts of business activities, which may indeed include considerable elements of creativity and at the same time does not exclude receiving commercial profit. There is no check in law prescribing who has the right of a decisive vote in case of any dispute. The chief reason of such a situation, quite impossible in Western democracies, is that the lengthy absence of legally protected private property and profits has left a considerable deficiency in the legal regulation of all matters at the junction of personal economic interests and civic duties. The Federal Law 'On Control over Incomes and Expenditures of State Officials' (SZ, 2012 No. 49) had been called for since the early 1990s but was adopted only on 3 December 2012 (as amended on 3 November 2015). Long awaited and desired by public opinion, that Law, however, is desired by the judiciary. And even apart from that, it is hard to argue that members of Federal Assembly are state officials (nominally they are not).

B. Guarantees of the Deputy's Activity

123. Under the provisions of Federal Law 'On the Status of the Member of the Council of the Federation and Status of the Deputy of the State Duma of the Federal Assembly of the Russian Federation', as amended on 3 May 2016, a deputy of the State Duma and a member of the Council of the Federation have the rights and duties that are traditional for deputies of legislative bodies.[37] They take part in the meetings of their Chamber, work in the commissions, committees and deputy caucuses, have the right of the legislative initiative, and work with electors. For the fulfilment of his or her duties, a deputy must receive the necessary information. In Parliament, he or she may ask oral and written questions and make inquiries. State and municipal bodies and organizations must submit relevant information within thirty days and consult the deputy on issues within their respective competence. A deputy has the right to take part in the meetings of those bodies and organizations regarding the examination of issues put in his question or inquiry. A deputy has access to the mass media when he needs to inform electors about matters decided or in preparation. The materials cannot be edited without his consent.

37. V.A. Chetvernin, 'Garantii deputatskoi deiatelnosti', in *Konstitutsia Rossiiskoi Federatsii. Problemni Kommentari*, ed. Chetvernin (Moskva: Jurispridentia 1997), 418.

C. Immunities

124. Deputies of the State Duma and members of the Council of the Federation enjoy immunity during their whole term of office. They cannot be arrested, searched or examined without the agreement of the corresponding Chamber, except if they are detained at the place of the commitment of the offence. The immunity of a deputy extends to his home, car, office, documents and communications. No deputy may be prosecuted or sued for the opinions expressed in the exercise of his functions. But a deputy is responsible for public insult or libel. A deputy may refuse to give testimony concerning his activity. A deputy may be deprived of his immunity by an order of the Procurator General of Russia with the consent of the Chamber.

D. Indemnity and Benefits

125. A deputy receives a salary equivalent to the salary of a federal Minister. The Chairman of the State Duma receives a salary equivalent to that of the Chairman of the Government. In the case of dissolution of the State Duma, a deputy is paid an allowance equivalent to three of his salaries. The deputies and their families who are not Moscow residents are supported by the State on their arrival to Moscow, during their residence in Moscow and on their way back. The law guarantees the labour rights of a deputy. After the end of his term, he may return to his previous place of work. Deputies of the State Duma and the members of the Council of the Federation must lodge annually tax declarations and information about all their income and property (but yet not about expenditures).

§3. COMPETENCE

I. Legislation

126. The legislative powers are the main powers of the Federal Assembly as a representative body. The Constitution names it a representative (and legislative) body. The leading role in the lawmaking is played by the Lower Chamber – the State Duma, as the Upper Chamber – the Council of the Federation must examine only some categories of acts adopted by it, and the State Duma may override the position of the Council of the Federation.

II. Supervision of and Control over the Executive

127. The number of powers of control depends upon the form of government. The Russian Parliament has different forms of control over bodies of executive power entrenched in the Federal Law 'On Parliamentary Investigation of the Federal Assembly of the Russian Federation' of 27 December 2005, as amended on 28 December 2010, and 'On Parliamentary Control in the Russian Federation' of 7 May 2013, as amended on 9 March 2016. Some of them have legal consequences (participation of deputies in the nomination of the Chairman of the Government, votes of non-confidence, and procedures of impeachment). Other forms of control are aimed at collecting information from executive bodies (questions, enquiry). The power of investigation of executive bodies is still not used by the Federal Assembly.

A. *Participation in the Appointment of the Prime Minister*

128. The State Duma exercises control over the executive powers giving consent to the appointment of the Prime Minister. The candidate and the programme are debated. The decisions concerning the candidate must be supported by the majority of all deputies of the State Duma.

B. *Vote of Non-confidence*

129. A vote of non-confidence in the Lower Chamber is a de facto censure vote, transplanted to the Russian constitutional model from the French Fifth Republic. The vote may be initiated by the State Duma, as well by the Government (Article 117 of the Constitution). The motion may be suggested by not less than one-fifth of the deputies of the State Duma. The State Duma takes its decision within seven days after the submission of the motion of non-confidence. After the submission the Chairman of the Government has the right to address the State Duma. The deputies may ask questions. The State Duma has a right to adopt resolution of non-confidence by a simple majority, by open or secret ballot. Usually the Chamber prefers to use a secret ballot. Up to the present date in the constitutional practice of Russian Federation, there is no case of resignation of the Government in connection with a resolution approved by the State Duma.

C. *Questions*

130. A deputy or a group of deputies may ask questions to a member of the Government of Russia. The State Duma determines the time for asking and answering questions. The questions may be oral or written. A member of the Government may be invited to the State Duma. If he is not able to come, the questions may be answered in written form. The Chairman of the State Duma reads the answer to the State Duma. Each Wednesday the State Duma has a so-called ‘government hour’ (a rough equivalent to ‘Question Period’ in many Parliaments). This time is used for taking the answers of the federal ministers or other state officials on questions and inquiries of the deputies. The conditions of ‘government hour’ are favourable to members of the Government. Over the course of ninety minutes the minister has twenty minutes for basic information, three minutes for an answer and five minutes for conclusions. During the ‘government hour’ the answers of ministers are not debated but the representatives of the caucuses may make their comments during five minutes.

The Government presents annually a report regarding the results of its activity to the State Duma. A report is made by the Head of the Government during the spring session. Beforehand the caucuses may formulate their questions to the Government. The questions approved by the Council of the State Duma are submitted to the Government.

D. Inquiry

131. This form of control may be used in both Chambers. A deputy or a group of deputies of the State Duma, a member or a group of members of the Council of the Federation may make inquiries concerning the activity or inaction of the Government as a whole, the Procurator General of Russia, the Chairman of the Central Bank, the heads of the federal executive bodies of Russia and entities of the Russian Federation, and local government bodies on issues within their respective powers. A deputy or a group of deputies may insist on introducing an inquiry in a Chamber. Such inquiry is introduced in written form only. The answer may be made in oral or written form.

There is in the Russian constitutional order a special Federal Law of 27 December 2005 (SZ, 2006 No. 1), as amended by the 28 December 2010 Law 'On Parliamentary Investigation of the Federal Assembly'. It stipulates that the Chambers of the Federal Assembly have the power to form Commissions on Investigation. The purpose is declared as the protection of human rights and freedoms guaranteed by the Constitution (Article 1 of the Law). An Investigation Commission is filled by equal numbers of persons from both Chambers, with two co-chairpersons. Such Commission must function on the basis of openness ('*glasnost*', transparency). All its materials have to be published afterwards without omissions. All persons summoned by the Commission must appear and cooperate. The Law contains relevant provisions regulating liability for a refusal to answer questions of the Commission members, for presenting false information, for avoiding explanations, and so on. At the same time, foreseen are rights for the persons summoned: a right against self-incrimination and having to testify against close relatives, and a right to counsel. This suggests to us that the Law aims to develop the Federal Assembly as a vital instrument of democratic control. Adopting the Law meant deviating from a totalitarian stereotype of parliamentary silence on public events occurring within the state. Without doubt, however, it is possible still to discover in the letter of the Law various indicia of the influence of the doctrine and practice of parliamentary supremacy.

Nevertheless, the spirit of the Law produces a steady stream of criticism from specialists and the public in general (as well as the one-party dominance in the State Duma). The subject of the Assembly's investigative powers is too narrowly defined. Outside of the sphere of parliamentary control remain all the situations occurring in Russia up to 2006, any activities of the President, activities of all the courts, action and inactions by regular bodies of preliminary investigation (police forces, Investigation Committee and personnel). Apart from this, it is unclear for example how to understand the expression 'activity' and whether the Commission has a power to investigate the activities of political parties, deputies at any level, private corporations, and so on. The Commission has no power to define independently the limits of official secrets. The Commission apparatus is recruited from the apparatus of the Chambers which contain too few lawyers by training. The Head of the Commission has no right to invite experts at his discretion. One-party dominance in the Lower Chamber, de facto established in the 2000s, limits potential Commission prospects. As a result, for the recent twelve years – a period marked by serious public events within Russia (a recent one occurring in the City of Kemerovo, Siberia, in March 2018, and the most fresh one, in the City of Magnitogorsk, Ural, on 31 December 2018) – the Chambers of the Federal Assembly have never established an Investigation Committee.

E. Procedure of Impeaching a President

132. The procedure was never foreseen in Russian Empire laws or in the USSR constitutional order either. Both chambers of the Federal Assembly take part in the procedure of Presidential impeachment (*see* paragraph 88). In theory, it appears to form a considerable check and balance to the vast powers of the Head of State. The procedure was used against President Boris Eltzin in the 1990s. After 1999, however, there was never any attempt to implement the procedure.

F. Control of the Central Bank of Russia

133. The relations between the State Duma and the Central Bank of Russia are regulated by the Constitution and by Federal Law 'On the Central Bank of the Russian Federation (Bank of Russia)' of 10 July 2002, as amended on 3 July 2016. All issues concerning relations of the State Duma with the Central Bank are initially examined by the Committee on budget and taxes, which makes a report to the State Duma. The Chamber appoints or dismisses the Chairman of the Central Bank on the proposal of the President of the Russian Federation (Articles 103.1(c), 83 of the Constitution). The State Duma appoints members of the Council of Directors of the Central Bank upon the proposal of the Chairman of the Central Bank and with the consent of the President of the Russian Federation.

The Central Bank presents every year an annual report to the State Duma, confirmed by the Council of Directors. The State Duma submits the report to the President and to the Government. Annually, the Central Bank presents before 26th of August a project and before 1st of December the basic guidelines of the state credit and monetary policy.

III. Power to Appoint Members of Other Bodies

134. The power of the Chambers to appoint or dismiss members of other bodies is determined by the principle of the separation of powers. The State Duma nominates the Chairman of the Audit Chamber, while the Council of the Federation nominates his deputy. The powers of either Chamber are balanced by the powers of other bodies or officials. Either the President appoints or dismisses an official with the consent of a Chamber (e.g., the Procurator General) or a Chamber appoints a candidate upon the proposal of the President. The Council of the Federation appoints, on the recommendation of the President, the judges of the Constitutional Court of the Russian Federation, of the Supreme Court of the Russian Federation (Article 102.1(g) of the Constitution, *see* below paragraph 95). The two Chambers use the power to appoint members of other bodies separately even when it concerns the same bodies, as in the case of the Audit Chamber and the Central Electoral Commission. Each Chamber has the power to appoint half of the members of the Audit Chamber and one-third members of the Central Electoral Commission. The candidates for office in the Audit Chamber are nominated by the President. Candidates must comply with the requirements of the Federal Law 'On the Audit Chamber of the Russian Federation' of 5 April 2003, as amended on 3 July 2016. The candidates for the Central Electoral Commission (except for its Head) are proposed by the deputies and deputy caucuses of the State Duma. There is a different procedure in the Council of the Federation: candidates for the Commission members posts are suggested by the legislative and executive bodies of the Federal Entities. The merits of the candidates are debated and a decision is taken on a basis of simple majority of votes.

IV. Foreign Affairs Power

135. International relations are within the powers of the President and the executive bodies of State power. However, these powers are exercised with the consent of both Chambers of the Federal Assembly. The President or the Government submits to the State Duma a draft law on the ratification, denunciation or suspension of any international treaty. The State Duma issues declarations on Russian foreign policy or international relations. They may be initiated by the subjects of the legislative initiative. Each Chamber adopts plans of international contacts with foreign Parliaments. The Chambers may conclude agreements with foreign parliaments and international parliamentary organizations.

V. Other Powers of the Council of the Federation

136. The Council of the Federation approves the changes of borders between the entities of the Russian Federation (Article 102.1(a) of the Constitution). It examines the matter with the mutual accord of the Federal Entities whose borders are going to be changed. The legislative (representative) bodies of those members take corresponding decisions. The issue is examined by the Committee on federation issues and regional policy. Within thirty days, the conclusion of the Committee is presented to the Council of the Federation. The representatives of the concerned Federal Entities and of the Government take part in the work of the Committee and in the meeting of the Chamber. The Federal Entities and the executive bodies are informed by the Council of the Federation about the decision within a week.

137. The Council of the Federation examines and approves or rejects the edicts of the President concerning a state of emergency and martial law (Article 102.1 of the Constitution). Those edicts of the President are immediately submitted to the Council of the Federation and must be examined by the Chamber within forty-eight hours in the case of a state of emergency and within seventy-two hours after its proclamation in the case of martial law. If the edict is not approved, the state of emergency is terminated after seventy-two hours after its proclamation.

The Council of the Federation gives (or rejects) its permission for using the Armed Forces outside the territory of the Russian Federation (Article 102.1(d) of the Constitution). This issue is debated at the initiative of the President. Initially, it is examined at the meeting of committees on defence and security, on international affairs and on the CIS of the Upper Chamber with participation of the plenipotentiary representative of the President of the Russian Federation. This issue is examined at the nearest meeting of the Chamber or at the extraordinary meeting. The President, the Chairman of the Government and the heads of the appropriate federal bodies of executive power (of Defence and of International Affairs) are invited to this meeting.

§4. Working

I. Parliamentary Proceedings

138. The proceedings are regulated by the Standing Orders (the code of rules of proceedings) adopted by each Chamber by the majority of their members (Decree of the State Duma of 22 January 1998 'On the Standing Orders of the State Duma of the Federal Assembly of the Russian Federation' (SZ, 1998 No. 7), as amended on 14 January 2011, Decree of the Council of the Federation of 31 January 2002 'On the Standing Orders of the Council of the Federation of the Federal Assembly of the Russian Federation' (SZ, 2002 No. 7), as amended on 15 December 2010). In both Chambers, their members, committees and commissions may suggest amending or revising the Standing Orders. This right is granted as well to the caucuses of the State Duma and to the group of members of the Council of the Federation. In order to ensure that the Standing Orders are respected, both Chambers form special committees: on the Standing Orders and parliamentary activity in the Council of the Federation and on the Standing Orders and organization of the work of the State Duma. Those committees may suggest revising the Standing Orders or amending them, consult the members and officials of the Chamber and interpret the Standing Orders.

A. *Sessions of the Chambers*

139. According to Article 99.1 of the Constitution, the Federal Assembly is a permanently functioning body (like the Senate in France). The State Duma convenes for its first session on the thirtieth day after the election. The President of the Russian Federation may convene a session of the State Duma before this term. The

State Duma has Spring and Autumn sessions. Usually they take place from 12 January until 20 June and from 1 September until 25 December. The Council of the Federation works from 25 January until 15 July and from 16 September until 31 December. The meetings of that Chamber must be held at least twice per month. The terms of the convocation are established by the Standing Orders that secure the independent character of the legislative body. The Chambers sit separately. However, a deputy of the State Duma has the right to present at the meetings of the Council of the Federation, and a member of the Council of the Federation has the right to present at the meetings of the State Duma. The Chambers hold joint sessions only to hear the messages of the President and of the Constitutional Court, and speeches of foreign leaders. In contrast with the Soviet representative bodies, the Federal Assembly does not have a joint body of the Chambers (like the Presidium of the Soviet or Chairman of the Supreme Soviet). Each Chamber has its own bodies and standing orders; there are no standing orders for joint meetings of the Chambers since they must take decisions separately.

140. The State Duma sits three times per week: on Tuesdays, Wednesdays and Fridays. The morning session lasts from 10.00 until 14.00 with a break from 12.00 until 12.30, the evening session from 14.00 until 18.00. A 'voting hour' takes place at 17.00. A 'government hour' (an equivalent to the 'Question Period') is held on Wednesday from 12.30 until 14.00. The meetings of commissions and deputy caucuses are held on Thursdays. The meeting of the Chambers may be open or closed. For instance, the President of Russia, the Chairman of the Government, the Chairman of the meeting of the Chamber, a committee or commission supported by at least twenty-five members may suggest an *in camera* meeting of the Council of the Federation. That is considered quite undemocratic and is applied therefore quite rarely.

141. Extraordinary meetings of the Council of the Federation may be convened upon the proposal of the President of Russia, Chairman or Council of the Chamber, committee or commission supported by one-fifth of the members of the Chamber on the issue within its jurisdiction, or a group of at least one-third of the members of the Council. In the State Duma, extraordinary sittings are called by the Council of the Duma at the proposal of the President, a demand of a deputies' caucus supported by at least one-fifth members of the Chamber, or the suggestion of the Chairman. Russian is the working language of the Chambers. If a deputy wishes to speak in his native language, the Council of the Duma must be informed, and the speech will be translated simultaneously.

B. The Chairmen of the Chambers

142. Each Chamber constitutes its own internal bodies, as the Federal Assembly is an independent body in the system of the separation of powers. The Chambers elect their Chairmen. The Chairman of the State Duma and his deputies are elected by secret ballot, but the Chamber may take a decision to hold open election too. In the State Duma, the candidates for this post are nominated by the caucuses, and their selection is debated in the Chamber. In the Council of the Federation, the candidates are submitted by members. The Chambers determine the number of vice-chairmen (in the Upper Chamber there is a post of the first deputy). In the State Duma, vice-chairmen of the Chamber must represent different parliamentary parties, and vice-chairmen in the Council of the Federation – different Federal Entities.

The Chairmen of the Chambers have similar functions: they lead the work of a Chamber, ensure the legislative process, represent a Chamber and direct the activity of its staff, conduct the meetings of a Chamber and keep order. The Chairmen are controlled by the Chambers. Any Chairman act may be abolished by the Chamber if it is not in conformity with legislation or the Standing Orders (up-to-date, there were no precedents).

C. The Council of the Chamber

143. Now both Chambers of the Federal Assembly have its internal Councils, which are formed to prepare and examine the issues of their activity (in the State Duma – only organizational issues). This body consists of the Chairman, deputy chairmen of the Chamber in both cases. In the Council of the Federation, the heads of the committees and commissions are its permanent members, but in the State Duma they may take part in the meeting of the Council with deliberative vote. A deputy or a member of the Council of the Federation may be present at the meeting of the Council and make suggestions concerning the agenda. The Council of the State Duma prepares a plan for the legislative work of the session, as well as a monthly thematic calendar and the agenda for the day's meeting. It convenes extraordinary sittings of the Chamber and decides to send a bill to the corresponding committee. In the Council of the Federation, this body approves the schedule of the meetings and their agenda, adopts declarations on political and socio-economic issues, convenes parliamentary hearings. A Chamber may repeal any decision of the Council. However, there were no such precedents in the Russian Federation parliamentary practice.

D. The Procedure of Voting

144. The decisions of the Chambers are taken by open or secret ballot. Open ballots may be by name. That procedure is used rarely. The electronic system, which has become a traditional in both Chambers since the 1990s, may be used for quantitative, alternative, qualitative and rating voting. 'Quantitative' voting means voting 'for', 'against', or 'abstention'. 'Alternative' voting means voting only for one version among several proposed. 'Rating' voting means quantitative voting on each question. 'Qualitative' voting means alternative voting for 'very bad', 'bad', 'satisfactory', 'good' or 'very good'. The decision on voting by name is made by a majority of the deputies taking part in the voting. In the case of voting by name, a deputy has the right to receive lists with results. As a rule, the decisions of the State Duma are taken by the simple majority of votes, if another procedure is not provided for by the Constitution. Procedural questions are decided by the majority of the deputies taking part in the voting. Every deputy has one vote and must exercise the right in person. The decision regarding the secret ballot is taken by the majority of deputies that took part in the voting. In the event of a secret ballot, a paper-ballot (used rarely) or electronic system (foremost) is used.

E. The Committees and the Commissions of the Chambers of the Federal Assembly

145. Both Chambers form internal profile committees for a term of mandate and permanent and temporary commissions. According to the Standing Orders, the Chairman of the State Duma may not be a member of any committee. In the Council of the Federation, the Chairman and deputy Chairman may be a member of the temporary commissions, but not a member of profile committee or permanent commission. A deputy of the State Duma may be member of only one committee, a member of the Council of the Federation – of one committee and two commissions. As an example of a parliamentary committee, the State Duma Committee on Ethics examines and resolves matters connected with conflicts of economic and political interests of the deputies.

The Chambers determine the number of members of these bodies: in the State Duma committees, as a rule, consist of not less than twelve and not more than thirty-five deputies, in the Council of the Federation committees (except on budget) consist of seven to fifteen members, commissions – of eleven to twenty-five members. In the State Duma the committees are organized according to the proportional representation of the deputy caucuses. Their chairmen and deputy chairmen are elected by the Chamber. The total number of deputies who are elected chairman or a deputy chairman of a committee may not exceed 50% of the total number of members of a caucus. In the Council of the Federation, a chairman and deputy chairmen are elected by the committees and commissions. Those persons may not represent the same Federal Entity. As a rule, the meetings of the committees are open, but they can also be closed. At the meetings of committees, deputies and members of the Council of the Federation who are not their members may be present with deliberative vote. Experts and mass media may be invited. The committees have their meetings at least twice a month. The committees may hold their meetings outside federal capital in other Federal Entities (up to the present date, there are no precedents). Meanwhile, Soviet constitutionalism had never known that right even on paper.

The committees of the Chambers have many powers. The committees of the State Duma conduct preliminary examination of bills; prepare reports to the State Duma as well as requests to the Constitutional Court; and organize parliamentary hearings. The committees may establish their own procedural rules. They may invite officials to take part in their meetings. State bodies and social organizations must present the required materials and documents to the committees.

II. The Legislative Process

146. The legislative process is regulated by the Constitution and the Standing Orders of the State Duma and the Council of the Federation. They establish different processes for drafts of federal laws and constitutional laws, financial laws, drafts on ratification, and denunciation or suspending of international treaties.

The right of legislative initiative belongs to the President of the Russian Federation, the Council of the Federation, its members, deputies of the State Duma, the Government of Russia and the legislative (representative) bodies of the entities of the Russian Federation. The right of the legislative initiative also belongs to the Constitutional Court of the Russian Federation and the Supreme Court of the Russian Federation on issues within their competence. In total, there are several hundreds of subjects of legislative initiative, including more than eighty bodies of State power, in the Russian Federation. It is much more than in the Russian Empire in 1905–1917 or in the USSR altogether. Probably it is a historical record among federal states of the world. Initially, the deputies introduced the greater part of the drafts, but now a government and presidential drafts are prevailing. For years, there are just a few initiatives of all other subjects combined.

Draft laws are submitted primarily to the State Duma. Under the provisions of Article 104.3 of the Constitution the draft laws on the introduction or abolishing of taxes, exemption from the payment thereof, on the issue of state loans, on changes in the financial obligations of the state and other draft laws providing for expenditures covered from the federal budget may be introduced only with the corresponding resolution of the Government of Russia. The Council of the State Duma includes a draft law into the legislative plan and informs all governmental bodies interested in the bill. Before first reading, a draft law is examined in committee, as determined by the Council of the State Duma. A draft law may be sent to governmental bodies or to research institutes for expert's review. The Council of the State Duma or the committee may ask the Legal Department of the State Duma to provide an opinion on the coherence of a draft law with the current legislation. Deputies of the State Duma may also submit their comments and opinions concerning a draft law to the committee. A party having the right of legislative initiative may make changes to the text of the draft law. The committee combines the amendments and reports to the Council of the State Duma not later than fourteen days before the hearing in the Chamber. The draft laws on the issues of the joint jurisdiction must be sent to the legislative and high executive bodies of state power of the constituent entities not later than forty-five days before its examination in the Chamber.

147. Although Russia never was and is not a parliamentary democracy yet, in some procedural issues the Chambers of the Federal Assembly follow the Westminster (British) parliamentary model. As a rule, draft laws pass three readings. On the first reading, the general concept of a bill is discussed. Then, a draft law is sent to the profile committee. On the second reading, a report is made by the chairman of the committee. Any amendments are debated and voted upon. A bill may be adopted, rejected or adopted in general. An adopted draft is directed to its committee for technical elaboration. On the third reading, the bill is debated in general. On some occasions deputy units, supported by the majority of the deputies, may suggest returning a draft law to a stage of second reading. A draft law is adopted by the majority of all deputies. The law adopted by the State Duma is sent to the Council of the Federation for review within five days.

The Council of Federation has limited legislative powers. According to the Constitution (Article 106), the following laws adopted by the State Duma must be examined in the Council of the Federation: the federal budget, federal taxes and duties, financial, currency, credit and customs regulations, laws regarding money emission, ratification and denunciation of international treaties of the Russian Federation, the status and protection of the state border, and war and peace. Other federal laws adopted by the State Duma may also be examined by the Council of the Federation. The law and corresponding documents are registered during an hour and within twenty-four hours distributed between the members of the Council of the Federation. The Chairman of the Council of the Federation or his deputy sends the act to a profile committee or to several committees. If a law is on the issue of joint jurisdiction the information regarding the position of bodies of state power of the constituent entities must be submitted as well.

148. The committee reaches a conclusion about the need to examine the act at the meeting of the Council of the Federation or approves an act without examination within seventy-two hours after its submission. If the Council of the Federation does not examine a law which compulsorily ought to have been examined within fourteen days, the law is considered to be approved and is sent to the President for signing and promulgating.

If the Council of the Federation decides to examine an act, it is considered to have been approved if over a half of the total number of members have voted for it. Federal constitutional laws must be adopted by three-fourths of the members of the Council of the Federation. An adopted law is directed to the President within five days. A law adopted by the State Duma which is not examined by the Council of the Federation within fourteen days is sent to the President on the fifteenth day.

If the Council of the Federation rejects the law adopted by the State Duma, it is sent back to the State Duma within five days. The State Duma may agree with the position of the Council of the Federation and adopt it in the wording proposed by the Council of the Federation. The corresponding committee of the Council of the Federation confirms this and suggests the Council of the Federation approve an act adopted by the State Duma for the second time without debate. If the State Duma agrees with only a part of the amendments of the Council of the Federation, the law is examined by the Council of the Federation again in the same way as the first time. The committee of the Council of the Federation may propose adopting the law as amended by the State Duma, or to refuse again to adopt it. A conciliatory committee may be organized on the initiative of the State Duma or the Council of the Federation. The committee analyses each position and may change the text of the law. Each position is voted on in the Chambers and adopted by the majority of the deputies. If the State Duma rejects the results of the work of the conciliatory committee and refuses the position of the Council of the Federation, the bill may be voted on again in the wording adopted by the State Duma. Such a bill is adopted by the two-thirds majority of members of the Chamber. The Chairman of the State Duma informs the Council of the Federation and sends the law to the President.

149. An adopted law is submitted to the President of the Russian Federation for signing and promulgation. The President must sign and promulgate it within fourteen days. However, the President may return a federal law without examination if to his mind the constitutional procedure was not followed. The President has the right of a suspensory veto. If the President rejects a law within fourteen days, it may be adopted in the version suggested by the President. If the State Duma decides to adopt an act as amended by the President, each option is voted. A law so adopted by the State Duma is sent to the Council of the Federation.

A vetoed act may also be adopted in the old wording. If the Chamber decides to vote an act in the first wording, it must be adopted by a majority of not less than two-thirds of the total number of members of the Council of the Federation and the State Duma.

A federal law adopted by the Federal Assembly and signed by the President must be published (*see* Federal Law 'On Procedure of Publishing Federal Laws' of 14 June 1994, as amended on 25 December 2012).

According to the data of the State Duma, during the summer session of 2009 the correlation between drafts introduced, adopted and rejected was the following: 697 drafts were introduced; 220 laws were adopted by the State Duma; 6 laws were rejected by the Council of the Federation; and 220 laws among which 3 constitutional laws and 28 laws on ratification were signed by the President. During the autumn session of 2009, 433 drafts were introduced; 174 laws were adopted by the State Duma; one such law was rejected by the Council of the Federation and one was rejected by the President; 174 laws (among which 6 constitutional laws and 26 laws on ratification) were signed by the President. Statistics on federal lawmaking for 2009–2014 give the following picture: in 2009 394 federal laws came into force; in 2010, 450; in 2011, 431; in 2012, 334; in 2013, 448; in 2014, 555 ones. For comparison, 225 federal laws were adopted in 2004. Meanwhile, in the 2010s, the lion's share of all laws (around 92%) adopted appeared to be amendments to legislative acts adopted earlier. This shows the necessity of improving the quality of lawmaking process as a whole.

§5. Miscellaneous

150. Like most modern states, Russian law is based on the general principle that laws have no retroactive effect. The Constitution especially indicates that a law, which introduces or increases liability, has no retroactive effect (Article 54.1). The Constitutional Court of the Russian Federation pointed out that laws limiting human rights also have no retroactive effect (Judgment of 23 June 1992, VKS, 1993 Nos 2–3). The problem of retroactive effect of laws is of particular importance in the criminal law sphere. In the Soviet period, criminal laws could have retroactive effect. The Constitution 1993 established that nobody may be liable for an action which was not regarded as a crime when it was committed. If, after an offence has been committed, the extent of liability is lifted or mitigated, the new law is applied (Article 54.2).

At the same time, a legislator may indicate in a law that it has a retroactive effect. For example, some provisions of the Law of the Russian Federation of 24 December 1992 'On the Basis of the Housing Policy' had retroactive effect.

Chapter 4. The Executive

T. Vassilieva

§1. The Organ of State

I. The Process of Forming a Government

151. Under the current system the President has a dominating influence upon the process of forming a Government.[38] As a rule, it begins after a newly elected President enters office (Articles 111.2, 116 of the Constitution). The Government does not lose its powers after the parliamentary elections. The President nominates a candidate for Chairman of the Government. A nomination is his personal choice; he does not conduct negotiations or consultations with representatives of political parties or state officials. The only restriction on the presidential power is a time limit established by the Constitution: a candidate must be submitted to the State Duma within two weeks after the President's entry into office.

However, the appointment of the Chairman of the Government by the President may take place upon the consent of the State Duma. At the meeting of the Lower Chamber of the Federal Assembly, a candidate presents his programme outlining the basic policy guidelines for a new Government, but this programme is not subject to approval. The Constitution of 1993 gives the President legal possibilities to insist upon his choice. First of all, he may propose candidates to the State Duma three times, and any proposal must be examined within a week following its submission (Article 111.3 of the Constitution). In August and September 1998, President Boris Yeltsin presented the candidacy of Viktor Chernomyrdin twice, and every time it was rejected by the State Duma. The Constitutional Court of the Russian Federation held in its Judgment of 11 December 1998 (SZ, 1998 No. 52) that the President is competent to determine whether he submits the same candidate or presents a new one. If the Chamber rejects the proposals three times, the President is entitled to appoint the Chairman of the Government nonetheless, dissolve the State Duma and call extra parliamentary elections (Article 111.4 of the Constitution). Nevertheless, the State Duma cannot be dissolved within the last six months of a presidency and during a state of emergency or martial law, or after having filed accusations against the President (Article 109.5, 4 of the Constitution). According to the previous (up to 1993) legislation, in case of disagreement upon the candidate for Chairman of the Government, the President is entitled to appoint acting Chairman for three months, and then recommend a new candidate to the Chamber.

---

38. *See* I.L. Bachilo (ed.), *Ispolnitel'naia vlast' v Rossiiskoi Federatsii. Problemy razvitia* (Moskva: Jurist, 1998); Nozdrachev & Yu.A. Tikhomirov (eds), *Ispolnitel'naia vlast' v Rossiiskoi Federatsii* (Moskva: BEK, 1996); A.G. Barabashev, 'Parlament i Pravitel'stvo v Rossiiskoi Federatsii', in *Konstitutsionnyi stroi Rossii.* 2nd ed. Glushko, Kozlov & Stepanov *(Moskva: Institut gosudarstva i prava, 1997)*, 77–84.

152. The Chairman submits to the President proposals regarding a structure of the federal bodies of executive power not later than a week after his appointment. Insofar as the Constitution does not enumerate those bodies or determine their types, the proposals are the basis for the structure of a new Government and future nominations. Under the provisions of the Edict of the President No. 314 of 9 March 2004 'On the System and Structure of the Federal Bodies of Executive Power' (SZ, 2004 No. 11) which is in force in the wording of 22 June 2010, the system of the federal bodies was reformed and several types of those bodies were abolished (state committees of Russia, federal commissions of Russia, supervisory inspectorates). In the current structure of the federal bodies of executive power, there are federal ministries, services and agencies. The Edict distinguishes two classes of federal bodies of executive power – those which are subordinated to the President directly and whose functions are determined by the Presidential edict, and those are subordinated to the Government and whose functions are determined by the Governmental decree.

Besides that, the Head of the Government presents the candidates for the offices of deputy chairmen and federal ministers (Article 112.2). The members of the Government must have no foreign citizenship or a residence permit in the foreign country. They are chosen in their personal capacity and not as representatives of political parties, though their political orientation may be taken into account. In the event of disagreements, the President takes a final decision. As a rule, he issues several additional edicts concerning the formation of the Government.

II. Composition and Organization of the Government

153. The Government is comprised of the Chairman, deputy chairmen and federal ministers who perform their functions in accordance with the Federal Constitutional Law of 17 December 1997 'On the Government of the Russian Federation' (SZ, 1997 No. 51) as amended on 3 July 2016. The composition of the Government can vary both in the number of ministers and in their designation. Currently there are two categories of deputies: 'first' and 'ordinary', though this division is not provided for by the Constitution or federal legislation either. A traditional member of the Government is the head of a ministry, while those who are responsible for specific functions are not so typical, although previously in several Governments there were ministers without portfolio. In accordance with an edict of the President, deputy chairmen and federal ministers may hold an office of a plenipotentiary representative of the President in a federal district.

The Russian system of organs of state power does not distinguish the Cabinet from the Government. A Presidium of the Government may be formed for taking operative decisions. The Chairman of the Government puts forward a proposal to this end that must be approved by the collegiate body as a whole. The status of the Presidium differs from that of the Cabinet, as any of its decisions may be rescinded by the Government.

154. According to the Standing Orders of the Government of 1 June 2004 (SZ, 2004 No. 23), as amended on 15 May 2010, issues within the competence of the Government are examined in plenary meetings or by coordinating and consultative bodies. According to federal constitutional law, plenary meetings may take place at least once per month, but as a rule, the Government meets weekly. Currently the representatives of Chambers of the Federal Assembly, highest judicial bodies, Procurator's Office, Investigation Committee, Audit Chamber and Central Bank and other persons may take part in meetings in accordance with the federal legislation and the procedure provided for by the Government.

The normal place of meetings of the Government is the Kremlin in Moscow. However, after 2010 there were several meetings of the Government in the peripheral areas of Russia. It is not excluded that precedents transplanted to Russia from the constitutional practice in some Western democracies may be transformed into Russian legal custom afterwards (*see* above Chapter 2).

Several matters may be decided only by the Government as a whole. This rule applies to the following issues: submission of the federal budget, report on its implementation, budgets of the state extra-budgetary funds, as well as draft laws to the State Duma, examination of draft programmes of economic and social development establishing free economic zones, programmes of privatization of the federal state property, conclusion of international treaties subject to ratification or agreements with Federal Entities, approval of the regulations on federal ministries or other bodies of executive power, adoption of the standing orders of the Government, as well as examination of the annual report to the State Duma on activity of the Government.

The Government forms different types of consultative and coordinating structures (such as governmental commissions, organization committees, interdepartmental committees and councils). They may work on a permanent or temporary basis. As a rule, a decision upon formation, reorganization or abolishment of such structures is adopted at the plenary meetings. These commissions and councils ensuring interdepartmental coordination may submit their proposals, if an issue is to be decided by the Government.

§2. Legal Status

155. Executive power is exercised by the Government as a collegiate body and not by individual ministers (Article 110.1 of the Constitution). As the Government is not a political body, the rule regarding the loyalty of a minister is not formulated very rigidly. While there is no provision in the Constitution and legislation that those members of the Government who disagree with its acts are obliged to resign, their activity 'must be consistent' with the official position of the Government.

The fulfilling of duties in the government (like in any legislative or judicial body) inescapably draws any person into issues of economic and political interests which may lead to a conflict with their own respective ones. According to federal legislation, the office of a Russian Federation Government member is incompatible with any concurrent posting in other bodies of state power or local self-government, businesses and with any activity except teaching, research or creative ones. The shortcomings of these conditions are the same as in the case of those covering the behaviour of deputies (*see* above paragraph 122).

It is necessary to mention that, for a short transitional period, some exceptions were admissible in this regard. The members of the Government could simultaneously be deputies of the first State Duma (1994–1998), but rules regarding the immunity of deputies were not applied to them (ninth Concluding Provision and Transitional Provision of the Constitution). On assuming office, ministers must arrange their affairs so that there is no conflict between their public duties (political interest) and private (economic) interests. After appointment, a member of the Government must inform the tax officials about his income and property situation and the situation of his wife (husband) and of his or her non-adult children. Thereafter, the minister submits this information annually. The tax authorities inform the President and Chambers of the Federal Assembly about a minister's obeying or not obeying that law. Recent legislation, the above-mentioned Federal Law 'On Control over Incomes and Expenditures of State Officials' of 3 December 2012, as amended on 3 November 2015, devotes multiple provisions to that issue. The recent version of the Law regulates scrupulously the order and procedures of financial accounts of any executive official, including members of the Government. Critics, however, emphasize considerable blanks in the regulations: particularly, the conditions mentioned are binding for officials themselves and their spouses, but do not cover adult children, other relatives (brothers, parents, grandparents, etc.) and divorced spouses.

Also any member of the Government of the Russian Federation cannot receive fees for his publications and speeches presented in an official capacity; go to business missions abroad at the expense of physical or legal persons, or be awarded the ranks and honours of other States without the permission of the President.

Federal ministers are subordinated to the Government, and to the President regarding the issues within his competence. On a strictly literal reading of Constitutional articles without considering the practice of their application, the President cannot bypass the Chairman of the Government and dismiss them. However, in practice, Presidential powers in this field are far from nominal. For example, the President has a power to dismiss any minister on the basis of 'loss of confidence'. It was based on this that the federal Minister of Economic Development, Alexey Uliukaev, was fired in December 2016.

As for special rules regarding the criminal liability of the members of the Government or the granting of a pardon to them, there are no such provisions in the Russian law.

156. The Chairman defines the basic guidelines for the activity of the Government and organizes its work (Article 113 of the Constitution) and determines the spheres of competence of his deputies. At the same time de jure his position is not very strong, for the President has the opportunity to influence the activity of the Government via its formation, the determination of the basic guidelines of the external and internal policy and the adoption of important decisions in the sphere of executive power. But de facto it depends upon the personalities of the President and the Chairman and their personal relationship.

When the Chairman of the Government is unable for some reason to perform his functions, he is temporarily substituted by a deputy chairman. The President may remove the Chairman of the Government from office on the basis of a letter of resignation or in the event of an inability to perform his duties. In that case, the President informs the Federal Assembly on the very day when a decision is adopted. The removal of the Chairman from office means the resignation of the Government as a whole. At the same time, the common practice is that after the dismissal of the Chairman, the majority of federal ministers and even several deputy chairmen may continue to perform their functions as members of a newly formed Government. During the Presidency of Boris Yeltsin and Vladimir Putin, the cases of the dismissal of the Chairman of the Government were not very rare. In a year and a half, the President Yeltsin removed from office four Chairmen (on 23 March 1998 – V. Chernomyrdin, on 23 August 1998 – S. Kirienko, on 12 May 1999 – E. Primakov and S. Stepashin in August 1999). In those cases, the President entrusted a deputy chairman to take care of the Chairman's duties for a transitional period not longer than two months. Sometimes the President did not follow this rule very carefully. For instance, in August 1998 (after the dismissal of S. Kirienko), the President empowered V. Chernomyrdin (who was not a member of the Government at that time) to serve as an acting Chairman until a new one took office.

157. The Constitution of 1993 establishes a new balance of powers between the governmental bodies of the Russian Federation. Under the previous Constitution, the Government was subordinated directly to the President who was the head of executive power and to the Parliament which was empowered to form it. At present, it is an independent federal organ of state power at the head of a unitary system of executive power that exercises guidance and control over the federal bodies; coordinates and controls the activity of the bodies of the Federal Entities within the jurisdiction of the Russian Federation and joint jurisdiction; and resolves disputes between the bodies of executive power of the Federation and its entities. Currently, the Government may repeal or suspend the operation of an act of certain federal bodies. As for organs of the Federal Entities, the Government may only submit proposals to the President regarding the suspension of certain acts.

158. There are several procedures for removing the Government from office in the Constitution (Article 117) that are important to note. First, the Government may offer its resignation to the President, who either accepts or rejects it. Insofar as federal constitutional law does not include this matter in the list of issues subject to compulsory examination at plenary meetings, it may be decided by its Chairman. Second, the President may take a decision to discharge the Government at any time and on the basis of any reason, i.e., at his discretion. He is not obliged to notify in advance the Chairmen of the Government or the Chambers of the Federal Assembly or explain the motives of his decision. It should be remembered that according to the previous legislation, such decisions could be made only by consent of the Parliament.

Third, the State Duma may, by means of a majority of votes of the total membership of deputies, adopt a motion of non-confidence in the Government (de facto, it is a censure vote), but applying this power is restricted by the Constitution. The Chamber would need to be very persistent to make the President discharge the Government. Even after the approval of the motion of non-confidence in the Lower

Chamber, the President is not obliged to fulfil the Chamber's will. He announces the dismissal or disagrees with the decision. He must dissolve the State Duma or discharge the Government only if the Chamber expresses non-confidence in the Government for a second time within three months. As a motion of non-confidence may cause the early dissolution of the Chamber, the reasons for initiating such proceeding must be very serious. Usually, a proposition by minor party caucuses to approve that motion cannot collect a majority of votes in the Chamber.

Fourth, the Chairman of the Government may submit to the State Duma a motion of confidence in the Government. If the Chamber refuses to approve it, the President has seven days to take a decision. He may dismiss the Government or dissolve the Chamber. In the event of its resignation or losing its powers, the Government continues to perform its functions until a new Government is formed.

§3. Competence

159. The Constitution determines the main areas of responsibility of the Government (Article 114.1). The constitutional list may be broadened by other provisions of the Constitution, federal laws and edicts of the President. At present it includes financial, credit and monetary policy, and state policy in the sphere of culture, science, education, health protection, social security and ecology. The activity of the Government aims at ensuring legality, the rights and freedoms of citizens, the protection of property and public order and the control of crime. In addition, it manages federal property. Several other areas of its responsibility are determined by federal legislation. Particularly, the Law of Russian Federation of 21 July 1993 'On the State Secrets', as amended on 8 March 2016, gives to the Government, along with the President, a power to overview regime of protection of state secrets in the limitations of powers established by the Constitution, federal constitutional laws and ordinary federal laws. The order and procedures of that protection, norms of access to the state secrets are regulated by the Government, too (Articles 27, 30 and 30.1 of the Law).

I. Regulatory Powers

160. The Government may issue decrees having normative character, and orders dealing with operative matters. Before submission to the Government, draft normative acts are examined by the Ministry of Justice. Execution of governmental acts is mandatory; nevertheless, the President may repeal them if they are not in compliance with the Constitution, federal laws or his edicts. Decrees are subject to official publication not later than fifteen days after their adoption, in the case of necessity they are made public through the mass media without delay. This rule does not apply to those acts which contain state secrets or confidential information. Decrees with the exception of affecting human rights come in force on the day of their signing by the Chairman of the Government if a decree does not provide otherwise. Orders come in force on the day of their signing. The acts of the Government may be subject to judicial review.

II. National Defence and Foreign Affairs

161. The Government adopts measures to ensure the country's defence and state security, organizes the supplies of arms and military equipment to the armed forces, ensures the implementation of the state programmes and plans on the development of arms and on citizens military training, adopts measures for the protection of the State border, ensures the social guarantees for military personnel and exercises guidance over civil defence. It develops and submits to the State Duma proposals regarding the defence expenditures of the federal budget, organizes the elaboration and enforcement of state programmes on arms and on the development of the defence industry, mobilization plans, defines the goals and organization of the civil and territorial defence and ensures general planning in this field. Furthermore, it is empowered to determine grants and uses of natural resources for the purposes of the armed forces; regulate the procedure of transfer, leasing, sale and liquidation of arms and military equipment; and organize the system of control over the state defence order, export of arms and military equipment, strategic materials, technology and double-use products.

In the sphere of external relations, the Government adopts measures for the implementation of the foreign policy of the Russian Federation, guarantees the representation of Russia in other States and international organizations; within its jurisdiction concludes international treaties and ensures the fulfilment of obligations stipulated by them, defends geopolitical interests of the country and ensures the protection of citizens abroad; regulates the external economic activity and international scientific, technical and cultural cooperation. The federal bodies of executive power coordinate international and external economic contacts of the Federal Entities. The Federal Government gives permission for establishing contacts with the governmental bodies of other countries whereas missions of a Federal Entity may be opened outside the Russian territory upon the consent of the Ministry of Foreign Affairs. A draft of any agreement by a Federal Entity is submitted to the Ministry of Foreign Affairs at least a month before its signing.

III. Relations with the President

162. The Head of State ensures concerted functioning and interaction of the Government and the other bodies of state power. There is division of powers/functions between the Head of Government and the Head of State. Both of them are not head of the executive. But, though the President is not the head of the executive power (as well as in France and Latin American republics and unlike US), he may chair the meeting of the Government and its Presidium. He exercises guidance over the activity of the so-called 'institutes of force' – federal bodies of defence, security, internal and external affairs, justice, law enforcement, prevention of emergency situations and termination of their consequences. A number of deputy ministers, inner departments and size of staff of every such institution are defining by the Presidential Edicts. However, the President approves the regulations regarding the status of those bodies and appoints their heads only on the recommendation of the Chairman of the Government.

The Chairman of the Government informs the President at regular meetings of its general business. The common practice is that drafts and overall plans of legislative work of the Government are examined and coordinated by the President. In the event that an edict of the President provides for the adoption of a governmental act or the President was a chair at the meeting when the decision was taken, the Government submits the draft act to the Administration of the President. The Government ensures the generalization of practice of state registration of normative acts of the federal bodies of executive power affecting rights, freedoms and obligations of human person and the citizen, establishing the legal status of organizations or having interdepartmental character, and informs the President.

The independence of the Government has certain limits: its policy must be consistent with the basic guidelines determined by the President and loyal to the interests of the Head of State. In that connection it should be remembered that the Chairman of the Government acts as a President if the latter is not able to perform his functions.

IV. Relations with the Federal Assembly

163. The Government enjoys the right of legislative initiative and it is empowered to submit drafts of the federal budget to the State Duma (Articles 104.1, 114.1(a)). So, in 2008, the Government submitted 427 draft laws to the State Duma; in 2009, their number was 471, in 2010 – 638. As a rule, draft laws are subject to legal and anticorruption review by the Ministry of Justice, the experts of the Institute of Legislation and Comparative Law Studies under the Government of the Russian Federation must submit their opinion upon those acts within fifteen days after they have received a draft. Draft laws within the joint jurisdiction must be as well send to the bodies of state power of the Federal Entities. The Constitution establishes several cases when the presentation of an opinion of the Government is a compulsory condition for the examination of a draft law (Article 104.3). This opinion must be presented to the State Duma and to those introducing the draft law within a month after the Government has received a draft.

In 2004, the Government established the Commission on the law-drafting activity (Decree No. 264 of 2 June 2004, SZ, 2004 No. 23, which is in force in the wording of 27 December 2010) in order to improve the quality of legislation and coordination with the Federal Assembly. The Commission which meets weekly examines preliminary draft laws and opinions to be submitted to the meeting of the Government, determines the position of the Government on draft laws which are examined by the Chambers. According to Decree No. 94 of 1 February 2000 (SZ, 2000 No. 6), as amended on 28 March 2008, the Government has its plenipotentiary representatives in the Chambers of the Federal Assembly who coordinates the activity of other persons representing its interests in the Chamber. The Government may appoint its regular representative who presents a draft law of the governmental initiative in the Chambers, or a special representative who expresses and supports the position of the Government regarding opinions and amendments submitted to a Chamber.

Since 2009, the Government presents annual report on its activity to the State Duma. The members of the Government may participate in the meetings of the Chambers, but they are not personally responsible to them. Although federal constitutional law establishes the obligation of a member of the Government to appear in a Chamber at its invitation, and answer questions in person, this rule is not followed very strictly. An invitation must be submitted at least five days before the parliamentary meeting. If a federal minister cannot attend it, he notifies the Chamber in good time about the reasons and appoints a person who may attend the sitting and answer the questions (usually it is one of the Deputy Ministers who are civil servants). The institution of Parliamentary Secretaries to Ministers, operating successfully in Britain, Canada, Japan and India, is unknown to both Russian legal doctrine and the constitutional practice of Russia.

§4. Working

164. The work procedure of the Government is defined by a federal constitutional law (Article 114.2 of the Constitution). The governmental activity is a planned one. As a rule, closed meetings of the Government are not so common. Usually a decision is taken on the basis of a consensus. But voting may take place at the decision of the chair of a meeting. In that case, a majority of the votes of those present is required; when votes are equally divided, the position of the chair of the meeting is decisive.

§5. Miscellaneous

165. Under the provisions of the Federal Law of 27 May 2003 ‘On the System of the State Service of the Russian Federation’ (SZ, 2003 No. 22), in the wording of 5 February 2014, and the Federal Law of 27 April 2004 ‘On the Civil State Service in the Russian Federation’ (SZ, 2004, No. 19), as amended on 30 December 2015, the state service is a professional activity aiming to ensure the implementation of the powers of the Russian Federation and its Entities, federal and regional state bodies, state officials of Russia and its Entities. There are two levels of that service: the federal one and that of the Federal Entities. According to data of the Federal Service of State Statistics, on 1 October 2009 there were 6,348,000 federal civil servants and 2,333,000 regional civil servants. The Federal Law provides for the following general principles of state service: federalism, which ensure unity of the state power and implementation of the constitutional delimitation of jurisdictions between Russia and the Federal Entities, legality, priority of human rights, equal access of citizens to the state service, unity of legal and organizational foundations of the state service, its transparency and accessibility for public control, professionalism and competence of state servants, protection of state servants from illegal interference of state bodies and officials as well as other persons into their professional activity.

Chapter 5. The Judiciary

I. Bogdanovskaia & S. Danilov

§1. Judicial Organization

166. After the Soviet period, the conception of the judicial power has been revised according to the principles of the rule of law and of separation of powers.[39] The concept of the judicial reform, proposed by the President of Russia, was adopted in 1991 by the Supreme Council of the RSFSR. Several important steps were taken to secure legally the judiciary as an independent branch of power. In contrast with the previous period, when the judiciary was organized by the Soviets in the constitutional model, the third branch is formed now by the legislative power and the Head of the State. The courts (except the higher instances) are established by the Federal Assembly while the judges (except the judges of the higher instances) are nominated by the President. Such a balance of powers is intended to safeguard the independence of the judicial power.

The status of the courts in the modern Russian constitutional order is defined and protected much more clearly and scrupulously than at any time before. The Constitution stipulates that the courts, as well as the President, the Federal Assembly and the Government, exercise the state power (Article 11). The decisions of the courts as state bodies are binding across the territory of Russia. In the system of the separation of powers only courts administer justice. The judiciary, as an independent branch of power, is subordinated only to the law. It also balances other powers, both legislative and executive (e.g., checking of the legality and constitutionality of their acts, exercising judicial review).

167. In Russian Federation, justice is administered solely by the courts established by the Constitution and the federal constitutional law, the creation of extraordinary courts is forbidden (Article 118 of the Constitution). The Constitution establishes and regulates the basic elements of status of two (up to 2014 – three) higher courts of Russia – the Constitutional Court and the Supreme Court. These courts may be abolished only by introducing of constitutional amendments. All other courts are set up and abolished by the federal legislation, given that the organization of courts is within the jurisdiction of the Federation (Article 71(n) of the Constitution). The procedure for setting up and abolishing courts is regulated by the Federal Constitutional Law of 31 December 1996 'On the Judicial System of the Russian Federation' (SZ, 1997 No. 1), which is in force in the wording of 5 December 2014, and by the Federal Constitutional Law 'On the Arbitration Courts in the Russian Federation' of 28 April 1995, as amended on 6 December 2011. For example, in accordance with provisions of the latter, one more judicial instance, the Court of Intellectual Rights of the Russian Federation, was established in 2011 (that body began to function in 2013).

39. V.M. Zhuikov,*Problemy Dostupa k Pravosudiu* (Moskva: Norma, 2006); M.I. Kleandrov & D.A. Krasnov, *Sudeiskoie Soobschestvo v Rossii i Drugih Stranah SNG* (Moskva: Norma, 2014)

At present the legal position of the courts of the Russian Federation at the federal level is regulated by several laws (Federal Constitutional Law of 21 July 1994 'On the Constitutional Court of the Russian Federation' (SZ, 1994 No. 13), as amended on 14 December 2015; Federal Constitutional Law of 28 April 1995 'On the Arbitration Courts in the Russian Federation' (SZ, 1995 No. 18), as amended on 6 December 2011; Federal Constitutional Law of 23 June 1999 'On the Military Courts of the Russian Federation' (SZ, 1999 No. 26) as amended on 3 July 2016; Federal Constitutional Law of 7 February 2011 'On the Courts of General Jurisdiction in the Russian Federation' (SZ, 2011 No. 7), as amended on 21 July 2014; Federal Constitutional Law of 9 November 2009 'On the Disciplinary Judiciary Board', as amended on 4 June 2014; Federal Law of 17 December 1998 'On Justices of the Peace in the Russian Federation' (SZ, 1998 No. 51), as amended on 5 April 2014).

168. An important guarantee of the independence of the courts is that they are financed out of the federal budget (Article 124). No less important is that salaries of judges are protected from inflation by statutorily stipulated increases. To achieve a better organization of the judiciary activity and control over financing, the Court Department has been created (Federal Law of 8 January 1998 'On the Court Department under the Supreme Court of the Russian Federation' (SZ, 1998 No. 2), in force and as amended on 5 October 2015). This federal state body ensures organizationally the activity of courts, bodies of the Judiciary and justices of the peace. It supplies the courts with equipment and decides on matters of personnel, but does not interfere with adjudication. As observers and judges themselves recognize, a task of maintaining adequate judicial salaries was fulfilled in Russia around 2010.

The General Director of the Court Department is appointed by the Chairman of the Supreme Court of Russia with the consent of the Council of Judges of the Russian Federation. During the established by the Government time term he submits to the Government suggestions regarding the financing of the courts for a fiscal year, which were agreed with the Chairman of the Supreme Court and the Council of Judges of Russia. In the process of the elaboration of a draft of the federal budget the General Director of the Court Department may take part in those meeting of the Government where the matters within the Department's jurisdiction are discussed. That participation may be seen as one more example of a checks-and-balances system in the relations among the different branches of State power in the constitutional practice of modern Russia.

At the same time it worthwhile to note that whereas the Executive, in the person of the Justice Ministry, reviews the implementation of the laws, the courts have a right to review only judicial practice.

I. Court System

169. The judicial system of the Russian Federation has a unitary nature, though it consists of federal and regional courts. According to the provisions of the Federal Constitutional Law 'On the Judicial System of the Russian Federation', as amended on 5 February 2014, the federal courts include the Constitutional Court of the Russian Federation, courts of general jurisdiction, arbitration courts and the Disciplinary Judiciary Board.[40] A separate case are the justices of the peace – nominally they are not part of the judicial system. Constitutional review is done by the Constitutional Court of the Russian Federation. The courts of general jurisdiction, resolving criminal, civil, administrative and other cases, are:

- the Supreme Court of Russia, Supreme Courts of the republics;
- courts of *oblasts*, *krays*, cities of federal significance, autonomous *oblast* and autonomous *okrugs*;
- *raion* courts;
- military and specialized courts.

For a system of specialized courts, often referred to, for example, are the arbitration courts. The system of arbitration courts, resolving cases in the field of commercial and economic activity, has operated in Russia since the late 1980s. It received definitive legal status in 1995 and consists of federal District Arbitration Courts, Arbitration Appellate Courts and the Arbitration Courts of the Federal Entities.

Since the 2000s, the matter of establishing a juvenile justice system in Russia is on agenda. The Disciplinary Judiciary Board is the judicial body acting as an appeal instance towards the decisions of the High Qualification Board of Judges and other qualification boards of judges regarding the pre-schedule termination of powers of judges for committing disciplinary offences. It consists of six judges of the Supreme Court of Russia elected by secret ballot on a competitive basis at the Plenum of the latter. A Standing Order of the Disciplinary Judiciary Board is approved by the common ruling of the Plenums of the Court. The Federal Entities may have constitutional (charter) courts which do not form a unitary system with the Constitutional Court of the Russian Federation, and justices of the peace, whose powers and procedure for activity are established by federal and regional legislation.

A. The Supreme Court of Russia

170. According to the Constitution (Article 126) the Supreme Court is the highest judicial body on civil, criminal, administrative and other cases triable by courts of general jurisdiction, it carries out judicial supervision over their activity in line with federal procedural form and gives explanations on issues of judicial practice. It hears cases as a Court of First Instance, appellate, cassation or supervision instance, and examines cases in which new circumstances have come to light. It has the right of legislative initiative within its jurisdiction (Article 104.1 of the Constitution), decides issues regarding international treaties within its jurisdiction, makes

40. V.M. Savitski, *Organizatsia Sudebnoi Vlasti v Rossiiskoi Federatsii* (Moskva: Jurist, 1996); *Sud i gosudarstvo*. Golovko L.V. et al., eds. Moskva: Statut, 2017.

public decisions of the Supreme Court and ensures the access of public to information on the activity of the Court. The Supreme Court works at the levels of the Plenum, Presidium and Chambers. Currently, the Supreme Court of the Russian Federation has 170 judges altogether (*see* Federal Constitutional Law 'On the Supreme Court of the Russian Federation', as amended on 5 February 2014).

The Plenum of the Supreme Court consists of the Chairman, his deputies and judges. It gives explanations to the courts of general jurisdiction on issues of judicial practice to ensure its unification; decides to use the right of legislative initiative; elects the Secretary of the Plenum, following the proposal of the Chairman; approves on the basis of the motion of the President the composition of the judicial panel which ought to give a conclusion on the presence of indicia of crime in the actions of the Chairman of the Investigation Committee or Procurator General; submits annually to the High Qualification Board of Judges the composition of judicial panels which will hear cases on administrative liability of judges, following the nomination by the Chairman of the Court; approves the Standing Orders of the Court; form the Chambers of the Court.

The Presidium of the Supreme Courts consists of the Chairman, Deputy Chairmen and judges of the Supreme Court, whose number is determined by the Standing Orders. The members of the Presidium are approved by the Council of the Federation following the nomination by the President of Russia with consent of the Chairman of the Court, if there is a positive conclusion of the High Qualification Board of Judges. The meetings of the Presidium are held at least once per month. The Presidium acts as a supervision instance and examines cases in which new circumstances have come to light. It decides issues concerning the organization of the activity of chambers, judicial panels and staff of the Supreme Court.

The Supreme Court has in the present time six Chambers: an Appeal Chamber, Civil Chamber, Criminal Chamber, Economic Disputes Chamber (established 2014), Administration Chamber and Military Chamber. The membership of the Chambers is approved by the Plenum of the Supreme Court upon the proposal of the Chairman of the Court. Each Chamber is headed by a Chairman. Within each Chamber the judicial panels are formed. The Chambers may act as a Court of First Instance, an appellate or cassation instance; and examine cases in which new circumstances have come to light. The Chairman of the Supreme Court organizes the activity of the Supreme Court and of the whole system of the courts of general jurisdiction; arrange a work regarding the examination and generalization of judicial practice and the analysis of judicial statistics; calls and chairs the meetings of the Plenum and the Presidium; forms the judicial panels and appoints their chairmen; represents the Court in relations with other bodies.

B. Other Courts of General Jurisdiction

171. Supreme Courts of the republics, courts of *oblasts*, *krays*, the cities of federal significance, autonomous *oblast* and autonomous *okrugs* act within the territory of an appropriate constituent entity. In remote localities may be established the permanent judicial boards, the separate subdivisions of those courts. These courts hear cases as courts of first, appellate and cassation instances and examine cases in which new circumstances have come to light. *Raion* court is established in the judicial *raion*, the territory of which includes *raion*, town or other appropriate administrative-territorial unit of a constituent entity. It hears all the criminal, civil and administrative cases, except those which are within the jurisdiction of other courts of general jurisdiction according to the federal law. Justices of the peace hear cases individually. Their territorial jurisdiction extends over judicial districts with population of 15,000–23,000 persons. The total number of justices of the peace and their judicial districts are defined by the federal law initiated by the appropriate constituent entity with consent of the Supreme Court or by the Supreme Court with consent of the constituent entity.

Judicial districts and posts of the justices of the peace are established by a law of the Federal Entity. Justices of the peace, acting as a Court of First Instance, may hear criminal cases in which the maximum punishment does not exceed three years' imprisonment, on issuing judicial orders, some categories of family cases concerning divorce (if there is no conflict about children), division of property between husband and wife, small claims cases, labour cases, cases about land use, and administrative offences.

C. Arbitration Courts

172. In the USSR since the 1930s to mid-1980s there was no legal private enterprise. In modern Russia, business disputes are resolved by the arbitration courts. The arbitration courts were established at the end of the 1980s to resolve 'economic' cases (i.e., disputes between entrepreneurs registered as legal persons or as individual entrepreneurs) and ensure the judicial control in the administrative sphere. The protection of rights and lawful interests of enterprises, institutions, organizations and citizens and strengthening of legality and prevention of law breaking in the sphere of entrepreneurial and other economic activity are the main tasks of the arbitration courts. These courts may hear cases in which foreign organizations or foreign citizens are parties. The list of issues within the jurisdiction of the arbitration courts is open and may be enlarged.

Now virtually all the Russian arbitration courts, in contrast with courts of general jurisdiction, do function in a regime of openness (including permanent and complete electronic records of the proceedings). This complies completely with provisions of the Federal Law of 22 December 2008 'On Access to the Information about Courts Activities'. Every arbitration court is equipped with all relevant computer facilities. The Russian public also benefit from the current general rules of procedure in these courts because they are more democratic and libertarian in the comparison with all another judicial bodies. In the 2010s it was determined that, significantly, the Russian people *per capita* began to seek protection of their interests in arbitration courts more than in the courts of general jurisdiction. At present, arbitration courts appear to be a truly popular component of the Judicial Branch in Russia. It is necessary to add that the abolishing of the High Arbitration Court in 2014 has not stopped this process.

Within system of arbitration courts, there is in operation since 2013 a new body: the Court of Intellectual Rights (albeit established by law in 2011). The analyses of cases note that the scope of action for the arbitration courts is moving steadily from the field of purely 'economic' matters to a wider spectrum of legal issues.

173. An Arbitration Court of a Federal Entity is a Court of First Instance. There are Arbitration Courts of the Republics, *krays*, *oblasts*, cities of federal significance, autonomous *oblast* and autonomous *okrugs*. An Arbitration Appellate Court acts as an appellate instance for the decisions of the first instance arbitration courts of the Federal Entities. The Plenum of the Supreme Court of Federal Entity may provide for the establishment of permanent judicial boards, which are not situated where the Arbitration Appellate Courts have a permanent seat. A federal District Arbitration Court is a cassation instance for the decisions of the arbitration courts of the Federal Entities and Arbitration Appellate Courts entered into force.

II. Legal Status of the Judges

174. The legal status of judges is established by the Constitution and Russian Federation Law of 26 June 1992 'On the Status of Judges in the Russian Federation' (Ved. Russian Federation, 1992, No. 30), as amended on 14 December 2015. According to the Law, a judge is a person empowered in the constitutional order to administer justice who fulfils his duties on the professional basis. In his activity, a judge is not accountable to anybody, his orders in the exercise of his powers have binding force. Contempt of a court is a prosecutable offence. All judges have equal status, but in the same time you may find easily some specifics in the legal position of the judges of the Constitutional Court, justices of the peace and of military courts judges.

175. The judges of the Supreme Court and the Constitutional Court are appointed by the Upper Chamber of the Federal Assembly, the Council of the Federation (Article 128 of the Constitution) on the recommendation of the President taking into account the opinion of the Chairman of appropriate court. In that mechanism we may see division of powers in action. Judges of the other courts are appointed directly by the President on the recommendation of the Chairman the Supreme Court. The appointment of judges may take place only if there is a positive conclusion of the relevant qualification board of judges. The Chairmen and the Deputy Chairmen of the highest courts are appointed by the Council of the Federation for a six-year term following the nomination by the President of the Russian Federation. Under the provisions of the Federal Law of 17 December 1998 'On the Justices of the Peace in the Russian Federation' (SZ, 1998 No. 51) as amended on 5 April 2014, those justices may be appointed (elected) by the legislatures of the Federal Entities or elected by the population of an appropriate judicial district in accordance with the regional legislation.

176. A candidate for the post of a judge must be a Russian Federation citizen, having a university legal education. A person as well may not have another citizenship or a residence permit in another country, convictions, be registered as alcoholic, drug-addicted or a person with mental disorder or have any other diseases that prevent him or her from the functioning as a judge. The Law 'On the Status of Judges in the Russian Federation', as amended on 14 December 2015, sets out the age and professional qualifications necessary for appointment to the post of a judge: at least forty years of age and fifteen years of experience in the legal profession (for the Constitutional Court of the Russian Federation); at least thirty-five years of age and ten years of professional experience for the Supreme Court of the Russian Federation; at least thirty years of age and seven years of professional experience for the Supreme Court of the Republics, and courts in an *oblast*, *kray*, city of federal significance, autonomous *oblast* and autonomous *okrug*, district military court, federal District Arbitration Court, Arbitration Appellate Court, and at least twenty-five years of age and five years of professional experience for the Arbitration Court of a Federal Entity, a constitutional (charter) court or a justice of the peace. Also prescribed are retirement ages for judges. Currently, the age maximum for judges is defined at 65 years (*see* Article 14 of the Federal Constitutional Law 'On the Judicial System of the Russian Federation', as amended on 5 February 2014). An exemption from that age limit is made for members of two superior courts of the Russian Federation: the Supreme and the Constitutional Courts, respectively.

177. The candidates to the post of a judge are selected on competitive basis as well as in most states. They have to pass qualifying exams, for which an examination commission is formed under the corresponding qualification board of judges.[41] The results of the examination remain valid for three years or during the whole term of office after the appointment to the post of a judge. A commission may not refuse a person who submitted all the documents to take the exam. Under the provisions of the Federal Law of 14 March 2002 'On the Bodies of the Judicial Community in the Russian Federation' (SZ, 2002 No. 11) as amended on 5 February 2014, the members of qualification boards are judges of federal and regional courts, representatives of public (the latter term admits of many interpretations) and the President of the Russian Federation. The High Qualification Board of Judges of Russia consists of twenty-nine members, among which eighteen represent the judicial community (four members from the judges of the Supreme Court, two members from the judges of the federal District Arbitration Courts, two members from the judges of the Arbitration Appellate Courts, four members from the judges of the Supreme Courts of the Republics, courts of *oblasts*, *krays*, cities of federal significance, autonomous *oblast* and autonomous *okrugs,* three members from the judges of the arbitration courts of the Federal Entities, and three members from the judges of district military courts. Ten of the Board's twenty-nine members are nominated by the public and one by the President of Russia.

The members of the High Qualification Board of Judges of Russia, representing the judicial Community, are elected by the separate vote of the delegates of appropriate courts at the Congress of judges. The representatives of public are appointed by the Council of Federation. Those members may be at least 35 years old, have higher legal education. They must not discredit themselves, be municipal or civil

41. N.F. Kuznetsova, 'A sud'i kto? (K voprosu o professionalnom otbore na sudebnuiu rabotu)', *Gosudarstvo i Pravo,* no. 8 (1994): 128.

servants, a head of any organization or institution, barrister or notary. A representative of the President must be a civil servant. This board is formed for four-year term. The qualification boards play an important role in the judicial corpus since they secure the independence of the judges. They form an exam commission, which makes recommendations based on the result of the exams. The qualification boards make decisions concerning the institution of proceedings or the arrest of a judge; may decide to revoke the powers of a judge and examine complaints against judges.

178. Judges are independent and subordinate only to the Constitution of Russia and federal law (Article 120 of the Constitution). According to the Russian Federation Law their independence is guaranteed by the law-stipulated procedure for administration of justice, the established order of suspension and termination of their powers, the right to retire, immunity, the system of bodies of judicial community and by granting of material and social maintenance corresponding to their high status (including 'adequate shelter conditions'). Interference in the activity of the court is forbidden (Article 294 of the Criminal Code).

179. Judges of the courts of general jurisdiction and of arbitration courts are irremovable (Article 121), they may not be transferred to another post or to another court without their consent and the grounds for suspension or termination of their powers are regulated by federal law. Under the provisions of the Russian Federation Law 'On the Status of Judges in the Russian Federation', the powers of a judge of a federal court are not limited by a definite time term, but he or she may perform his or her functions until 70 years. In the same time, the term of office of justices is determined by the regional legislation, may not exceed five years. It is necessary to note that justices may be re-elected.

The powers of the judge may be suspended or terminated by a decision of the appropriate qualification board of judges. There are three grounds for suspension of judge's powers (participation in the electoral campaign as a candidate, a criminal charges or status of defendant in a criminal proceeding, recognition as absent for unknown reasons by a court decision). Among the grounds for termination of the judge's powers there are written application for retirement or termination of powers, incapability to perform his functions, the cessation of the Russian citizenship or acquirement of a citizenship or a residence permit of a foreign country, activities incompatible with the status of judge, conviction, refusal to be transferred to another court in the case of reorganization.

It is necessary to note that the powers of a judge of the Constitutional Court may be terminated if he or she did not take part in proceedings, or did not vote in more than two cases without motivation. The termination of powers may be connected with the committing of a disciplinary offence (a violation of the provisions of the Russian Federation Law 'On the Status of Judges in the Russian Federation' of 26 June 1992, as amended on 14 December 2015, and of the Code of the Judicial Ethics). These decisions of the qualification boards may be appealed against to the Disciplinary Judiciary Board. All judges have the right to retirement. A retired judge has rights to pension or allowance.

180. Under the constitutional provisions, judges possess immunity (Article 122.1) that presupposes personal inviolability, inviolability of his or her home, office, property, documents and means of transport, as well as the secrecy of correspondence and other forms of communication. The Federal Law of 20 April 1995 'On the State Protection of the Judges, Officials of the Law-Enforcement Bodies and Control Bodies' (SZ, 1995 No. 17), as amended on 3 July 2016, provides for special measures aimed at personal security (protection of health, life and property, including the right to have personal guard and a weapon); legal (more severe punishment for encroachment on life and health of a judge) and social protection (material compensation in case of injury) of those persons. Under the provisions of the Criminal Code, a divulgence of information regarding the state protection of a judge is punishable by the law (Article 311). A judge is not prosecuted for an opinion expressed in administrating justice or for decisions adopted by a court except if this decision constituted an abuse of power.

According to the Constitution, criminal proceedings may not be brought against a judge except as provided for by federal law (Article 122.2). These proceedings may be instituted by the Chairman of the Investigation Committee of the Russian Federation (until 2007 – the Procurator General) with the consent of the appropriate judicial body (the Constitutional Court – with respect to its judges; the High Qualification Board of Judges of the Russian Federation – with respect to a judge of the Supreme Court, Supreme Courts of republics, courts of *krays*, *oblasts*, cities of federal significance, autonomous *oblast* and autonomous *okrugs*, military courts and federal arbitration courts; qualification board of the appropriate constituent entity – with respect to a judge of any other court). The decisions of the qualification boards may be appealed against to an appropriate court. A criminal case instituted against a judge is considered by the Supreme Court of Russia.

The Constitutional Court in its Judgment of 7 March 1996 (SZ, 1996 No. 14) ruled that the inviolability of a judge is an exception to the principle of the equality before the law, since society must establish additional guarantees for judges. The aim of this rule is to secure the foundations of the constitutional order, to protect the public interest and the interests of justice. The Constitutional Court found that the agreement of the qualification board for the institution of proceedings against a judge is an element that guarantees the inviolability of judges. Sometimes the position of the qualification boards was criticized as a protection of 'regimen honour', since they have often refused to allow the institution of the proceedings. During the first half of 2010, the High Qualification Board of the Judges of the Russian Federation gave its consent to bringing a criminal proceeding against four retired judges, qualification boards of constituent entities – against six judges (in four cases they did not allow to institute the proceeding).

181. Judges of all courts, including justices of the peace, may not hold other state or municipal offices, be civil or municipal servant, arbitrator or arbiter. A judge is not able to have a business or additional paid work, but he may give lectures and carry out research. The problem of political neutrality is especially important for those persons. They may not belong to political parties, support them materially, take part in political actions and other forms of political activity, express publicly their attitude towards political parties and other public associations. A judge is not able as well to express an opinion concerning a matter which is the subject of a case before the Court, before the final decision.

III. Judicial Proceedings

182. Due process is an important factor of the activity of the judiciary.[42] Therefore, the Constitution declaring the right to judicial protection (Article 46) provides for the procedural rights which guarantee its realization, including the right to have the case heard in court, the right to qualified legal assistance, the right against self-incrimination, as well as the presumption of innocence (Articles 47–53). Under the constitutional provisions judicial power is exercised through constitutional, civil, administrative and criminal proceedings (Article 118.2), and the matters of procedural legislation are within the jurisdiction of the Russian Federation (Article 71(b)). At present the procedure of constitutional justice is regulated by the Federal Constitutional Law 'On the Constitutional Court of the Russian Federation' of 21 July 1994, as amended on 14 December 2015; civil justice by the Civil Procedure Code; administrative justice by the Administrative Liability Code; criminal justice by the Criminal Procedure Code; arbitration by the Arbitration Procedure Code.

183. The Constitution declares the basic principles of the judicial proceedings: open hearing, the ban of hearing criminal cases in absentia, adversarial and equal trial, participation of citizens in the administration of justice through the jury trial (Articles 123, 32.5). The hearing in camera may be held only in the cases established by law (e.g., if open proceedings are contrary to the interests of state secrecy; if an accused is younger than 16 years old; sex crimes; to preserve secrets of private life, and in some other cases).

The principle of open proceedings is connected with the matters regarding language of judicial proceedings and records keeping in courts. The judicial proceedings in the Constitutional Court, the Supreme Court, arbitration courts and military courts are held in the Russian language as the official (state) language. The judicial proceedings in other courts of general jurisdiction may be held in the state language of the republic on the territory of which a court is located. Judicial proceeding with justices of the peace or in the constitutional (charter) courts of the constituent entities may be held in Russian or in the state language of a republic. Persons taking part in a case may request the help of an interpreter if they do not know the language of the proceedings. The help of the interpreter may be free.

184. Hearing criminal cases in absentia is not permitted except in cases indicated in the law: if the defendant is outside of the State or asks to have a case heard in his absence and if the court agrees. In civil cases, the case may be heard in the absence of the respondent if he was informed about the place and time of the court hearing and if the plaintiff agrees.

42. V.A. Rzhevski & N.M. Chepurnova, *Sudebnaia Vlast v Rossiiskoi Federatsii: Konstitutsionni osnovi Organizatsii i Deiatelnosti* (Moskva: Jurist), 1998.

185. The citizens may take part in the administration of justice as assessors or juries. Under the provisions of the Federal Law of 30 May 2001 'On the Arbitration Assessors of the Arbitration Courts of the Federal Entities' (SZ, 2001 No. 23), as amended on 19 December 2016, an arbitration assessor may be citizen not younger than 25 years and not older than 70 years, having higher professional education and at least five years professional experience in the sphere of economy, finance, law, administration or entrepreneurial activity, as well as unstained reputation. The lists of arbitration assessors are formed by the arbitration courts of the constituent entities upon the proposals of the Commerce Chambers, employers' associations, other public and professional associations. Those lists are approved by the Plenum of the Supreme Court. Two assessors may take part in the proceeding together with the judge of the arbitration court of the first instance upon the initiative of the parties. Assessors have the same rights as judges. Decisions are taken by simple majority. Assessors may perform their functions during two years and be enlisted later. In the courts of general jurisdiction, assessors took part in proceedings until 2004.

186. The jury ('*sud prisiazhnykh zasedatelei*'), which was used successfully in the Russian Empire at the end of the nineteenth century/the beginning of twentieth century, was restored in the Russian Federation in 1993, initially as an experiment in nine constituent entities.[43] On 1 January 2004, it was established in all the Federal Entities except the Chechen Republic, where juries started to be empanelled as of 2010. According to the Federal Law of 20 August 2004 'On the Jury Members of the Federal Courts of General Jurisdiction in the Russian Federation' (SZ, 2004 No. 34), as amended on 3 July 2016, a jury trial may be held in the Supreme Court of Russia, Supreme Courts of the republics, courts of *krays*, *oblasts*, cities of federal significance, autonomous *oblast* and autonomous *okrugs*, district military courts. The lists of jury members and a reserve list are composed by the high executive body of state power of the Federal Entity. Both lists are published in local newspapers. Complaints concerning the lists are examined by the High Executive body of State power; its decision may be appealed before the court. A list may include citizens not younger than 25 years old, who have no previous convictions, are not registered as alcoholics, drug-addicted or persons with a mental disorder. A person who is under indictment in a criminal case does not know the language of a court, or has physical or mental problems preventing them from taking an active part in the hearing may not be a jury member. The High Executive body of State power of the Federal Entity may exclude from the lists of jury members, certain persons at their request: if they are aged 60 years or more, perform functions of state officials, are civil servants, judges, military personnel, investigators, barristers, notaries, and so on. As a rule, a jury member may perform his or her functions over ten days once per year. In the 1990s and 2000s, persons, enlisted in the army or employees of law enforcement and state security bodies had no right to be put on the lists of potential jury members. That restriction is now abolished.

43. N. Radutnaia, 'Prisiazhnii zasedatel' v Ugolovnom Protsesse', *Rossiiskaia Ustitsia*, no. 3, 4 (1994).

§2. Judicial Review

187. In Russian constitutional theory, constitutional review is considered as an organic element of the Constitutional State, which ensures the supremacy of the Constitution and prevents arbitrary activity of the governmental bodies and restoration of a totalitarian regime.[44] The Constitutional Court is an important actor in the establishment of constitutional values.[45]

I. The Constitutional Court

188. The Russian Constitutional Court has gone through two periods of development. The first (1991–1993) was the period of judicial activism. After the adoption of the Constitution in 1993 and the Federal Constitutional Law of 21 July 1994 'On the Constitutional Court of the Russian Federation', as amended on 14 December 2015, the structure and the jurisdiction of the Constitutional Court were changed. The judges of the Constitutional Court in the present period are more known for their self-restraint. As well as many other supreme judicial instances in various states across the world, the Constitutional Court of Russia tries to find a balance between non-interference in political questions and questions of law.

The Constitutional Court is considered an integral part of the judicial system. It is a specialized court which has a jurisdiction established by the Constitution and the Federal Constitutional Law 'On the Constitutional Court of the Russian Federation'. The Constitutional Court does not adjudicate on the legitimacy and reasoning of the decisions in the ordinary courts, while the ordinary courts are not able to decide on the constitutionality of an act. If a judge is not sure of the constitutionality of an act, he must suspend examination of the case and appeal to the Constitutional Court for a review of the constitutionality of the act. The problem of the divided jurisdictions of the Constitutional Court and the ordinary courts has been the subject of discussion. The reason is that the Constitution is directly enforceable and all courts may take decisions based on the Constitution (Ruling No. 8 of the Plenum of the Supreme Court of the Russian Federation 1995, 'Some questions on the enforcement of the Constitution of the Russian Federation by courts', Bulletin of the Supreme Court, No. 1, 1996). The Constitutional Court in its decision concerning interpretation of Articles 125, 126 and 127 of the Constitution reaffirmed that only the Constitutional Court has the right to check the constitutionality of a law and determine its invalidity. Other courts are not able to decide whether a law contradicts the Constitution. The Constitutional Court must follow its previous decisions as a rule. However, that principle is not an absolute one. If the majority of the panel finds that it is necessary to take a decision not corresponding to previous decisions, the case must be resolved by a plenary session.

44. N.V. Vitruk, *Konstitutsionnoe Pravosudie* (Moskva: Jurisprudentia, 1998); Federalni Konstitutsionni zakon 'O Konstitutsionnom Sude Rosiiskoi Federatsii'. Commentarii (Moskva: Juridicheskaya literatura, 1996); A. Blankenagel, *'Detstvo, Otrotchestvo, Unost' Rosiskogo Konstitutsionnogo Suda* (Moskva: Prospekt, 1996).
45. B.S. Ebzeev, *Konstitusia. Pravovoe Gosudarstvo. Konstitutsionni Sud* (Moskva: Prospekt, 1997).

According to Article 3 of the Federal Constitutional Law, mentioned above, the Constitutional Court makes decisions on national legislation (federal and regional) evaluating not only content and sense of the act reviewed, but its official and other interpretation, and judicial practice too. So, this federal constitutional act recognizes as a norm not only text of the act reviewed but its sense (understanding) produced by its interpretation by other courts ('established practice of law implementation'). That provision means a certain departure from traditions of the positivist approaches to law, so strong in Russia. However, the expression about 'established practice of law implementation' in turn admits a lot of interpretations.

189. The decisions of the Constitutional Court also differ from decisions of the ordinary courts. They are extensively reasoned. The dissenting opinions of judges are also published though they do not have legal force. The Constitutional Court may adopt judgments (concluding decisions on the merit of questions concerning the constitutionality of acts, competence, individual complaints and interpretation of the Constitution), opinions (decisions concerning the legality of the procedure of impeaching the President for state treason or other offences), and decisions. The ruling of the Constitutional Court is final and comes into force immediately after pronouncement. Acts or certain provisions thereof which are recognized as unconstitutional become invalid and lose their legal force; international treaties of the Russian Federation which do not correspond to the Constitution of the Russian Federation are not implemented or used. If, as a result of the pronouncement that an act is unconstitutional, there would be a gap in the law, the task of the lawmaking bodies is to adopt a new act. Until then the constitutional provisions will apply.

190. The Constitutional Court has jurisdiction to check compliance with the Constitution of federal laws; normative acts of the President of Russia, of the Council of the Federation, of the State Duma and of the Government; constitutions of Federal Entities; normative acts of the Federal Entities adopted within their jurisdiction or within joint jurisdiction; and agreements between bodies of the Federation and of the Federal Entities. In these cases it realizes the following constitutional control. The Constitutional Court also checks the constitutionality of international agreements which are not yet in force. In this case, the Court exercises preliminary constitutional control. The Constitutional Court resolves conflicts between federal governmental bodies, between federal governmental bodies and bodies of Federal Entities, and among governmental bodies of Federal Entities regarding competence. For instance, those proceedings may be initiated by the President, if he has used the conciliatory proceeding to resolve disagreement between the governmental bodies of the federal and regional level in accordance with the Article 85 of the Constitution and those disagreements are in fact a dispute on the competence within the jurisdiction of the Constitutional Court.

The Constitutional Court gives an official interpretation of the Constitution of the Russian Federation; provides conclusions about the due procedure for accusing the President of state treason or another offence; and has the right of legislative initiative on questions within its competence. The Constitutional Court of the Russian

Federation, after receiving complaints about violations of the constitutional rights and freedoms of citizens and at the request of courts, reviews the constitutionality of a law applicable in a particular case.

191. The right to request decisions from the Constitutional Court is enjoyed by the President of the Russian Federation, the Council of the Federation, the State Duma, one-fifth of the members of the Council of the Federation or of the deputies of the State Duma, the Government, the Supreme Court of the Russian Federation, and the legislative and executive government bodies of constituent entities of the Russian Federation. According to federal constitutional law, the Human Rights Commissioner has a right to appeal to the Constitutional Court. The Constitutional Court in its Judgment of 18 July 2003 (SZ, 2003 No. 26) ruled that the Procurator General has the right as well to request decisions from the Constitutional Court – provision which probably has no analogue in the Western democracies across the world.

The courts may address themselves to the Constitutional Court if they doubt the constitutionality of a law which is used or to be used in a particular case. Individuals, as well as groups of citizens and associations also have the right to submit a constitutional complaint if their rights and freedoms are violated by an applicable law. The Constitutional Court informs the court or other body which examines the complaint. A court or body may (but is not obliged to) suspend the hearing of the case.

192. The cases are resolved in plenary sessions and in chambers. Two chambers, of nine and ten judges respectively, are organized. The judges are assigned for chambers by lots. The Chairman and the Deputy Chairman of the Court must not belong to the same Chamber. In plenary session, the Constitutional Court checks the constitutionality of Constitutions (charters) of the Federal Entities; gives interpretations of the Constitution of Russia; gives opinions about the constitutionality of the procedure for accusing the President; decides to exercise legislative initiative; and revokes the powers of judges. In plenary session, the Standing Orders are adopted, the panels are formed and the division of labour among chambers is made.

193. The Constitutional Court is established and acts in accordance with the following principles: independence, collective nature, openness, competitiveness and the parties' equality. Decisions of the Constitutional Court are made jointly by the judges in proceedings, the proceedings in camera are regulated by law. The Constitutional Court, whether in Plenum or by Chamber, is not able to examine another case until deciding on the case currently before it.

II. Constitutional (Charter) Court of a Federal Entity

194. In accordance with the horizontal division of powers within a federal state, constitutional justice is fulfilled in Russia by the Constitutional Court of the Russian Federation and by the constitutional (charter) courts in the Federal Entities. The constitutional (charter) court of a Federal Entity may be created by a Federal Entity to check whether its laws and the normative acts of its governmental bodies and local government bodies comply with its constitution (charter) and to interpret its constitution (charter). These courts are financed from the budget of the Federal Entity. The decisions of these constitutional (charter) courts cannot be reviewed by other courts.

Constitutional (charter) courts are foreseen by law in every Federal Entity. However, there is not enough clear-cut legal regulation of the status and financing of these courts. By the Constitution of the Russian Federation (Articles 72 and 76) issues of maintaining constitutional order and protection of human rights and freedoms are referred to the joint sphere of competence, whereas from Articles 71 and 74 it is easy to conclude that the structure of regional bodies of State power is within the Federal Entities' exclusive competence. Apart from that, Article 124 of the Constitution indicates in general form that in the Russian Federation 'all courts are financed from the federal budget' (but financing from regional budgets is not excluded or prohibited). In the result, constitutional (charter) courts currently function only in sixteen Federal Entities out of a total of eighty-five. Among the various reasons for the situation it is necessary to note the following ones: constant deficits in most Federal Entities budgets; an absence of interest in regional bodies of State power for creating independent instances enjoying a right to control the legality of local normative acts; and an overall 'managerial-born' prejudices and sceptical approach to the role and possibilities of judicial power.

It is sensible to add that the current judicial power in Russia does not have its own territorial structure in the form of judicial districts separate from executive ones. The internal borders of judicial jurisdiction (except for military courts) replicate those of the general administrative divisions of the State (Federal Entities, cities, *oblasts*, *raions*). That factor tends to expose courts and judges to pressure from executive bodies). It is especially important because a large number of suits are directed at local executives for abuse of power or non-action.[46]

46. *See*: V.B. Evdokimov & T.A. Tuchvatyllin. O neobhodimosti sozdaniya konstitutsionnykh (ustavnyckh) sudov v subiektakh Rossiyskoy Federatcii, *Pravo. Zhurnal Vysshey shkoly ekonomiki*, no. 2 (2015): 112–121; I.L. Latypova. Konstitutsionnyye osnovy finansirovaniya sudebnoy vlasti v Rossiyskoy Federatsii, *Pravo. Zhurnal Vysshey shkoly ekonomiki*, no. 3 (2015): 119–130.

Chapter 6. Independent Non-political Bodies: The Audit Chamber

T. Vassilieva

195. The Audit Chamber is a new structure in the system of state bodies of the Russian Federation which replaced the bodies of people's control typical of a socialist State. Its main task is to supervise compliance with the federal budget (Article 101.5 of the Constitution). Both Chambers of the Federal Assembly take part in the process of appointing the Audit Chamber. The State Duma appoints and removes from office the Chairman and half of the auditors (Article 103.1(d)), and the Council of the Federation appoints and dismisses the deputy Chairman and the other half (Article 102.1(i)). The legal status of this federal body is regulated by the Federal Law of 11 January 1995 'On the Audit Chamber of the Russian Federation' (SZ, 1995 No. 3), as amended by the Federal Law of 3 July 2016. The first auditors were appointed in 1995.

196. The Audit Chamber is composed of a Chairman, deputy Chairman, twelve auditors appointed for a six-year term, and staff. The Chairman, deputy Chairman and auditors may not have other citizenship or a residence permit in the foreign country. The auditors must have a higher education and professional experience in the field of state control, economy and finance. Moreover, the Chairman and deputy Chairman need professional experience in the sphere of state administration. The office of auditor is incompatible with any other paid activity except teaching and scientific or creative activity. As for the Chairman and deputy Chairman, they cannot be relatives of the President or the head of his administration, chairmen of the federal legislative, executive and highest judicial bodies, Investigation Committee or the Procurator General. The auditors must lodge information about their property situation and the property situation of a wife (husband) and under age children.

The Chairman, deputy Chairman and auditors may be removed from office for violation of the legislation or abuse of authority, if this decision is approved by the majority of the total membership of a Chamber, with a personal letter of resignation, for incapacity declared by a court, or when reaching the age of 65. Furthermore, a dismissal may be connected with the formation of a Chamber of the Federal Assembly, but this proceeding is not valid earlier than six months after the beginning of a Chamber's work. In that case, a decision must be approved by the majority of the total membership of a Chamber. The Chairman, deputy Chairman and auditors cannot be detained, arrested or charged criminally without the consent of the appropriate Chamber of the Federal Assembly. The Chairman of the Investigation Committee is the only person empowered to initiate a criminal proceeding against them.

197. The Audit Chamber supervises the management of the federal budget and of the federal extra-budgetary funds; monitors the efficiency and effectiveness of expenditures and the use of federal property; examines the realism of a draft of the federal budget, financial aspects of draft laws or acts providing for the expenditures funded from the federal budget or affecting budgetary creation or compliance. The supervisory body informs the Federal Assembly about federal budget management and submits to the Chambers quarterly reports regarding the state of revenues and expenditures, management failures and suggestions for correction. The powers of the Audit Chamber extend towards the accounts of the state bodies and institutions of Russia and federal extra-budgetary funds, state corporations and companies. Furthermore, it may supervise the financial activity of the local self-governmental bodies, enterprises, organizations, and banks and financial institutions if their respective expenditures are funded from the federal budget or if they use federal resources, utilize or manage federal property, or have tax or custom privileges or exemptions granted by the federal legislation or by federal governmental bodies. In the event of non-compliance or improper enforcement of the prescriptions issued by the Audit Chamber, its Board may decide, after consultation with the State Duma, to suspend financial operations with those enterprises, organizations and institutions whose activity was checked by the Chamber. A proscription of the Audit Chamber may be cancelled or changed only by its Board, or appealed to court.

Part III. The State and Its Subdivisions

S. Danilov & T. Vassilieva

Chapter 1. The Structure of the State: A Federal State

198. Russia is a federation that was originally and for a very long time, up to 1918, a unitary State with administrative entities of different special status within it: Finland, Poland, Bukhara, Cossack areas, etc.).[47] The process of federalization was initiated by the central authorities that delegated part of their powers to the constituent entities. Initially, the model of the state structure was based upon autonomy, and ethnic factors were the main criterion for the formation of the Federal Entities. The process of federalization was oriented towards plurality of types of constituent entities having different legal status. From 1922 until 12 December 1991, Russia was one of the members of the USSR, and its sovereignty was considerably restricted de facto and de jure (particularly, the biggest, most populated and economically most developed republic of the USSR had no its own capital, state anthem, Communist Party, Academy of Sciences, etc.).

Until 1992, the Federal Entities were established in the places of traditional settlement of non-Russian populations. The number of entities of the Russian Federation increased substantially after the conclusion of the Federation Treaty of 1992. The status of constituent entity was granted to fifty-seven territorial units – *oblasts*, *krays* and cities of federal significance. Arising was a tendency towards Russia's transformation into a Federation recognizing both the ethnic factor and regional diversities.

199. The current state structure has several distinctive features. The Russian Federation is characterized by the plurality of the centres of power. It is composed of eighty-three Federal Entities, an excessive number of which has a serious influence on the types and intensity of contacts between the federal authorities and the authorities of the Federal Entities. Another distinctive factor is the variety of types

47. *See*: I.A. Umnova, *Konstitutsionnie osnovy sovremennogo rossiiskogo federalisma* (Moskva: Delo, 1998); N.V. Varlamova, *Sovremennyi rossiiskii federalism: konstitutsionnaia model' i politiko-pravovaia dinamika* (Moskva: Institut prava i publichnoi politiki, 2001); A.N. Chertkov, *Territorial'noe ustroistvo Rossiiskoi Federatsii. Pravovye aspekti* (Moskva: Institut zakonodatel'stva i sravnitel'nogo pravovedenia, 2009).

of entities of the Russian Federation – republics, *krays*, *oblasts*, cities of federal significance, autonomous *oblast* and *okrugs*. In spite of the Constitution of 1993 proclaiming all the entities to be legally equal (Article 5.1), it is not only the title that distinguishes one from another. There are particularities in their legal status yet.

Among the Federal Entities, only republics are considered States (Article 5.2 of the Constitution), having constitutions (Article 66.1 of the Constitution) and systems of high bodies of state power, with the right to establish their own state languages (Article 68.2 of the Constitution). The wardship of the federal authorities over those constituent entities is less evident than in other cases. The differences between the other types of constituent entities that act on the basis of the charters adopted by their legislative (representative) bodies (Article 66.2 of the Constitution) are not so great. It is necessary to mention the specific legal position of the autonomous *okrugs*. Practically all of them, except Chukotka, are included in the territory of another constituent entity – a *kray* or *oblast*. The relationship between the interdependent constituent entities may be regulated by a federal law or a treaty between their bodies of state power (Article 66.4 of the Constitution). Moreover, the legislative and executive bodies of the autonomous entities – *okrugs* and *oblast* – may initiate legislative proceedings regarding the adoption of a federal law by individual autonomous *okrugs* or *oblast* (Article 66.3 of the Constitution).

200. After the adoption of the Constitution of 1993, there was a big gap between the constitutional and the real model of federal relationships in Russia. Within the partial vacuum of federal laws, regarding the organization of the system of power in the constituent entities and the interrelations between the governmental bodies of the Federation and its entities, the granting of special privileges to individual subjects was a common practice. A growing number of bilateral treaties and agreements devoted to the delimitation of spheres of jurisdiction and powers made asymmetry not only possible, but also inevitable. At that period, one could easily trace centrifugal tendencies within the Russian Federation. The extreme example was the Chechen Republic that was legally a constituent entity within the Russian Federation, but where in practice the federal governmental bodies were not able to ensure the implementation of their powers. Among the less evident examples, there were the insertions into the constitutions of several republics of provisions regarding ratification of federal laws in the sphere of joint jurisdiction or suspension of their validity in the territory of the constituent entity (e.g., Yakutia, Tyva, Komi, Ingushetia) or refusal to pay federal taxes (in 1991–1993 – Tatarstan, Bashkortostan, Yakutia, Chechnya). The federal authorities were, to a certain extent, catalysts of these tendencies for, at the beginning of *perestroika*, they put forward Boris Yeltsin's irresponsible slogan 'take as much sovereignty as you can' and used the same methods in their relationships with the authorities of the USSR. At the same time it should be recalled that there were evident economic reasons for centripetal tendencies. The majority of the constituent entities were recipients of federal grants.

In 1999, the federal bodies of state power began the reformation of the relations between the Russian Federation and the constituent entities. During that period, there were two important laws adopted that were aimed to restrict the self-dependence of the constituent entities, unify their competence and the system of the bodies of state power – the Federal Law of 24 June 1999 'On the Principles and the

Procedure of the Delimitation of Areas of Jurisdiction and Powers between the Bodies of State Power of the Russian Federation and the Bodies of State Power of the Entities of the Russian Federation' (SZ, 1999 No. 26, it is not in force since July 2003) and the Federal Law of 6 October 1999 'On the General Principles of the Organization of Legislative (Representative) and Executive Bodies of State Power of the Entities of the Russian Federation' (SZ, 1999 No. 42, as amended on 7 June 2017). After the presidential election, in which V. Putin was elected the president, the federal activity aimed to bring the regional legislation in conformity with the federal Constitution became systematic and persistent. In the Message to the Federal Assembly of 8 July 2000, the President pointed out that the federal authorities had moral right to demand the observance of the established rules and fix the possibilities of federal intervention in those situations, when the regional authorities were ignoring the Constitution and the federal law, violated rights and freedoms of the citizens. The President began to use his constitutional powers to suspend regional laws (Article 85.2 of the Constitution) more frequently, for instance in 2000 he issued eighteen edicts regarding the acts of the regional authorities of nine constituent entities. The Edict No. 1486 of 10 August 2000 'On Additional Measures to Ensure the Unity of the Legal Space of the Russian Federation' (SZ, 2000 No. 33) provided for the establishment of the federal register of the acts of the Federal Entities. The President set the task – to bring the regional legislation to conformity with the Constitution up to 1 of January 2001, and the other regional acts – during the first half of that year to the Ministry of Justice and the Procurator's Office.

In 2000, the post of the Plenipotentiary representative of the President in the federal district was established, and those federal officials were empowered to solve collisions between the federal and regional legal acts. It is necessary to note that during a short period of 2000–2001 the federal authorities succeeded in the correction of the regional legislation.

201. The status of a republic is determined by the Constitution of the Russian Federation and the constitution of that republic, whereas the position of the other constituent entities is determined by the Constitution of Russia and the charter of that component unit (Article 66.1, 66.2 of the Constitution). All the Federal Entities are granted legislative powers (Article 76.4 of the Constitution). Two ordinary federal laws in particular regulate the relationships in the sphere of the state structure and the status of the constituent entities: 'On the Fundamental Guarantees of the Electoral Rights and the Right to Participate in Referendum of the Citizens of the Russian Federation' of 12 June 2002 (SZ, 2002 No. 25), as amended on 28 December 2010, 'On the General Principles of the Organization of Legislative (Representative) and Executive Bodies of State Power of the Entities of the Russian Federation' of 6 October 1999 (SZ, 2011, No. 1), as amended on 7 June 2017, and the Federal Constitutional Law 'On the Procedure of Accession to the Russian Federation and Formation of a New Entity of the Russian Federation within it' of 17 December 2001 (SZ, 2001 No. 52), as amended on 31 October 2005. It should be mentioned that an act regarding a change of the status of a constituent entity (Article 66.5) is not adopted yet.

Chapter 2. Entities of the Russian Federation

§1. General Description

202. The Russian Federation consists of eighty-three Federal Entities, some of which are established on the basis of ethnic factors. This applies to twenty-one republics, an autonomous *oblast* and four autonomous *okrugs*. As a rule, the denomination of the component unit derives from the name of the ethnic group (e.g., Tatars – the Republic of Tatarstan, Nenets – the Nenets autonomous *okrug*, Jews – the Jewish autonomous *oblast*). Republics are established in the areas of historical settlement of the numerous peoples of Russia. Autonomous *okrugs* were established in areas traditionally inhabited by numerically small peoples of the North, Siberia and the Far East in order to provide favourable conditions for their development. An autonomous *oblast* differs in particulars of culture and national composition of its population, and is characterized by a certain economic integrity. The pyramid of Entities was too large whereas arguments for criteria of Entities classification were constantly open for critic. In 1991, most autonomous *oblasts* acquired the status of republics.

Until 1992, six *krays*, forty-nine *oblasts* and two cities of federal significance were considered administrative units within the Russian Federation. After the conclusion of the Federation Treaty, they acquired a status of constituent entity. Several *oblasts* (Irkutsk, Kamchatka, Perm, Tiumen and Chita) and the Krasnoyarsk *kray* included within them the territory of an autonomous *okrug*. As a rule, the name of a component unit derives from the name of its administrative centre (e.g., Rostov – the Rostov *oblast*) or from the geographic position of the constituent entity (e.g., the Primorie *kray* – maritime *kray*). Moscow and St. Petersburg (formerly Leningrad) should be qualified as the administrative centres of Moscow and Leningrad *oblasts*, but in 1991 the present and previous capitals of Russia became cities of federal significance and a year later acquired a status of Constitutional (Federal) Entities.

Following the classic doctrine of federalism, constituent entities are territorial ones. Under the constitutional provisions, no border modification within Russia is effectuated without the consent of the individual entities concerned (Article 67.3), but those modifications are subject to a compulsory examination of the Council of the Federation (Article 102.1(a)). In 1994, the Chamber adopted several decisions concerning border modifications (e.g., between the Ivanovo and Nizhny Novgorod *oblasts* of 3 February, as well as between the Kostroma and Vologda *oblasts* of 25 October). The list of the constituent entities may be corrected, for the Constitution includes provisions regarding the possibility of admission to the Russian Federation or creation within it of a new constituent entity. After the adoption of the Constitution the attempts of several territorial administrative units to acquire the status of constituent entity were not successful. The main reason was the lack of procedures of examination of those proposals, as well as precise criteria for the formation of a new constituent entity.

It is necessary to note that the Federal Law 'On the Procedure of Accession to the Russian Federation and Formation of a New Entity of the Russian Federation within it' was adopted only in 2001. According to its provisions the territorial changes must be voluntary and take into account the state interests, the principles of the federal structure, human rights and freedoms and the existing historical, economic and cultural connections between the component units, as well as the social and economic potential of the constituent entities. A new entity may be formed only by means of the unification of those units which have common boundaries. This process may be initiated by the interested Entities which submit the appropriate suggestion to the President of the Russian Federation. The suggestion must be well-founded and contain the basic characteristics of a new entity (denomination, status and borders) and the prognosis of social, economic and other consequences of its formation.

After the consultations with the President, the higher state officials of the interested component units put this issue to regional referendums. The decision to form a new entity must be approved in all the interested Federal Entities. In the case of failure, the next referendum with the same content may not take place within a year. The draft of the federal constitutional law regarding the formation of a new entity is introduced to the State Duma when the results of the regional referendums come in force. As it was mentioned earlier, on the basis of this law six autonomous *okrugs* specified in the Constitution in its original wording lost their status of constituent entities and became the integral part of *kray* or *oblast* in 2004–2007. The accession of the foreign state or its part is based upon the international treaty. The draft laws on the ratification of the treaty and on the accession to the Russian Federation are to be introduced to the State Duma simultaneously. A foreign state which is admitted to the Russian Federation is granted the status of republic.

§2. Delimitation of Powers Between the Federation and Its Entities

203. There are two methods of regulating the division of jurisdiction and powers between the Federation and its entities: through constitutional provisions and by treaty.[48] The Constitution of 1993 specifies the spheres belonging to the jurisdiction of the Russian Federation (Article 71) and those falling under the joint jurisdiction of the Federation and its constituent entities (Article 72). As for the constituent entities, they enjoy the residual powers. In accordance with Article 73, they possess the entire plenitude of state power beyond the areas of jurisdiction of the Russian Federation and of joint jurisdiction. The constitutional provisions were oriented towards the division of the areas of jurisdiction and did not regulate the division of powers. That led to serious problems in practice (*see* above paragraph 102 for example).

Unlike the Federation Treaty that guaranteed a special status of the republics, the Constitution of 1993 establishes identical spheres of jurisdiction and powers for all Federal Entities. The Constitution not only amplifies particular formulations of the Federation Treaty on the delimitation of powers, but also makes certain amendments to the areas of jurisdiction. The jurisdiction of Russia was extended over the following areas: protection of the rights and freedoms of man and the citizen

48. *See* S.L. Solnick, 'Federal Bargaining in Russia', *East European Constitutional Review* 4, no. 4 (Fall 1995): 40–46; E.W. Walker, 'Designing Center-Region Relations in the New Russia', *East European Constitutional Review* 4, no. 1 (Winter 1995): 14–19.

(Article 71(c)), the legal regulation of intellectual property (Article 71(n)), and naming of geographical objects (Article 71(p)). In addition, the following issues were assigned to joint jurisdiction: staffing of judicial and law-enforcement bodies (Article 72.1(k)), the establishment of the general principles for the organization of the system of the governmental bodies (Article 72.1(m)), issues of possession, use and disposal of land, the subsurface, water and other natural resources (Article 72.1(c)), and coordination of the international and external economic contacts of the constituent entities and fulfilment of the international treaties and agreements of the Russian Federation (Article 72.1(n)). In general, the constitutional model was adjusted to mitigate the 'asymmetry' of the Russian model of federation. The Federal Law of 24 June 1999 'On the Principles and the Procedure of the Delimitation of Areas of Jurisdiction and Powers between the Bodies of State Power of the Russian Federation and the Bodies of State Power of the Entities of the Russian Federation' prohibited the delegation, exclusion or any other method of redistribution of the jurisdiction of the Russian Federation and of the joint jurisdiction as established by the Constitution of the Russian Federation.

204. The process of concluding bilateral treaties within federation (absent in other federal states) began with the signing of the treaty with Tatarstan on 15 February 1994. Both sides had different approaches towards the establishment of new federal relationships in Russia. Representatives of Tatarstan considered that the delimitation of powers should proceed from the bottom up: each component unit should define areas of jurisdiction to be transferred to the central authorities. Like Chechnya, this republic did not sign the Federation Treaty and in fact boycotted the referendum and election conducted by the federal authorities. Only after the signing of the bilateral treaty did it fill the seats reserved for it in the Federal Assembly. The signing of the other treaties was not so well-motivated politically or legally. By virtue of treaties, the list of matters under joint jurisdiction was considerably extended in accordance with the interests of the Federal Entities. Those matters might include such issues as conversion, delocalization of military units, estimation of the quality of environment and guarantees of ecological safety, management of federal property in the territory of a constituent entity, creation of free economic zones, and coordination of budgetary, financial, taxation, monetary, credit and price policy. Several constituent entities attempted to accumulate as many powers as possible through the treaty-making process. For example, the authorities of Tatarstan and Bashkortostan obtained the right to pardon persons convicted within the territory of those republics, although according to the constitutional provisions this is a power of the President of the Russian Federation.

It is clear that in some cases, different solutions have to be accepted to cope with the specific problems of the Federal Entities. On the other hand, the expansion of the treaty-making practice and granting of special privileges resulted in a greater asymmetry and a decline of the universal character of the constitutional provisions in the field of federal relationships. The political compromises which accompanied the treaty-making process led to serious institutional problems. This prompted the President of the Russian Federation to sign Edict No. 370 of 12 March 1996 (RG, 14 March 1996) dealing with the due process for negotiating and elaborating treaty drafts. The President set certain limits on the autonomy of the contracting parties.

According to the Edict, the constitutional status of the Federal Entities could not be established or changed by a treaty. Furthermore, such treaties could not withdraw or redistribute matters within the areas of jurisdiction of the Russian Federation or joint jurisdiction enumerated in the Constitution of the Russian Federation.

As mentioned above the Federal Law of 24 June 1999 'On the Principles and the Procedure of the Delimitation of Areas of Jurisdiction and Powers between the Bodies of State Power of the Russian Federation and the Bodies of State Power of the Entities of the Russian Federation' restricted the treaty-making powers of the governmental bodies of the Federation and its entities. According to the new rules, a treaty might be concluded on issues belonging to the joint jurisdiction, if a federal law provided for it or if there was no federal law in this field. Further, a treaty might be concluded if its aim was to define completely the spheres of jurisdiction taking into account political, economic, social, geographical, ethnic and other particularities of an individual constituent entity. In accordance with the Federal Law, the government bodies of constituent entities that were not involved in the treaty might inquire into the draft of a treaty and submit their suggestions and observations in those cases when they considered that a treaty could infringe their rights and interests. Moreover, the procedure of examination of a draft treaty became more open. A draft was subject to examination by the legislative (representative) body of a constituent entity, as well by the Council of the Federation. The President of the Russian Federation was empowered to sign a treaty. He ought to be informed of the opinion of the Upper Chamber of the Federal Assembly and to make his decision taking into account the results of the discussion in the Council of the Federation, expressing the point of view of the Federal Entities. Such guidelines, underdeveloped or absent in Soviet constitutional practice, may be seen as an emerging model of checks and balances in the area of Federal Entities relations. At the same time, according to a majority of legal scholars, the treaties within a federal state are not necessary; the blanks in a constitutional text are better filled by agreement and federal laws.

At present the treaty-making powers are regulated by the above-mentioned Federal Law 'On the General Principles of the Organization of Legislative (Representative) and Executive Bodies of State Power of the Entities of the Russian Federation', as amended on 7 June 2017. Under the provisions of that Law, a treaty may be signed for a period not more than ten years in the case that it provides for the delimitation of powers which differs from established by federal law and is conditioned by the economic, geographic and other peculiarities of a constituent entity. A draft treaty must be approved by the legislative body of the entity and signed by the President of Russia and the high official of that entity. The President introduces a draft law on approval of the treaty to the State Duma within ten days after its signing. The federal law and the treaty come in force simultaneously, unless the law provides otherwise. The treaty may be amended or repealed in accordance with the same procedure. A court decision or the mutual agreement of the parties is the basis for its denunciation.

205. In Article 11.3 of the Constitution of the Russian Federation, federal laws are not indicated among the legal instruments regarding the delimitation of jurisdiction and powers. At the same time, the Federal Assembly and the Constitutional

Court interpret this provision loosely. The latter considers that interpretation of Article 76 of the Constitution presupposes that the principles of delimitation of power may be established by federal laws adopted within the joint jurisdiction (Decision of 4 February 1997). According to the Court, the federal legislator is empowered to make decisions affecting the constitutional status of the constituent entities if it takes into account the constitutional foundations of the federal structure. But, as mentioned in the Judgment of 15 July 1996 (SZ, 1996 No. 29), arbitrary restrictions of legal powers of the constituent entities are not admissible.

206. The Constitution defines a hierarchy of legal acts of the Russian Federation and its entities, providing for the delimitation of powers in this field (Article 76). It should be remembered that, in the Russian federal model, an integrated system of executive power is established which accordingly makes enforcement of federal laws one of the tasks of the regional bodies of executive power.

With regard to the areas of jurisdiction of the Russian Federation, the Constitution refers to only federal constitutional and ordinary laws and does not mention acts of the Federal Entities in this context. As for the areas of joint jurisdiction, it refers to both federal laws and laws and other normative acts of the constituent entities, but establishes the condition that an act of the Federal Entity must be in conformity with federal laws, which are given the priority in the event of conflict. The laws and normative acts of the constituent entities prevail outside the jurisdiction of the Russian Federation or the joint jurisdiction, but at the same time the possibility of adoption of federal laws in this field is not excluded.

Unlike the Constitution of Germany, that of Russia does not clearly define the cases in which the State Duma may adopt laws in the sphere of joint jurisdiction. Exploiting the lack of regulation, a number of the constituent entities used the tactic of the 'unoccupied field'. Initially, the Federal Law of 24 June 1999 'On the Principles and the Procedure of the Delimitation of Areas of Jurisdiction and Powers between the Bodies of State Power of the Russian Federation and the Bodies of State Power of the Entities of the Russian Federation' determined the basic rules in this field. At present those matters are regulated by the Federal Law 'On the General Principles of the Organization of Legislative (Representative) and Executive Bodies of State Power of the Entities of the Russian Federation', as amended on 7 June 2017. The federal laws regarding issues belonging to the sphere of joint jurisdiction may aim to establish the basic principles of regulation, as well as to ensure the exercise of the powers of the federal bodies of state power. The constituent entities may adopt their own acts on the issues belonging to the spheres of joint jurisdiction before the adoption of a federal law in this field. After that the legal acts of the constituent entities must be brought into conformity with it within three months. Acts not in compliance with the federal law are not enforceable.

At the same time it is necessary to mention that the constitutional model of delimitation of powers opens the possibility of paternalistic tendencies. The existence of broad areas of joint jurisdiction raises the possibility of excess federal legislation leaving insufficient room for regional experiments or preferences. The integral system of executive power may also provide an excuse for continued administrative control by federal governmental bodies.

§3. Cooperation Between Federation and Entities of the Russian Federation, Prevention and Settlement of Conflicts

207. The existing model of federal relations opens possibilities for the coordinate functioning and collaboration of the governmental bodies of the Federation and its entities. The constituent entities are represented at the federal level. Each Federal Entity, irrespective of its population size or territory, has two representatives in the Council of the Federation. The high state officials at the head of the executive branch of power in constituent entities ex officio take part in the meetings of the State Council, established by the President of Russia in 2000 as deliberative body, the heads of the legislative branch of power are members of the Council of Legislators, a deliberative body too, established at the federal level and acting under the auspices of the Chambers of the Federal Assembly. Each Federal Entity has its official representative in Moscow.

The Federal Entities have the opportunity to participate directly in the decision-making process at the federal level. According to the Constitution, their legislative bodies of state power have the right of legislative initiative at federal level (Article 104.1) and may as well initiate proposals of amendments and revision of constitutional provisions (Article 134). In that respect, Russian federalism is unique one. There are no comparable provisions in constitutions, legislative acts or conventions of overwhelming majority of federal states abroad. After their submission to the State Duma or after the first reading, draft laws on issues belonging to joint jurisdiction are sent to the constituent entities, which may present their suggestions and observations. If the bodies of state power of at least one-third of the constituent entities oppose the adoption of that law, a conciliatory commission must be formed. The representatives of the Federal Entities may take part in the process of elaboration or examination of draft laws on the issues belonging to joint jurisdiction in the committees and commissions of the State Duma. However, usually these powers of the Entities remain unimplemented.

The Government as well submits its draft acts on issues within joint jurisdiction to the legislative (representative) and executive bodies of state power of the constituent entities, and their suggestions are subject to compulsory examination by the Government. If an international treaty affects matters relating to joint jurisdiction or jurisdiction of the Federal Entities, their position must be taken into account. The federal bodies of executive power make decisions regarding the participation of representatives of a Federal Entity during the process of the elaboration of a draft, or when negotiating or signing a treaty in agreement with the bodies of state power of a constituent entity.

The constituent entities may take part in the process of the formation of the federal bodies or appointment of federal officials, for example submit proposals to the President of Russia regarding the candidates for a post of a judge of the Constitutional Court in the case of the vacancy. Prosecutors of constituent entities are appointed by the Prosecutor General after consultations with the bodies of State power of appropriate federal entity (Article 129.3). Prosecutors of that level may be dismissed by the Prosecutor General or by the President directly either.

208. The closest of contacts exist between the bodies of executive power. The Constitution of 1993 established a uniform system of executive power (Article 77.2) with a rather flexible mechanism for the redistribution of powers (Article 78.2–3) on the basis of agreements. The bodies of executive power of the Russian Federation and those of the constituent entities are empowered to delegate to each other a part of their powers. The practice of transfer of powers existed earlier, but it was based upon the decrees of the Government of the Russian Federation. The intergovernmental agreements concluded so far, like those implemented in federal states such as Australia, Canada, and Germany, provide for various means of cooperation. Among them are the coordination of actions and draft enactments, joint programme elaboration and financing, formation of intergovernmental commissions, involvement of the regional representatives in the examination and decision-making process regarding issues of federal importance, and participation of the representatives of the constituent entities in delegations or intergovernmental commissions formed by the Government of the Russian Federation to hold external contacts with appropriate bodies of other States or international organizations.

According to the above-mentioned Federal Law of 6 October 1999 'On the General Principles of the Organization of the Legislative (Representative) and Executive Bodies of State Power of the Entities of the Russian Federation', the intergovernmental agreements are concluded if the delegation of certain powers may not be realized by the adoption of federal law. These agreements are signed by the head of a federal body of executive power and the high official of the constituent entity (governor). The agreement defines conditions and procedure of delegation, including the term of action, financial aspects of the delegation of powers, grounds and procedure of denunciation. A body of state power of a constituent entity which is not a party of an agreement may receive a draft, if it applies for it.

209. The Constitution provides for several procedures of settlement of conflict between the authorities of the Russian Federation and of the constituent entities. The President may use conciliation proceedings to resolve disagreements in this field (Article 85). This procedure has universal character: it may be applied in the event of a conflict of interests or competence and irrespective of the substance of the disagreements. When it is difficult to reach a solution, the President may refer the dispute to the appropriate court for resolution (until now, there were no precedents).

As a rule, the plenipotentiary representative of the President in the Federal District participates in the conciliatory proceedings on behalf of the President, if the Federal Entities of this district are involved. Sometimes other officials performed those functions. For instance, in January 1999 the Secretary of the Security Council participated in the conciliatory proceedings with the President of the Ingush Republic on behalf of the Head of State. The governmental bodies of that constituent entity were claiming the transfer of the federal *raion* (district) courts to regional subordination and the power to appoint all procurators acting within the territory of Ingushetia with the consent of the governmental bodies of the component unit. The conflict was resolved by the conclusion of an agreement on 19 February 1999. In the case of a constitutional dispute and conflicts of competence, the Constitutional Court is the main arbiter empowered to resolve the dispute between the authorities of the Russian Federation and of the constituent entities (Article 125 of the Constitution).

In accordance with the current model of constitutional justice, the Court is not empowered to initiate a proceeding itself; an authorized body must submit an appropriate request. It is necessary to mention that the bodies of state power of the Federation and its entities do not apply to the Court very frequently, preferring informal contacts for resolution of disagreements.

§4. Financial Position and Relations Between the Federation and the Entities of the Russian Federation

210. The financial aspects of the federal relationship are not so well developed in the Russian Federation. In the process of the elaboration of the constitutional draft those problems were not taken into account, and the Constitution contains few provisions in this field. This approach was not typical for previous Constitutions. The Constitution of 1978, in its original wording, contained a special chapter on the state budget of the RSFSR. At that time, the delimitation of expenditures and revenues between the budgets of different levels was regulated by law in conformity with the general constitutional rule that the Federation was empowered to administer the implementation of the state budgets of the autonomous republics, budgets of *krays* and *oblasts* and cities of federal significance (Article 72.8). Nevertheless, the budgetary system of Russia was a highly centralized one based upon federal property and the redistribution of national income. Until 1991, the regional authorities were not empowered to create an independent budgetary or tax policy. The prosperity of one, and decline of another, region was a result of the concentration of the resources in accordance with the decisions adopted by the central authorities.

According to the Constitution of 1993, federal taxes and levies belong to the jurisdiction of the Russian Federation (Article 71(h)), whereas the establishing of general principles for levying taxes and levies in the Russian Federation belongs to the joint jurisdiction (Article 72.1(i)). At the same time the Constitution requires that the system of taxes collected for the federal budget and the general principles of levying taxes and levies in the Russian Federation are established by federal law (Article 75.3).

The Constitutional Court of the Russian Federation has determined the main rules regarding the delimitation of the tax powers. According to the Judgment of 21 March 1997 (VKS, 1997 No. 4) taxes and levies may be established by federal governmental bodies, governmental bodies of the constituent entities of the Russian Federation and by local self-government bodies. The federal lawmaker, according to the Court, independently defines the list of taxes and all elements of tax obligations. The right to establish taxes enjoyed by the constituent entities of the Russian Federation is of a derivative nature; they may decide whether to introduce a corresponding tax in their territory or not. According to the Judgment of 8 October 1997 (VKS, 1997 No. 5) the list of the regional taxes and levies which may be established by the governmental bodies of the Federal Entities is an exhaustive one, and that presupposes certain limitations regarding the introduction of additional taxes and the increasing of the taxation rates. In conformity with the Part One of the Tax Code of 31 July 1998 (SZ, 1998 No. 31), as amended on 27 July 2010, the representative bodies of the constituent entities and of the local self-government may determine the following substantial elements of fiscal obligations: tax rates, the procedure and the deadline for the payment of a tax, if these elements are not provided for by the Code.

The tax system in the Federation consists of federal, regional and local taxes, and levies. The federal taxes and levies include value-added tax, excise tax, personal income tax, tax on profit of organizations, tax on subsoil use, water tax, levy for the right to use fauna and aquatic biological resources, state duty. The Tax Code defines as regional taxes tax on property of organizations, tax on the gambling business, transport tax, and as local taxes – land tax and personal property tax.

It is necessary to mention that the established regional taxes are not sufficient for the activities of the regions. The fiscal system is based upon four federal taxes: value-added tax, tax on profits, excise taxes and personal income tax which together account for more than 80% of consolidated fiscal revenues and are distributed between the budgets of various levels. In 1997, the total amount of federal grants and transfers exceeded the federal tax revenues in every third constituent entity. If grants to the pension fund and expenditures for regional purposes funded from the federal budget are included, the total number of net recipients is above two-thirds of the constituent entities. The fund for financial support of the regions was established in 1994. According to the data of the Ministry of Finance, only eighteen of eighty-five constituent entities did not receive support from the fund. Since 2007, this fund grants the subsidies for the equalization of the budgetary provision of the constituent entities, its resources are distributed in accordance with a criterion of budgetary supply for every resident of the constituent entity taking into account the structure of population, socio-economic, geographical and climatic factors and conditions which influence upon the costs of the public services.

In the period of 1998–2005, the budgetary policy of the Government of the Russian Federation evolved from the distribution of the budgetary resources to the division of powers and responsibilities between the Russian Federation and its constituent entities. This process resulted in the formation of the legislative base for the division of the spending powers between federal, regional and local bodies. Particularly, in the Message 'On the Budgetary Policy in 2011–2013' the President of the Russian Federation declared the broadening of the financial independence of the constituent entities and municipalities as one of the priorities.

211. The budgets of the constituent entities are within the sphere of their own jurisdiction. The regional authorities may independently decide on the methods of their compilation or spending. At the same time the differences between the economic potentials of the constituent entities are substantial, and the budgetary relationships within the Federation are frequently based upon individual accords and not general rules. The conclusion of bilateral agreements regarding budgetary issues led to the establishment of specific budgetary regimes. The edicts of the President or decrees of the Government gave authorization for tax experiments in the territory of an individual entity. One of the serious problems in the fiscal relations between the Federation and its entities is the typically Russian phenomenon of 'mutual non-payments' when both sides do not fulfil their financial obligations in time. The common practice is that even those entities that have fulfilled their obligations regarding tax collection for the federal budget cannot receive money funded from the federal budget for their purposes in time.

In 2004, the new Chapter 19.1 was added to the Budgetary Code (Imposed by the Federal Law 'On the Budgetary Code of the Russian Federation' of 31 July 1998, SZ 1998 No. 29, as amended on 30 November 2011). The chapter is concerning the temporary external financial administration. This regime may be introduced in the constituent entity for a period up to a year upon the decision of the Supreme Court of the Russian Federation initiated by the Government of Russia in order to restore the solvency of that entity. A federal or regional executive body empowered by the Government of the Russian Federation carries out the financial administration. The temporary financial administration may not be introduced during a year after the beginning of the term of office of the legislative body of the constituent entity. Since 2007, The Budgetary Code includes the closed list of transfers and other types of financial assistance funded from the federal budget. These transfers are granted to the constituent entities if they observe the budgetary and tax legislation of the Russian Federation. As well in many other federal states, at least half of the Russian Federation Entities seek and receive federal grants, and even since the 1920s it was a permanent practice in the USSR too.

§5. Internal Structure of the Constituent Entities

212. The Constitution of 1993 tried to depart from the previous practice of centralized unified regulation of the system of the governmental bodies of the constituent entities, effectively granting autonomy to the Federal Entities in this field. The system of such bodies is established by the Federal Entities independently (Article 11.2 of the Constitution) in conformity with the foundations of the constitutional order of the Russian Federation and the general principles governing the organization of representative and executive bodies of state power laid down by federal law (Article 77.1 of the Constitution).

The Constitutional Court determining the basic guidelines concerning the system of the governmental bodies of the constituent entities has set some limits on the autonomy of the regional authorities. According to its Judgment of 18 January 1996 (VKS, 1996 No. 1), the state power in the Federal Entities must be based upon the principles of a democratic federal legal State having the republican form of government, the unity of the state power and the separation of the legislative, executive and judicial powers. Furthermore, the constitutional principle of the unity of state power requires that the systems of governmental bodies of the constituent entities conform basically to the federal model of relations between the executive and legislative powers. Moreover, in its Judgment of 24 June 1997 (VKS, 1997 No. 1), the Court pointed out that the introduction by constituent entities of a residence requirement as a condition for election to state office is contrary to the provisions of the federal Constitution which guarantees the equality of all citizens, particularly in respect of passive electoral rights, regardless of the place of residence or other circumstances.

213. The multiplicity of the historical and cultural traditions of the population and the particularities of the political situation in the regions presupposed a variety of systems of governmental bodies. The constitutions of the republics established various models of executive power. In Bashkortostan, the Prime Minister was the head of the cabinet of ministers, whereas in Buriatia the President performed the functions of the head of the republic and the chairman of the government. In Daghestan, the executive power was headed by a collegial body, the State Council, that formed the government subordinated to it. It should be noted that the possibilities of the other constituent entities were substantially limited by the adoption of several presidential edicts in 1993–1994. Particularly important was Edict No. 1969 of 3 October 1994 'On Measures for the Entrenchment of a Unitary System of Executive Power in the Russian Federation' (RG, 25 February 1994). Pending the adoption of federal laws and laws of constituent entities defining the mechanism of enforcement of the provisions of Article 77 of the Constitution, as well as principles and procedures for the formation of the governmental bodies of the Federal Entities, the President took the responsibility for making appointments and removing from office the heads of administration of those entities, as well as applying disciplinary sanctions to them and deciding to call elections to fill the vacancies. After the elections of the heads of administration took place, the President lost those powers.

One of the serious problems was the dual subordination of bodies of executive power of the constituent entities of the Russian Federation. The Constitutional Court in its Judgment of 10 December 1997 (VKS, 1998 No. 1) stated that the federal body of executive power at the head of the appropriate system has priority deciding issues regarding the cadre resources included in the unitary system of executive power of Russia. At the same time, some of those bodies have a dual nature insofar as they belong to the bodies of executive power of the Federal Entities, and that dual subordination presupposes the necessity to make the candidacy of the head of that body acceptable to the appropriate constituent entity. Under the provisions of the Federal Law of 6 October 1999, the system of regional bodies consists of legislative (representative) body, the high executive body of state power and other bodies provided for by the constitution (charter) of a constituent entity. For instance, it may establish the post of the high official of the constituent entity. The list of the standard state posts of the constituent entities is approved by the President of the Russian Federation. The restrictions concerning the inviolability of the members of the Government of the Russian Federation are applied to all persons who hold regional state posts, except deputies of the legislative bodies and justices of peace.

A number of deputies of the legislative body of a constituent entity depends upon the number of registered electors in this region (15–50 deputies, if the number of electors is less than 500,000; 25–70 deputies, if it is more than 500,000 but less than one million; 35–90 deputies, when it exceeds one million but less than 2 million; 45–110 deputies in those cases when a number of electors is more than 2 million). At least half of the deputies must be elected on the basis of a proportional system in a regional electoral district. The high official of the entity (often called a governor) is elected now by direct popular vote. Up to 2015 this official had been appointed by the legislative body upon the proposal of the President of the Russian Federation. Then the Head of State selected a candidate among the persons nominated by the political party which had enjoyed the best results at the most recent regional elections. The number of terms in power for high officials of entity Federal Entity was and is not restricted.

A candidate for that office must be at least 30 years old, not have foreign citizenship or a certificate for residence in a foreign state, be eligible to run in any Russian election, and must be supported officially by 5% to 10% of members sitting in the Entity's Legislative Assembly. To own a residence or to live in the territory of the Entity is not obligatory for a candidate or acting governor either. Like the President, the Head of a Federal Entity filling the office must take an oath of office. Currently the high official of a Federal Entity holds office for up to five years.

The person elected to the office of high official of a Federal Entity must not be a member of the Legislative Assembly, but has a right to be present and even to participate in its sessions – but with a determinative vote. Usually the heads of Federal Entities do not use that right. The structure of the executive bodies of the Federal Entity is established by its high official in accordance with the Constitution (charter) of that Entity.

The Head of State may terminate on a presumptive, preliminary basis the powers of regional bodies in cases established by federal legislation. He may dissolve a legislative body of a Federal Entity which adopted an Act which contravened the Constitution and federal legislation and did not bring it in conformity with the necessary legislation during a period determined by court decision and three months after the warning of the President of the Russian Federation. The regional parliament may be dissolved as well by the Head of State if it twice rejected approving a candidate for the post of high official of that Federal Entity. The powers of a high official of a Federal Entity, like a federal Minister and other federal high officials, may be terminated on a presumptive and preliminary basis by the President because of 'loss of confidence'. For instance, this was the grounds for dismissing Jurii Luzhkov, for years the high official (mayor) of Moscow City, in 2010. Around ten high officials (governors) of Federal Entities have followed him this way between 2014 and early 2018. Also the Head of State has currently the power to appoint at will to any Federal Entity a temporary governor. That power of the Head of State first was established by Presidential Edict No. 1969 mentioned above and later was entrenched by Amendments to the Federal Law of 6 October 1999.

According to legislation, the federal bodies of State power may temporarily substitute regional bodies if they do not perform properly budgetary or debtor's obligations or functions financed by the federal transfers on the basis of the edict of the President of the Russian Federation agreed with the Council of Federation.

Since the 1990s there was a notable gap in the legislation in the defining of number of terms of office for the high officials of the Entities. As a result, in many Federal Entities – Bashkotostan, Kalmykia, Tatarstan, Chitinskaya, Kemerovskaya, Sverdlovskaya oblasts, Moscow City – high officials (governors) won elections handily for decades with growing corruption as a consequence. The 2015 amendments to Federal Law of 6 October 1999 have imposed restrictions upon terms of office for high officials of the Entities. Since then, they have a right to hold office for no more than two consecutive five-year terms. However, an overall number of terms in office are still not established by law.

214. The constitutions and charters of several constituent entities have provided for the establishment of the constitutional (charter) courts of the Federal Entities. The federal legislator approved this idea. According to the provisions of the Federal Constitutional Law of 31 December 1996 'On the Judicial System of the Russian Federation', as amended on 5 February 2014, these courts are classified as the courts of the constituent entities established by their laws in order to make decisions on the compliance with the constitution (charter) of a constituent entity of laws and normative acts at a regional level, as well as enactments of local bodies of self-government and to interpret their constitution (charter). Currently, twenty-six Federal Entities have regional laws regarding constitutional (charter) courts, and those courts exist in sixteen Federal Entities including Tatarstan, Bashkortostan, Yakutia, Daghestan, Buriatia, Kabardino-Balkaria, Mari El, Komi and Karelia.

215. The office of human rights commissioners may be established in the constituent entities in accordance with their constitutions (charters) and laws. At present those officials perform their functions in fifty-one Federal Entities, the office of child rights commissioner is established in twenty-three entities.

Chapter 3. Local Self-government

216. The Constitution of 1993 provides for new approaches towards local self-government that is classified as not belonging to the system of bodies of state power and as independent within its field of competence (Article 12). Those provisions, included in the chapter devoted to the foundations of the constitutional order in the Russian Federation and detailed in the Federal Law 'On the General Principles of the Organization of the Local Self-Government in the Russian Federation' of 6 October 2003, as amended on 3 July 2016 (SZ, 2003 No. 44), are in contrast with the previous practice in this area. The Soviet model of self-government was based upon the following general rules. Local councils were included directly in the system of bodies of the state power, itself characterized by the hierarchy of the representative bodies, the rigid subordination of its different levels and the absence of any specific local issues excluded from examination by higher authorities.

Establishing general principles of organization of the system of local self-government (Article 72.1(m) of the Constitution) belongs to the joint jurisdiction of Federation and its Entities. As a rule, a Federal Entity adopts a special law regarding local self-government, whereas the particularities of a municipality are reflected in its charter.

217. According to the legislation previously in force, the boundaries of the local formation coincided with the boundaries of the territorial administrative units. At present this rule is not applied so strictly. A municipality may be established in accordance with historical and other local traditions, and the structure of local self-government bodies is determined by the population independently. The Constitution does not determine rigidly the territorial levels of self-government, indicating only urban and rural settlements and other areas (Article 131.1). According to the legal positions of the Constitutional Court, municipalities may be established at different territorial levels, that depends upon the specific characteristics of a constituent entity (Judgment of 24 January 1997, SZ, 1997 No. 5), and the territorial area of the local self-government must be determined on the basis of such conditions as the maximal proximity to the population, effectiveness with due regard for the specificity of the legal and factual situations (Judgment of 15 January 1998, SZ, 1998 No. 4). The opinion of the local population must be taken into account in the event of changes to the territorial administrative bodies (Article 131.2). The Constitutional Court in its Judgment of 24 January 1997 interpreted this provision loosely and held that in the setting up or changing of the territorial administrative structure and types of self-governing territories, it is unacceptable to terminate prematurely the powers of local self-government bodies without taking account of the opinion of the population of those territories.

218. According to the Federal Law of 6 October 2003 'On the General Principles of the Organization of the Local Self-Government in the Russian Federation', as amended on 3 July 2016, the basic territorial-political structure ensuring the enjoyment of the right of self-government is a municipality. Urban or rural settlements, as well as municipal district, urban circuits and inside territories of the city of federal significance having a common territory, municipal property or local budget, and elected bodies of the local self-government may be deemed a municipality. The Federal Law mentioned provides for two-level system of local self-government without direct subordination (the high level includes municipal district and urban circuit). Each formation has a charter adopted by the representative body or approved by popular vote and subject to state registration. The local government is exercised through various forms of direct expression of the will of the population including referenda and elections and through elected and other bodies (Article 130.2 of the Constitution). Any agency created in compliance with the Constitution and other legislative acts in urban and rural settlements and other territories in order to ensure the independent solution of local issues or the possession, use and disposal of municipal property by the population may be deemed a local self-government body. According to the Federal Law, the structure of the bodies of local self-government consists of a representative body, a head of a municipality, local administration and a control body.

The bodies of local self-government are empowered to administer municipal property; formulate, approve and implement the local budget; establish local taxes and duties; ensure the protection of public order; and resolve other issues of local importance (Article 132.1 of the Constitution). The complete list of those issues is determined also by the Federal Law of 6 October 2003, as amended on 3 July 2016. The Constitution does not exclude the possibility of delegation of some state functions to local authorities but that can only take place with the transfer of adequate financial and material resources (Article 132.2). Since 2006, the state functions may be delegated even to municipalities of the lower territorial level. Up-to-date the implementing these provisions is not frequent one. At the same time, the transformation of local self-governmental bodies into governmental bodies and the exercise by the latter of local government is not admissible, as far as local issues must be solved by the bodies of local self-government or directly by population (Judgment of 24 January 1997). One of the basic guarantees of local self-government is the right to judicial protection and compensation for any additional expenses arising from the decisions passed by the bodies of state power formulated in Article 133 of the Constitution.

Part IV. Citizenship and the Administration of Justice

T. Vassilieva

Chapter 1. Rules Regarding Citizenship and the Relevance of Citizenship

§1. Constitutional and Statutory Provisions Regarding Citizenship

219. In accordance with the Constitution of 1993, the Russian Federation citizenship is equal and uniform irrespective of the grounds of its acquisition (Article 6.1).[49] A citizen may alter the country of his affiliation, but nobody can be deprived of Russian citizenship or of the right to change it (Article 6.3). Any permissible dual citizenship does not lead to the diminution of the rights and freedoms or release from obligations deriving from the Russian citizenship (Article 62.1,2).

Citizenship in the Russian Federation falls under federal jurisdiction (Article 71(c)). Its acquisition and termination are regulated by a federal law (Article 6.1), whereas dual citizenship may be also regulated by an international treaty of the Russian Federation (Article 62.1).

220. The RSFSR Law of 28 November 1991 'On the Citizenship of the RSFSR' (Ved. RSFSR, 1992 No. 6) was adopted a month before the break-up of the Soviet Union. It was based upon the state-centrist concept of citizenship, and some of its provisions conflicted with the USSR practice in this field. This law which was in force for a decade identified citizens of the newly independent State. Under its provisions, the former USSR citizens permanently residing in the territory of Russia on the day the Citizenship Law came into force were deemed citizens of the Russian Federation unless they declared otherwise within a year. As a legal successor to the Soviet Union, the Russian Federation accepted its obligations towards the former USSR citizens, especially if they became stateless persons after the break-up of the Soviet Union. Furthermore, the fact that a person had the USSR citizenship in the past facilitates admission of Russian Federation citizenship. The overwhelming majority of those who acquired Russian citizenship under the RSFSR Law were

49. *See* S.A. Avak'ian, *Rossia: grazhdanstvo, inostrantsi, vneshniaia migratsia* (Sanct-Peterburg: Juridicheskii tsentr Press, 2003); O.E. Kutafin, *Rossiiskoe grazhdanstvo* (Moskva: Jurist, 2003).

former USSR citizens – 99% in 1998 (RG, 18 May 1999). At the same time its provisions differed from provisions of the Constitution of 1993 (e.g., the RSFSR Law provided for the citizenship of republics within the Federation) and did not establish restrictions for persons applying for naturalization. The new Citizenship Law – Federal Law 'On the Citizenship of the Russian Federation' – was adopted on 31 May 2002 (SZ, 2002 No. 22), in force and as amended on 28 June 2009.

The Citizenship Law provides for the priority of the international treaties in this field; guarantees the right to citizenship irrespective of the marital status or the country of residence; bans the restrictions of citizens' rights by virtue of social, racial, ethnic, language or religion belonging.

I. Attribution of Russian Federation Citizenship

221. Russian Federation citizenship may be obtained by attribution or by acquisition. Attribution of citizenship is a result of birth. Descent or place of birth has influence on the attribution of citizenship. According to Russian law, mother and father have equal possibilities to give their citizenship to a child. If, by the date of a child's birth, single parent or both parents are Russian citizens or one of them is a Russian citizen and another is a stateless person, a child is considered a citizen of the Russian Federation irrespective of the place of birth. When the parents hold different citizenships, a child is a Russian citizen in the event that it was born in Russian territory or if otherwise it may become a stateless person. A child born in Russian territory is a Russian citizen if its parents are stateless persons or citizens of those States that would not grant it citizenship. Also, any child of unknown parents found on the territory of the country is considered a citizen if his parents fail to appear within six months after the time the child was found.

II. Acquisition of Russian Federation Citizenship

222. There are several possibilities for the acquisition of Russian citizenship: admission, registration, reinstatement or option. According to data of the Federal Service of State Statistics, 362,100 persons acquired Russian citizenship in 2008 (with 368,600 in 2007, 371,800 in 2006 and 508,500 in 2005). The Citizenship Law establishes restrictions for persons applying for naturalization which are quite moderate ones. A residence qualification – five years of continuous residence since the day a person receives the residence permit prior to the filing of the application – is the precondition for admission. This term is reduced to one year for persons having high achievements in the field of science, technology and culture or a profession or qualification of the interest of the Russian State.

In an order of exclusion that provision may be mitigated even more. In such a way Russian citizenship was granted in 2014–2017 to several noted foreign persons like businessman and actor Gerard Depardieu (France), actress Ornella Muti (Italy), and sport stars Roy Johns and Jeff Manson (US). The same rule is applied to those who were granted asylum or refugee status. Furthermore, citizens of the states which have once formed part of the USSR may apply for naturalization without observation of the residence condition if they served in the Russian Armed Forces for at least three years on a contract basis. In order to apply for naturalization a person ought to have a legal source for the means of subsistence, have command of the Russian language, renounce his previous citizenship and undertake to observe the Russian Constitution and laws.

The registration requirement is applied if an alien has personal connections with the Russian Federation (e.g., his spouse or direct ancestor is a Russian citizen or the person himself has been born on the territory of the RSFSR and has been a citizen of the former USSR). This rule also applies to former USSR citizens who have resided in the other Republics of the Soviet Union and moved to Russia, if they declare an intention to acquire Russian citizenship before 1 January 2006, if they are veterans of the Great Patriotic War 1941–1945, or disabled or stateless persons. This rule is also applied to citizens of those states which have previously formed a part of the USSR and who have received secondary vocational or higher vocational education at educational institutions of Russia after 1 July 2002. It is necessary to note that the Constitutional Court in its Judgment of 16 May 1996 (VKS, 1996 No. 3) came to the conclusion that acquisition of citizenship by registration may be applied only to those former USSR citizens who are not Russian citizens by birth. Those who have had Russian citizenship before may be reinstated into Russian citizenship under the procedure provided for naturalization by the Citizenship Law. But in that case the residence term is reduced to three years. According to Russian law, opting for citizenship is connected with the transfer of sovereignty over a territory where a person resides. It may take place only on the basis of an international treaty of the Russian Federation.

III. Loss of Russian Federation Citizenship

223. As a rule, the Citizenship Law connects the termination of citizenship with the acquisition of citizenship of another State. A person may withdraw from citizenship on application or by registration. The latter takes place if a person resides in another country. The Citizenship Law provides for temporary suspension of those proceedings in several cases. A person cannot terminate his citizenship if he has undischarged obligation to the Russian State. The same rule is applied to those situations when a person is under indictment in a criminal case or is already convicted. An application may also be rejected when a person has no other citizenship or guarantees of its acquisition. Under the provisions of the Citizenship Law, a decision concerning the admission of a certain person to Russian Federation citizenship may be reversed if it has been made on the basis of false information or forged documents and if that fact was proved in legal proceedings. Another ground for termination of Russian citizenship is by option, which is connected with the transfer of sovereignty over a territory where a person resides. It may take place only on the basis of an international treaty with the Russian Federation.

224. The present Citizenship Law prohibits deprivation of citizenship, which was admissible and implemented often enough in the Soviet Union. Under the provisions of the USSR Citizenship Law of 1938, deprivation of citizenship could result from a court decision or an edict of the Presidium of the Supreme Soviet. From 1978, criteria for deprivation were defined more exactly: the Presidium only could deprive those persons of citizenship who 'discredited its status or caused damage to the prestige and national security of the Soviet Union'. Deprivation of citizenship might also occur as a result of emigration. In accordance with the Edict of the Presidium of the Supreme Soviet of 1967, persons moving to Israel for residence lost their citizenship after their exit from the country, independently of their will. Those who have been deprived of citizenship or have lost it against their will were reinstated into Russian citizenship automatically by the RSFSR Citizenship Law.

IV. Dual Citizenship

225. Under the provisions of the Federal law, a citizen of the Russian Federation who also have another citizenship is deemed as a Russian citizen, except the cases stipulated by an international treaty of the Russian Federation or by a federal law. Such treaties were concluded with Tajikistan and Turkmenistan (the treaty with Turkmenistan de facto ceased its effect since 2003). According to these treaties, persons who hold a dual citizenship have the right to call upon the protection of the country of their residence when abroad, but the other country of citizenship may also grant protection upon the person's request. As a rule, those persons perform military service in the country of their residence. In July 1999, Poland and Russia signed a protocol in this matter.

According to data of the national population census of 2002, 43,648 Russian citizens had the citizenship of another State. During the last decade the legislator restricted the access of those persons to several elective and official posts or activities. At present those who have another citizenship may not hold the office of the President of the Russian Federation, member of the Government, Parliament, Audit Chamber, Security Council, as well as of a judge or procurator. These provisions are in conflict with the principles established by the European Convention on Nationality, though it is necessary to note that the Russian Federation does not ratify it.

The USSR Citizenship Law of 1938 contained no provisions concerning dual citizenship. In 1956–1958 the Soviet Union concluded several international treaties with former socialist countries (Albania, Bulgaria, Hungary, China, Mongolia, Czechoslovakia, Yugoslavia), according to which persons holding the dual citizenship had to choose for one of them within a year after entry into force of that treaty. Under the provision of treaties with Poland and Bulgaria on the averting of dual citizenship concluded in 1963–1964, a person could not acquire citizenship of another country without the consent of the governmental bodies of the country of original affiliation. The USSR Citizenship Law of 1978 prohibited the holding of citizenship of another country by a Soviet citizen.

V. Proceeding

226. Applications for registration are filed with governmental bodies which exercise migration control in the place of residence in the Russian Federation or with the diplomatic or consular institutions. Petitions on citizenship matters are submitted to the President of the Russian Federation through the same bodies. The term for examination is six months for applications and twelve months for petitions. A refusal to accept an application or petition, denial of registration, violation of terms for examination or other procedural aspects established by law may be appealed to the court.

§2. Relevance of Citizenship

227. Russian citizenship has several benefits. Under the constitutional provisions, the concept of citizenship is legally important mainly in the following respects:

(a) Non-citizens do not enjoy political rights. As a rule, electoral rights and the right to participate in referenda are granted to citizens of the Russian Federation. The exception is provided for by the Charter of the Union of Belarus and Russia of 1997 (BMD, 1997 No. 9). Citizens of Belarus, permanently residing in the territory of the Russian Federation, may participate in municipal elections and be eligible as candidates. Russian citizenship is a precondition for access to the civil service (Article 32.4), participation in the administration of state affairs or justice (Article 32.1, 32.5), and enjoyment of the right to assembly (Article 31) and the right of petition (Article 33).
(b) In the economic sphere, only citizens and their associations may hold land in private ownership (Article 36).
(c) Russian citizens cannot be forced to leave their native country insofar as they are not subject to deportation or extradition. At the same time they have a right to call upon the protection and defence of the Russian Federation when they are abroad (Article 61.2).
(d) Citizenship carries with it the fundamental duty to protect the Fatherland and adult male conscription (Article 59.1, 2).

Chapter 2. Fundamental Rights and Liberties

I. Bogdanovskaia & T. Vassilieva

§1. General

228. In Russia, the institution of human rights developed in different political regimes and forms of government. It began to form at the beginning of the century when Russia took its first steps towards the rule of law, and some basic rights were granted to the people by the Russian Tsar. Though the Soviet constitutions proclaimed human rights and freedoms, they were not secured.[50] The State was free to determine the content of human rights since they were relative to the activity of the State. An individual had few ways to defend himself against the voluntary actions of the State. The Soviet system of government was based on strong control over society, which was permitted only limited freedom. The limitations first of all concerned political rights. At the same time, the paternalistic Soviet State was able to secure for human person small but stable salaries, or old-age pensions and allowances.

The transitional period began with the democratization of the social and political spheres and the revision of the sphere of human rights. First of all political rights and freedoms – the right to demonstration, freedom of press and other mass media, freedom of thought and speech, electoral rights – were given real content after the Soviet period. The State took several steps to restore social justice and adopted acts on the rights of repressed peoples or persons. The changes in the conception of human rights and freedoms were expressed in the Declaration of the Rights and Freedoms of Man and Citizen 1991 (Ved. RSFSR 1991, No. 52). It formed one of the cornerstones of the Constitution of 1993. New approaches[51] may be summarized as follows.

Russia has begun to orient itself towards international standards in the sphere of human rights.[52] The present list of constitutional rights, in general, corresponds to the main international acts on human rights. According to Article 17.1 of the Constitution, in Russia human and civil rights and freedoms are recognized and guaranteed according to the 'universally recognized principles and norms of international law'. The Constitutional Court of Russia uses international acts for interpretation of constitutional provisions. International acts have priority in the spheres of law in which domestic legislation does not secure human rights to the same extent as international law. For example, the Constitutional Court in the 1990s found that the International Convention on Civil and Political Rights offers more

50. B.N. Topornin, 'Introduction', in *Konstitutsia Rossiiskoi Federatsii*, ed. Topornin (Moskva: Jurist, 1997), 39–45.
51. E.A. Lukasheva, *Obshaia Teoria Prav Cheloveka* (Moskva: Statut, 1996).
52. V.A. Kartashkin, *Prava Cheloveka v Mezdunarodnom i Vnutrigosudarstvennom Prave* (Moskva: Institut Gosudarstva i Prava, 1995); idem. *Prava Cheloveka i Vooruzhennye Konflikty* (Moskva: Norma, 2007).

possibilities for defence than the current Criminal-Procedural Code and thus has priority over domestic law (Judgment of 2 February 1996, VKS, 1996, No. 2). The previous conception, according to which human rights were a result of the benevolent activity of the State, was rejected. The new conception is based on natural law. Basic human rights are considered inalienable and belonging to people by birth. According to the principle of the rule of law, human rights determine the meaning, content and implementation of laws, the functioning of legislative and executive authorities, and the local government (Article 18 of the Constitution).

The State has the obligation to recognize, observe and protect human rights and freedoms. No laws may abolish or diminish human and civil rights and freedoms (Articles 2, 55 of the Constitution). Human rights are of supreme value (Article 2 of the Constitution). The Constitutional Court of the Russian Federation, giving interpretation to this Article in its Judgment of 2 February 1996, held that the status of human rights as being of basic value entails the obligation of the State to secure effective mechanisms for restoration of violated rights (VKS, 1996, No. 2). The provisions on human rights are contained in Chapter 1 of the Constitution 'On the Foundations of the Constitutional Order' and in Chapter 2 'On Human Rights and Freedoms'. These chapters may be changed only according to special procedure, and that represents an additional legal guarantee. The rights and freedoms contained in the Constitution are considered as basic or fundamental ones, but they do not exclude the existence of other rights. The enumeration in the Constitution of the Russian Federation of basic rights and freedoms should not be interpreted as a denial or diminution of other universally recognized human and civil rights and freedoms (Article 55.1 of the Constitution).

The Constitution, following the Declaration of the Rights and Freedoms of Man and Citizen, recognizes a division of rights and freedoms of man and the citizen. The articles contain the first group of rights granted to everybody ('everybody may ... ', 'everybody has the right ... ', 'everybody is guaranteed ... '). The second group of rights and freedoms are guaranteed only for Russian citizens. As a rule, political rights are included in this list: the right to hold meetings, demonstrations or picketing; the right to participate in the state government and justice; and electoral rights. Only Russian citizens have the right to have land in their private ownership. Traditionally for Russia, the human rights and freedoms are declared together with the obligations. The Constitution revised the list of obligations contained in the Soviet constitutions. For example, labour is a right but no longer an obligation. Among the obligations included into the Constitution are the obligation to pay taxes (Article 57 of the Constitution; there was no such civil duty in the Soviet constitutional model where taxes were deducted from salaries automatically), a duty to preserve nature and the environment (Article 58), and the duty to defend the home country (Article 59). The latter duty was entrenched with specifications in socialist constitutions since 1918. In general, the rights, freedoms and obligations constitute the constitutional status of man and the citizen which is the basis of legal capacity.

In the Soviet period, the articles on human rights were to be detailed in ordinary laws, otherwise it was impossible to realize them. At present human rights, as well as the Constitution, have direct force. For example, the Constitution permits an alternative to military service, but before the adoption of the Federal Law of 25 July

2002 'On the Alternative Civil Service' (SZ, 2002 No. 30), as amended on 25 November 2013, this right was not institutionally protected. Nevertheless, the Constitutional Court of Russia in its Decision of 26 September 1996 (SZ, 1997 No. 2) ruled that the lack of a law regulating the conditions and the procedure of the alternative civil service may not prevent from the realization of that right if a citizen has the grounds for it in accordance with the constitutional provisions. Later in the Judgment of 23 November 1999 (SZ, 1999 No. 51) the Court pointed out that the right to the alternative civil service has direct force and should be secured independently of whether or not a law details its realization.

I. The Protection of Human Rights

229. The Constitutional Court ruled that an individual in his or her relationship with the State acts not as an object of a state activity but as an equal person who may defend his rights by any means not prohibited by law as well as dispute with it (Judgment of 3 May 1995, SZ, 1995 Nos 2–3). The Constitution establishes the system of guarantees for the realization of human rights and freedoms.[53] An individual may defend his rights (Article 45.2 of the Constitution) by any means not prohibited by law. Citizens of Russia may appeal to state bodies with proposals, applications and complaints.[54] Different state bodies and officials are responsible for the protection of human rights: the President as guarantor of the Constitution, the Human Rights Commissioner (*see* below paragraph 263), ordinary courts and the Constitutional Court. The Constitution enlarges the role of courts as guarantors of human rights and freedoms. In the Soviet period, people in many cases were not able to appeal to the courts for resolving conflicts, as the administrative system prevailed under which an individual had to appeal to a higher standing body of executive power. This system was not effective and depended heavily on the discretion of officials. The Constitution guarantees court protection of human rights and freedoms (Article 46.1 of the Constitution). The decisions and actions (or inaction) of governmental bodies, local government bodies, social associations and officials may be appealed to the Court. The Constitutional Court found unconstitutional several acts limiting the right of defence in court.[55] International protection of human rights and freedoms is strengthened. An individual may appeal to international bodies for defence of human rights after all available domestic means have been exhausted and if there is an international treaty.[56] Since Russia became a member of the Council

53. E.A. Lukasheva, 'Effectivnost Uridicheski Mehanismov Zaschiti Prav Cheloveka: Politicheskie, Economicheskie, Sotsialno-Psihologitscheskie Aspecti', in *Konstitutsia Rosiiskoi Federatsii i soverschenstvovanie Mechanisma Zaschiti Prav Cheloveka*, ed. Lukasheva (Moskva: Juridicheskaya literatura, 1994), 10.
54. N.U. Hamaneva, 'Konstitutsionnoe Pravo Grazdan na Podachu Obrascheni', *Gosudarstvo i Pravo*, no. 11 (1996): 10.
55. T.G. Morschakova, 'Sudebnaia Zaschita Osnovni Prav Grazdan v Obschem i Constitutsionnom Sudoproizvodstve', in *Sudebni control i prava cheloveka: materiali rossiisko-britanskogo seminara* (Moskva: Institut gosudarstva I prava RAN, 1996).
56. V.A. Kartashkin, 'Rossia i Evropeiskaia Conventsia o Zaschite Prav Cheloveka i Osnovni Svobod', *Moskovski Zhurnal mezhdunarodnogo prava*, no. 3 (1996): 21.

of Europe, citizens may apply to the European Court of Human Rights after suing unsuccessfully within the home country (there are many precedents in the 2000s and 2010s). Citizens may apply as well to the Committee on Human Rights of the Organization of the United Nations.

II. The Restriction of Human Rights and Freedoms

230. The problem of restriction of human rights is of theoretical and practical importance[57]. Some restrictions exist in the nature of rights and freedoms, because the exercise of them must not violate the rights and freedoms of other people (Article 17.3 of the Constitution). As mentioned above, some rights and freedoms depend on citizenship. Russian citizens may have full rights and freedoms at the age of 18 (Article 60 of the Constitution), but some rights may be exercised later (e.g., a candidate for a deputy to the State Duma must be not younger than 21 years old; a candidate for the President, not younger than 35 years old). The Constitution prohibits all forms of restriction of human rights on social, racial, national, linguistic or religious grounds (Article 19.2). Human rights may be restricted by the federal law only to extant required for the protection of the fundamentals of the constitutional system, morality, health, rights and lawful interests of other persons, for ensuring the defence of the country and national security (Article 55.3). These provisions are detailed in the decisions of the Constitutional Court which is of the view that the basis for restriction of human rights cannot be given a broad interpretation (Judgment of 20 December 1995; SZ, 1996 No. 1). According to the legal position formulated in the Judgment of 13 June 1996 (SZ, 1996 No. 26), the principle of proportional restriction of human rights provided for by Article 55.3 means that enumerated public interests may justify legal restriction of human rights if these restrictions are adequate to socially justified aims. Therefore, the Constitutional Court of Russia, when assessing the restriction of human rights and freedoms, reviews the correspondence of the restriction to its aim, as well as the proportionality of the restriction and its aim (Judgment of 4 April 1996 (SZ Russian Federation, 1996 No. 16). The restriction may be established only by the federal legislative body and this power cannot be delegated to the Federal Entities, otherwise it will be impossible to establish equal standards. Under the provisions of Article 71 of the Constitution, the jurisdiction of the Russian Federation includes regulation and protection of the human rights and freedoms while the Federal Entities according to Article 72 of the Constitution only defend human rights. Executive bodies may not restrict human rights by their acts. The Constitutional Court found an act of the Government concerning bank deposits of citizens unconstitutional because it limited human rights. Following Article 29 of the Universal Declaration of Human Rights, the Constitution contains the next grounds for possible restriction of human rights and freedoms: in a state of emergency, in order to ensure the safety of citizens and the

57. *See* V.M. Zhuikov, *Prava Cheloveka i Vlast Zakona* (Moskva: Rossiskaia Pravovaia Academia), 2000.

protection of the constitutional order and in accordance with federal constitutional law (Article 56 of the Constitution). In such a case, the period for which human rights will be limited must be indicated.

231. Human rights and freedoms may be restricted during a state of emergency. The Constitution, following the International Convention on Civil and Political Rights, defends some rights – the right to life, human dignity, personal inviolability, privacy, freedom of conscience, the right to use freely and properly one's abilities for entrepreneurial and other economic activities, the right to a home, and procedural rights (Articles 20, 21, 23.1, 24, 28, 34.1,40.1, 46–54 of the Constitution), the exercise of which cannot depend on the aims of the governmental bodies during the state of emergency. The restriction of rights may depend on the 'public status' of a person. For example, a person who decided to be a deputy must accept some limitations connected with the status of deputy, such as the interdiction to own an enterprise. In such a case, the decision regarding the restriction of some rights is taken consciously. The Constitutional Court does not consider such restriction a violation of human rights (Judgment of 19 April 1996, SZ, 1996 No. 18).

III. Equality

232. The Constitution contains provisions on equality before the court and the law, state guarantees of the equality of rights and freedoms regardless of sex, race, nationality, language, origin, property and employment status, place of residence, attitude to religion, convictions, membership in public associations and other circumstances, as well as of equal rights and opportunities for men and women (Article 19). There is no equality or non-discrimination legislation in Russia, but a lot of federal laws have an equality clause (Labour Code, the Foundations of Health Care Legislation, federal laws on education, trade unions, state civil service). The Criminal Code provides for a criminal liability in the case of discrimination actions.

The Constitutional Courts examined a lot of complaints regarding the non-observance of this principle on the grounds of sex, age, professional occupation, place of residence or religion and formulated the basic legal positions in this field[58]. According to the Court, the constitutional list of grounds which exclude any discrimination is not a closed one, it may be concretized by legislation or law-enforcing practice (Judgment of 4 February 1992, VKS, 1993 No. 1). The principle of equality serves as a constitutional criterion of evaluation of the legislative regulation of human rights, and its application may have different manifestations: in the field of personal rights as a rule it means the formal equality, but in the field of socio-economic rights that may result in material inequality (Decision of 2 February 2006). The Constitutional Court, examining the problem of equality in the social State, considered that equality before the law and the court does not exclude factual differences (Judgment of 3 May 1995, SZ, 1995 No. 19). Social equality is achieved

58. A.L. Kononov, 'Zaschita Prav i Svobod Cheloveka i Grazdanina', in *Konstitutsionni Sud Rossiiskoi Federatsii*, ed. Morschakova (Moskva: Jurist, 1997), 185–198.

by positive actions such as equitable redistribution of income and proportioning of taxes (Judgment of 4 April 1996, SZ, 1996 No. 16).

It is necessary to mention that the discrimination cases are very rare in the courts of general jurisdiction. The main reason for that is that the basic concepts of the Western equality law are unknown to Russian legal system, and it is very difficult to prove the fact of discrimination. At the same time the official reports of federal and regional human rights commissioners reflect the existence of facts of discrimination on the basis of sex and religion, systematic latent discrimination on the basis of ethnic origin in several Federal Entities (Annual Report of the Russian Human Rights Commissioner for 2004, RG, 31 March 2005), as well as discrimination on the basis of sex and age in labour relations (Annual Report of the Bashkortostan Human Rights Commissioner for 2007, Special Report of the Sverdlovsk oblast Commissioner 'On Infringement of Constitutional Rights of Citizens on the Grounds of Sex and Age in the Sphere of Labour' of 2005).

§2. Civil and Political Rights

233. The rights and freedoms contained in the Russian Constitution are not directly divided into groups but according to their content they may be classified as civil (in Russian legal doctrine they are also called 'personal'[59]), political and socio-economic rights. In the elaboration of the conception of civil and political rights and freedoms, Russia follows international acts. These rights are natural and inalienable. People have them from birth and independent of their national status. Only those political rights which are directly connected with the exercise of the state power are enjoyed by the citizens of the State (e.g., right to participate in the administration of the state affairs, electoral rights and right to take part in a referendum, equal access to state service, right to participate in the administration of justice). These rights were not among the top priorities of the Socialist State, and the rudiments of that approach may be seen in the actions of the modern officials and state bodies.

234. The Russian Constitution guarantees the right to life as an inalienable right (Article 20). At the same time the Constitution provided for the death penalty as an exclusive punishment for particularly serious crimes against life that may be instituted by the federal law until its abolition with the accused having the right to hear his case by a court with the participation of a jury. In the Judgment of 2 February 1999 (SZ, 1999 No. 6) the Constitutional Court interpreted this right of an accused as a special procedural guarantee of the judicial protection of the right to life. At present the Criminal Code, however, continues to establish the death penalty for five criminal offences – murder with the aggravating circumstances, assassination attempt against state official or public figure, attempt on the life of a person administering justice or preliminary investigation, attempt on the life of a law-enforcement officer and genocide, but it may not be applied. Though the Federal

---

59. M.V. Baglai, *Konstitutsionnoe Pravo Rossiiskoi Federatsii* (Moskva: Norma, 1997), 164.

Assembly did not ratify the Protocol No. 6 to the European Convention, the President of Russia had issued an Edict of 16 May 1996 No. 724 'On the Gradual Decrease of the Application of the Death Penalty in Connection with the Accession to the Council of Europe' (SZ, 1996 No. 21) that provided for a moratorium on the death penalty. That approach of the Russian Federation bodies of State power remains unchanged since then, despite the different attitudes of the popular majority. Quite recently, the Constitutional Court of Russia in its decision of 7 March 2017 (SZ, 2017 No. 12) has stated once more that 'the Russian Federation has a legitimate constitutional regime, taking into account foreign obligations of the state and trends occurring within international legal development. For a long time Russia uses prohibition upon death sentences; therefore, it is going an irreversible process designated for abolishing death penalty'. The terms of the process of transforming a moratorium into a legally valuable policy remain undefined. Such position means that the death penalty is not abolished completely, while not being implemented either in Russia.

It bears noting that Russia has substantial experience in abolishing corporal punishment or strong restrictions upon death sentences. Legally, the Russian Empire did not implement it between the 1740s and 1860s in the peacetime. Across its sixty-nine years of existence the USSR cancelled the death penalty two times (1922 and 1947) and twice restored it (1932 and 1950).

In 1993, a jury was established in nine Federal Entities as an experiment, and as a result the position of accused persons in different regions of the country has become unequal. Therefore, the Constitutional Court in the Judgment of 2 February 1999 ruled that the death penalty may not be applied until coming into force a federal law which guarantees any person accused of committing a crime punishable with a death penalty in any part of the country the right to hear his case by a jury. In 2004, a jury was introduced in all Federal Entities except the Chechen Republic. In 2009, the Supreme Court asked the Constitutional Court to explain the provisions of his Judgment of 2 February 1999 taking into account the fact that jury trial is to be introduced in 2010 in the Chechen Republic where a strong tradition of capital punishment exists. The Constitutional Court in the Decision of 19 November 2009 (SZ, 2009 No. 48) pointed out that at present in Russia there is a complex moratorium concerning the application of the death penalty, the stable guarantees of the right not to be subject to a death penalty are formed, exists the legitimate constitutional regime in the framework of which – in accordance with the international tendencies and obligations of the Russian Federation – the irreversible process is going on aimed at abolition of death penalty and realization of the goal proclaimed in Article 20.2. The Court ruled that the establishment of a jury trial on all the territory of the Russian Federation does not open the possibility to apply the capital punishment, even on the basis of the verdict of a jury. The fact that in 2017 the Constitutional Court must reproduce, word for word, its decision of 2009 shows that the vast majority of public opinion - and not only within the Chechen Republic – does not understand or approve of a moratorium policy.

235. The Constitution protects human dignity (Article 21) and the right to liberty and personal inviolability (Article 22). The Constitutional Court interprets the dignity as an inalienable characteristic of a person, the basis of the recognition and respect of all his or her rights and freedoms (Judgment of 27 July 2000, SZ, 2000 No. 27). It is necessary to note that the Court ruled that deprivation or temporarily termination of lawfully acquired citizenship (Judgment of 16 May 1996, SZ, 1996 No. 3), restriction of the right of the convicted to try to achieve the mitigation of his fate (Decision of 11 July 2006), as well as deprivation of a possibility to restore the person's right violated as a result of a terrorist act (Decision of 27 December 2005), violate the human dignity. Protecting human dignity, the Russian Federation Constitution forbids torture, violence or other severe or humiliating treatment or punishment; no person may be as well subject to medical, scientific or other experiments without his or her free consent (Article 21.2). Being bound by international treaties, Russia is changing its system of prisons and custody in accordance with international standards. The right to personal inviolability is broadly interpreted in the Russian legal doctrine. According to the Constitutional Court, the right to physical inviolability presupposes as well the legal protection of the body of the dead person, that includes the right to be buried in accordance with his will (Judgment of 28 June 2007, SZ, 2007 No. 27).

The Constitution establishes the control of the court over legality and validity of decisions on arrest and detention (Article 22.2; since the 1920s to early 1990s it was exclusively a power of the bodies of the Public Procurator's Office). Russian law distinguishes administrative arrest (up to fifteen days, in the case of a state of emergency up to thirty days, according to the decision of a judge or court); arrest as a form of criminal punishment; and disciplinary arrest used in the army. Any detention without the decision of the court may last only forty-eight hours. However, according to the interim provisions of the Constitution, as long as criminal-procedural legislation of the Russian Federation has not been brought into line with the provision of this Constitution, the previous procedure for the arrest, detention and keeping in custody of persons suspected of committing a crime applied.

236. Article 27.1 of the Constitution guarantees everyone who is legally present on the territory of the Russian Federation the right to free movement and freedom to choose their place of temporary or permanent residence. In the Soviet period, this right was seriously restricted by *propiska* – the system of registration and control of the residents, which presupposed the administrative (de facto the police) permission of the governmental bodies to choose a town, city, or village as a place of residence. *Propiska* which was a basis for limitation of other rights (e.g., labour rights) was proclaimed invalid by the Committee of the Constitutional Review of the USSR in 1991. The Russian Federation Law of 25 June 1993 'On the Right of Citizens of the Russian Federation to Freedom of Movement, Choice of the Place of Residence within the Russian Federation' (Ved. Russian Federation, 1993 No. 32), as amended on 2 June 2016 provides for registration of residents that presupposes the obligation of the citizen to inform the governmental bodies about the place of their stay or residence and the obligation of the registration body to register a person if that person has documents provided by law. The right to choose the place of stay or residence may be restricted in a border area, in closed cantonments or administrative-territorial formations, in zones of ecological disaster, in territories where the state of emergency, martial law or special regime in case of danger of infections and mass diseases or poisoning has been introduced. The Constitutional Court pointed out that the right to choose a place of residence is an integral part of the freedom to constitute oneself, and therefore the registration may not have a permissive character or serve as a basis for the restriction of rights (Judgment of 4 April 1996, SZ, 1996 No. 16). Nevertheless, it is necessary to note that the law-enforcement bodies do not follow this legal position very strictly.

Under the constitutional provisions, a person is free to leave the boundaries of Russia, and the citizen has the right to return freely into the country (Article 27.2). According to the Federal Law of 15 August 1996 'On the Procedure of Exit and Entry into the Russian Federation' (SZ R, 1996 No. 34), as amended on 20 October 2016, the right to exit from the country may be restricted only in the cases enumerated in the law, for example when a person who has access to state secrets signed an employment contract providing for the temporary restriction of his right to exit or evades performing his obligations imposed on him by a court decision. In all cases of temporary restriction of that right a migration control body issues a notification indicating the reason and the term of a restriction. Decisions in this field are subject to judicial control. The Constitutional Court ruled that the restriction of the right to leave the Russian Federation may not be interpreted broadly or resulted in the derogation of the civil, political or other rights guaranteed by the Constitution or legislation, as well as in the criminal liability for flight abroad (Judgment of 20 December 1995, SZ, 1996 No. 1).

237. Freedom of expression has important communicative meaning as a condition for the due functioning of the democratic society. Article 29 contained guarantees for freedom of speech and thought, freedom of information and freedom of mass media. The Constitution limits freedom of thought and speech by prohibiting propaganda or agitation which arouses social, racial, national or religious hatred and hostility. There are other limits, for example, propaganda of hostility to any language is prohibited. Responsibility for such actions made in public or by using mass media is set out in the Criminal Code. In memory of the previous socialist development, section 3 guarantees that nobody shall be forced to express thoughts and convictions or deny them.

The freedom of mass media was announced at the beginning of *perestroika*. The membership of Russia in the Council of Europe influences the content of the freedom of mass media. In the Soviet period, the mass media were owned and controlled by the State completely. At present, the State does not interfere in the activity of mass media to such an extent. According to the Russian Federation Law of 27 December 1991 'On Mass Media' (Ved. Russian Federation, 1992 No. 7), as amended on 9 February 2009, censorship in any form is forbidden and there is a solid list of those official materials that are to be published by the state periodicals anyway. Particularly, all judgments and decisions of the Constitutional Court of Russia are published currently in its own Gazette ('*Vestnik Constitutsionnogo suda*' – VKS), in the official Russian State Gazette ('*Rossiyskaya gazeta*'), and on the State Internet-site: http://www.pravo.gov.ru. At present, mass media may express and defend different positions and do so. Modern Russian legal doctrine and the courts recognize that is a vitally necessary condition for democratic government.

In 1994–2000 a Chamber on information conflicts was established under the President's office to settle conflicts in the sphere of the mass media. It was not a judicial body and its decisions had the character of recommendations, therefore they could not be effective or popular either. Since 2001, after abolishing the Chamber on Information Conflicts, mass media owners and activists had sought the protection of the courts.

238. Under the provisions of Article 29.4 of the Constitution, everyone has the right to seek, receive, transmit, produce and disseminate freely information by any lawful means independently of the form of its presentation. The Federal Law of 27 July 2006 'On Information, Information Technologies and Protection of Information' (SZ, 2006 No. 31 (P.1)) as amended on 1 May 2017, contains the list of information access to which cannot be restricted (e.g., legislation concerning the human rights and freedoms, legal status of state bodies and bodies of local government, information about conditions of environment, the activity of bodies of state power and of local government, the use of budgetary resources, etc.). The right of information according to the Declaration of the Rights and Freedoms of Man and Citizen may be limited for protection of personal, family, professional, commercial and state secrets and morality, according to the general provisions of the Constitution prescribing restrictions of human rights and freedoms.

The Constitutional Court confirmed that the freedom of information might be limited by a law in which a list of state secrets could be enumerated (Judgment of 20 December 1995, SZ, 1996 No. 1). The Federal Russian Federation Law of 21 July 1993 'On State Secrets' (RG, 1993, 21 September), as amended on 8 March 2015, determines the list of data containing state secrets, as well as those data which may not be recognized as state secrets. It is forbidden to classify as secret information regarding: accidents, catastrophes and calamities; situation in the sphere of ecology, health care, demography, education, culture, agriculture and crime; privileges, compensations and social guarantees of citizens, officials, enterprises, institutions and organizations; facts of violations of human rights or principle of legality by bodies of state power and officials; amounts of the state currency reserves and gold reserves: the health conditions of the high state officials of the country. It means indeed a break with Soviet standard of maintaining maximum secrecy regime in every area. The list of data containing state secrets is prepared by the Commission on the protection of state secrets which is appointed by the President on the proposal of the Government.

The Constitution guarantees the right to privacy of correspondence, of telephone conversations and of postal, telegraph and other communications. This right may be restricted only according to a court decision. Articles 23 and 24.1 establish that everyone has the right to the inviolability of private life, personal and family privacy and protection of honour and good name. Collecting, keeping and disseminating information about the private life of a person is not permitted without his or her consent. Professional secrets (of doctors, lawyers, priests and representatives of other professions who are responsible for the divulging of the information they received fulfilling their professional duties) are regulated by several laws: medical secrets are regulated by the Foundations of the Legislation on the Health Care of citizens of Russian Federation, and the rights of lawyers are defended by the criminal-procedural legislation. For example, they cannot be interrogated as witnesses on information they received while giving legal assistance.

239. A particular form of the freedom of information is the freedom of creative activity (freedom of literary, artistic, scientific, technical and other types of the activity) and of teaching. This information is intellectual property and is protected by law. Since 2013 the specialized Court for Intellectual Rights, created in 2011 for the protection of copyright, is sitting in Russia. The functioning of that Court, along with success of arbitration courts, appears to be indicators of a positive development in judicial power in the Russian Federation.

At the same time, the rising importance of information in the world and terrorist attacks and other social menaces to state (national) security are the reasons for strengthening state overview/control guidelines over the information sphere. The Presidential Edict No. 646 of 5 December 2016 has imposed a 'Doctrine of Information Security of the Russian Federation'. The instrument prescribes national interests contained in the area of information security: (1) maintenance and protection of constitutional rights and freedoms of individuals and citizens; (2) maintaining the sustainable functioning of critical informational structures; (3) innovative development of Russian-made information technologies and electronics industry, and their transformation into competitive models; (4) promoting trustworthy information covering the State policies of Russia and its official position on socially meaningful events within the Russian Federation and across the world; (5) assistance for building a system of international information security; (6) neutralization of informational influences tending to the erosion of traditional Russian spiritual and moral values; (7) forming a personal informational security culture in Russian society.

The Doctrine contains a description of fundamental information threats. Among them are included the following ones: (1) low potential and not enough efficiency of Russian academic elaborations in the field, and their weak implementation; (2) use by foreign powers of their technological superiority for dominance in all the information space; (3) strengthening possibilities of Western information and technical influence upon information infrastructure for military purposes; (4) activation of technical intelligence directed against Russia from abroad; (5) politically and socially destabilizing efforts of separate States in various regions of the world; (6) increasing prejudicial evaluations of Russian policies in the foreign mass media field; (7) discrimination measures against Russian mass media and their personnel abroad; (8) a rise in cyber crimes and widening its scope and sophistication, especially in the spheres of credit and finance and in the form of attacks on critical information infrastructures.

The essence and conclusion of the Doctrine appeared to be the following ones: at the present time the management of the Internet network on the basis of justice and mutual confidence between different States seems impossible.

Several provisions of the Doctrine have been implemented and were entrenched in amendments introduced recently into the Federal Law 'On Communication' and Federal Law 'On Information, Information Technologies and Protection of Data'. Both legislative acts as amended on 1 May 2017 are in force currently. According to the amendments, postal and telegraph/phone operators, as well as internet providers, now have to retain texts of messages and any other information (photos, oral information, video, etc. transmitted by users) for six months, and the metadata of transmitting, delivering and processing of any information exclusively in the territory of Russia for three years. Also all operators employed in the communications sphere have to submit any of the above-mentioned information to the investigation bodies or to state security bodies, whereas Internet operators, messengers, etc., furthermore, are obliged to assist in decoding of the transmitting, delivering and processing e-messages, too. Between March and June 2017 and March and May 2018 once again, there was a fierce dispute between Roskomnadzor and the messenger enterprise 'Telegram' for refusing to collaborate and concerning the constitutionally entrenched right for secrecy of correspondence.

However, the amendments mentioned above, while worsening the situation of the telecoms operators (especially those connected with cloud technologies), do not cancel or diminish directly the basic constitutional right of the individual for information which has come to play an enormous role in contemporary social fabric.

240. Under the constitutional provisions, the freedom of association including the right to establish trade unions is guaranteed for everyone (Article 30). It presupposes as well the right not to be coerced into joining any association or into membership thereof. The Constitution provides for the freedom of public associations activities (Article 30.1) and the equality of associations before the law (Article 13.4). At the same time it sets certain limits, prohibiting the establishment and the activities of those associations, whose aims and actions are directed at forcible alteration of the fundamentals of constitutional governance, violation of the integrity of Russia, undermining of the security of the state, the forming of armed units and incitement of social, racial, national and religious strife (Article 13.5).

The constitutional provisions are detailed in the Federal Law of 19 May 1995 'On Public Associations' (SZ, 1995 No. 21), as amended on 2 June 2016. The specific aspects of creation, functioning and liquidation of particular associations may be regulated by special laws. At present, several laws are adopted in this field: Federal Law of 11 August 1995 'On Charitable Activities and Organizations' (SZ, 1995 No. 33), as amended on 5 May 2014, Federal Law of 12 January 1996 'On Nonprofit Organizations' (SZ, 1996 No. 3), as amended on 3 July 2016, Federal Law of 12 January 1996 'On Trade Unions, Their Rights and Guarantees of Their Activity' (SZ, 1996 No. 3), as amended on 3 July 2016, Federal Law of 11 July 2001 'On Political Parties' (SZ, 2001 No. 29), as amended on 9 March 2016. According to the Federal Law of 19 May 1995 'On Public Associations in the Russian Federation', any voluntary, self-governing, non-profit formation, set up at the initiative of individuals who have united on the basis of the interests to realize common goals, indicated in their charter may be deemed a public association. Those associations may have different organizational and legal forms: non-governmental organizations, mass movements, public funds, non-governmental institutions, local community bodies or political parties. In accordance with the territorial sphere of activities, there are all-Russia, interregional, regional and local public associations.

All-Russia associations have structural subdivisions and carry their activity in more than half of the Federal Entities, interregional ones – in less than half of those entities. The State may not interfere in the internal affairs and activity of associations, but it may render support for their activity in the form of target-oriented financing of particular programmes of these associations or social order for the implementation of various state programmes, conclusion of contracts of any type with these organizations. Public associations are set up at the initiative of at least three individuals, who, as a rule, are not younger than 18 years old. For acquiring the rights of legal entity a public association is subject to state registration by the federal body of state registration or by a territorial agency thereof. State registration may be refused if a statute of that association contradicts the Constitution or federal law, if not all necessary documents are presented, if these documents are presented not in proper form or contain wrong information, if name of that association insults the morality or outrages national and religious feelings of citizens. The refusal to register an association may be appealed against to the court. According to data of the Ministry of Justice, on 1 January 2012 in the Russian Federation there were registered 119,247 public associations; among them were: 54,113 non-governmental organizations, 1,808 mass movements, 6,972 public funds, 626 non-governmental institutions, 185 local community bodies and 7 political parties. By 2018 the Ministry of Economic Development has counted in Russia around 140,000 non-commercial associations with almost one million persons employed.

The activity of a public association may be suspended for a period not exceeding six months in the case of violation of the Constitution and current legislation of the Russian Federation or performing actions contradicting its statutory goals. The federal registry body of a state or a territorial agency thereof, the Procurator General of Russia, or a public prosecutor make a presentation regarding those violations to the leading body of the association and fix a time term for their elimination. If those violations are not eliminated within that period, a state body which made the presentation may suspend the activity of the association. The decision on suspension may be appealed against to the court. Violation of rights and freedom of persons, repeated or serious violations of the Constitution, federal legislation and other legal acts, systematic actions contradicting its statutory goals or non-elimination of violations within a fixed term may lead to the liquidation of that public association. An appropriate application regarding international or All-Russia association is filed with a court by the Procurator General request or by the federal body of state registration (*Roskomnadzor*).

As far as it is forbidden to create public associations and to allow them to function if goals or activity of those organizations are aimed at the performance of the extremist activity, the activity of an association may be suspended or it may be liquidated in accordance with the provisions of the Federal Law of 27 July 2002 'On the Counteraction of Extremist Activity' (SZ, 2002 No. 30), as amended on 23 November 2015. In the case of disclosing facts concerning the presence of extremism in the actions of a public association or its territorial subdivision the Procurator General or a public prosecutor, the federal body of state registration or a territorial agency thereof may give a warning and fix a time term (at least two months) to eliminate them. That warning may be appealed against to the court. An organization is subject to liquidation or ban (if it is not a legal entity) by a court if a warning was not appealed against or it was recognized as legal by the court, if that organization or its territorial subdivision did not eliminate the violations or if within twelve months after the warning the new facts of extremist activity were revealed. The procedure may be initiated by the Procurator General or a public prosecutor, the federal body of state registration or a territorial agency thereof. They as well may suspend its activity pending the examination of a court of the statement on its ban or liquidation if the extremist activity resulted in the violation of rights and freedoms of persons, the infliction of damage to their personality and health, environment, public order, national security, property, lawful economic interests of individuals or legal entities, society and State or pose a real threat of inflicting such damage. The list of liquidated or banned public associations is made public on the sites of the federal body of state registration body or territorial agencies thereof or in the official periodicals determined by the Government of Russia.

In 2005 there was established and formed the Public Chamber whose main aim was to facilitate coordination between the Russian citizens, public associations and bodies of state power and local self-government in order to discuss and help to solve the most important problems of the country. Under the provisions of the Federal Law of 4 April 2005 'On the Public Chamber of the Russian Federation' (SZ, 2005 No. 15), as amended on 28 November 2015, it may put forward and support civil initiatives 'of national importance' (however, that vague expression still is not explained by courts or legal doctrine either), hold the public reviews of the draft laws and legal acts, execute the public control over the activity of the federal and regional bodies of executive power, as well as over the observance of the freedom of expression in mass media, draw up recommendations to governmental bodies. Annually the Public Chamber prepares a report on the state of civil society in the Russian Federation. Among the functions of the Public Chamber it is possible to discover a considerable number of intersection points with the powers of the State Duma, the Commissioner for Human Rights, the Public Procurator's Office and mass media (TV channels, Internet, newspapers).

The Chamber consists of 126 members, among which 42 are appointed by the President of the Russian Federation, 42 are elected from All-Russia public associations and other 42 from interregional and regional public associations. There are no members of the Chamber elected by direct popular election. The Chamber has no offices and budget of its own, and its members work on free-of-charge basis.

241. The right to gather peacefully (Article 31 of the Constitution) belongs to citizens of Russia. The right is regulated by the Federal Law of 19 June 2004 'On Rallies, Meetings, Demonstrations, Marches and Picketing' (SZ, 2004 No. 25), as amended on 9 March 2016. Amendments to the Law have extended considerably the powers of police formations and other laws-protecting forces in the field of counterstrikes against potential extremist menaces.

According to the provisions of the Federal Law mentioned above, a public event may be organized by a citizen, political party or association. The promoter of a public event notifies a regional executive authority or a local self-government body not earlier than fifteen and not later than ten days prior to this event. In case of a picketing this term is reduced to three days before this event (four days, if there is official holiday or Sunday within this period). A public event may be held at any place where such event creates no threat of collapse of building and structures or to the security of participants. It is prohibited to hold rallies and meetings in certain places, for instance – on the territories directly adjacent to residences of the President, buildings accommodating courts or prisons. The promoter may not hold a meeting if the notice was not filed in due time or no agreement was reached with the authorities as to the alteration at their motivated proposal of the place or time of holding this event. It is necessary to note that the Human Rights Commissioner submitted in 2007 the Special report regarding the respect of the constitutional right to gather peacefully on the territory of the Russian Federation, where pointed out that the practice of 'agreement' of place or time of the public event has the political and not the legal character. In the dissenting opinion to the Decision of the Constitutional Court of 2 April 2009 (VKS, 2009 No. 6) the Judge A.L. Kononov stressed that there are mass violations of that right in different parts of the country, and according to the administrative and judicial practice, the agreement is interpreted as a consent or permit to hold a public event, and in many cases the public bodies consider to have powers to appraise not only time and place of a public event, but its goals, forms, amount of participants and expediency.

242. The Constitution contains guarantees for participation in the activity of the State (Article 32). Citizens have the right to participate in managing state affairs directly (through elections and referenda) or through representatives. The Constitutional Court of the Russian Federation ruled that regional legislator may not introduce additional conditions for the passive electoral rights including term of residence on the territory of the constitutional entity and fluency in the state language of the republic (Judgment of 27 April 1998, SZ, 1998 No. 18; Decision of 13 November 2001). At the same time, according to the legal position of the Court, the ban of eligibility for those citizens who have as well foreign citizenship does not violate their rights as far as the Constitution admits the possibility of regulating the peculiarity of their status by a federal law (Article 62.2) and therefore does not obstacle the special regulation of their political rights (Decision of 4 December 2007). The Russian citizens have equal access to the state civil service. This right is regulated by the Federal Law of 27 July 2004 'On the State Civil Service of the Russian Federation' (SZ, 2004 No. 31), as amended on 30 December 2015. A person may become a civil servant if he/she is a Russian citizen, not younger than 18 years and not older than 60 years, knows the state language and has necessary professional qualifications, including a certain education, knowledge, skills and experience. Access to the state civil service is prohibited for those persons who are citizens of another State, have medical contraindications, do not submit information regarding their income or property situation, or have submitted false information. This right may be restricted by a court for some time.

§3. Social and Economic Rights

243. During the Soviet period these rights were among the top priorities of the State, which guaranteed to its citizens the free-of-charge gradual education, health care and medical assistance in state and municipal institutions. At the same time the term 'social state' was not known to legal doctrine and practice either. The present Constitution proclaimed Russia a social State whose policies are aimed at creating conditions for a dignified life and free development of a person (Article 7). It is necessary to note that coordination of policy on health issues, motherhood, fatherhood and childhood, social protection, including social security allowances, are within the joint jurisdiction of the Federation and its Entities (Article 72.1(g)).

The current legislation, in general, corresponds to international standards in this sphere: in 2009 the Russian Federation ratified the European Social Charter. At the same time social-economic rights depend on the activity of the State, its positive actions and economical resources. After the break-up of the Soviet Union and of the Soviet economic system the level of the social guarantees declined, and the enforcement of these rights (payment of salaries, pensions, benefits) became a serious problem. At the same time that encouraged the State to look for new mechanisms to secure the social-economic rights, for example, now several social services may be granted not in material but in monetary form.

244. In contemporary Russian legal doctrine the right to property is interpreted as an economic right, but it has different nature than social and economic rights. It is natural and inalienable right, one of those basic rights that guarantee the freedom of a person. The socialist State rejected the right to private property, but under the provisions of the modern Constitution that right is protected by law (Article 35). According to the Judgment of the Constitutional Court of 20 May 1997 (SZ, 1997 No. 21), the Constitution guarantees the protection of private property in the sphere of private relations and in the relations of State and a person in public sphere. The Court pointed out (Judgment of 20 July 1999, SZ, 1999 No. 30) that property relations in the Russian Federation must be regulated in accordance with the principles of the State governed by the rule of law on the basis of justice and legal equality. Under the constitutional provisions, nobody may be arbitrarily deprived of his or her property except on the basis of a court order. Forced expropriation of property for state needs may take place only on condition of a preliminary and fair compensation. The Constitution as well guarantees the right of inheritance. In spite of it, several federal and regional laws adopted in the 2000s and 2010s do not comply with these constitutional norms. For instance, the Federal Law of 1 December 2007 'On Preparing Winter Olympic Games at City of Sochi and on Amendments to Some Legislative Acts of the Russian Federation' (SZ, 2007 No. 51), as well as the Federal Law of 15 June 2017 'On Renovation of Shelters in Moscow City' recently approved by the Federal Assembly both have produced a wide and sharp critical resonance, in particular because of a lack of respect and guarantees for private property rights and for the human right to a residence.

245. The constitutional provisions regarding the labour rights correspond to international law and reflect the changes of attitude towards compulsory and forced labour. The Soviet legislation established different forms of liability for 'sponging' (parasitism). Now the corresponding provisions are excluded from the Codes. An individual is free not to work. Compulsory labour is forbidden, except during a state of emergency, military service or on the basis of the court decision. The Constitution proclaims simultaneously the right to work and free labour (Article 37). The Constitutional Court pointed out that it does not follow from these provisions that a citizen has the right to be placed in a certain job, that means only the contractual character of work (Judgment of 27 December 1999, SZ, 2000 No. 3). At the same time, according to the Court, the State is obliged to guarantee the just conditions of employment and dismissal, including the proper protection of rights and legal interests of an employee who is economically more weak party in the labour relations, in the case of dissolution of a contract on the initiative of an employer (Judgment of 15 March 2005, SZ, 2005 No. 13). The right to work is interpreted broadly by the Constitution as far as it presupposes the right to make free use of individual's abilities for work and choose the type of activity and occupation, including entrepreneurial and other economic activity not prohibited by law. The Constitution guarantees due labour conditions and protection against unemployment. Federal law establishes a minimum wage which is binding on all employers and is revised from time to time in accordance with the rate of inflation and economic situation.

246. The right to individual and collective labour disputes with the use of means of resolution thereof established by federal law, including the right to strike, is recognized by the Constitution (Article 37.4). The Constitutional Court pointed out that in the process of regulation of that right it is necessary to find a proper balance between the protection of professional interests, the means of which is a strike, and public interests, that may be damaged by it, the ensuring of which is a duty of the legislator (Judgment of 17 May 1995, SZ, 1995 No. 21). The grounds for restriction of the right to strike are enumerated in the Labour Code. It may be restricted during a state of emergency or martial law, in the bodies or organizations of the Armed Forces, military or militarized organizations whose direct responsibility are defence, national security and emergency protection, law-enforcement agencies, as well as organizations directly connected with the life-support system. That right may be restricted as well if a strike was announced not in conformity with the procedure prescribed by the Code.

247. According to the Constitution, everyone has the right to education (Article 43). The State guarantees access to free pre-school, secondary and secondary vocational education in governmental and municipal educational institutions and at enterprises. Basic general education is compulsory and free. Access to higher education may be received on a competitive basis. According to the provisions of the Russian Federation Law of 10 July 1992 'On Education' (Ved. Russian Federation, 1992 No. 30), as amended on 3 July 2016, in force since 1 September 2016, the State supports different forms of education.

248. Social security is regulated by Article 39 of the Constitution. Everyone is guaranteed social security for old age, in case of illness, disability and loss of the bread-winner, and in other cases indicated in the law. Everyone has the right to health protection and medical care. Medical care in the governmental and municipal health institutions is to be rendered to citizens free of charge and funded by the appropriate budget allocation, insurance premiums and other proceeds. Following the European Social Charter, Russia gives additional guarantees to children and women. Article 38 establishes that maternity, childhood and the family is protected by the State. (There were no provisions protecting fatherhood rights yet). The State develops federal programmes for protection and improvement of the public health and supports municipal and private health care systems. The concealment by officials of facts and circumstances which pose a threat to the life and health of people is a prosecutable offence.

249. Under the provisions of Article 40, everyone has the right to a home, and no one may be arbitrarily deprived of a home. According to the legal position of the Constitutional Court, registration or a lack of it may not be a basis for restriction or a condition for realization of that right (Judgment of 25 April 1995, SZ, 1995 No. 18). The temporary absence of a person in the case of imprisonment in itself does not testify to improper realization of the tenant's rights and obligations (in the case of social rent) and may not be deemed an individual ground for its deprivation (Judgment of 23 June 1995, SZ, 1995 No. 27). The housing privatization was one of the most successful reforms of the Russian government. The Constitutional Court ruled that the prohibition of privatization of some objects of the state or municipal housing funds may be conditioned only by the peculiarity of their legal regime (Judgment of 15 June 2006, SZ, 2006 No. 26). The restriction of the right to home by determination of a range of objects not subject to privatization is admissible only in the case that their purpose, location or other circumstances which condition the peculiarity of their legal regime exclude the possibility of their assignation (Decision of 10 December 2002).

Chapter 3. Constitutional Problems of Minorities

T. Vassilieva

§1. Constitutional and Statutory Provisions Regarding National Minorities

250. The Constitution of 1993, unlike the constitutions of several Central and East European countries, does not include a special chapter regarding the protection of national minorities.[60] At the same time, it contains several significant provisions in this field. The State guarantees the equality of rights and freedoms of man and citizen and prohibits any form of individual restriction on the grounds of racial, national, linguistic or religious affiliation (Article 19.2). Everyone has the right to determine and indicate his ethnonational affiliation, but nobody may be forced to do so (Article 26.1). In order to understand the significance and meaning of these provisions, it is necessary to take into account the previous practice. For a long time the Soviet citizens had to indicate their ethnic origin in any form filled up by them. The ethnic origin was determined on the basis of the parent's affiliation which was stated in their internal passports. If the mother and father had different nationalities, a person could choose one of them. At present the determination of a nationality is a personal choice, which cannot be regulated by state enactments.

After the break-up of the Soviet Union the enjoyment of native languages became the top priority in the cultural and political sphere of the republics. According to the research of ethnologists in Yakutia, Tatarstan, North Ossetia and Tuva, the values of a civil society for Russians were more important than the development of national culture or language, whereas for non-Russians the order of priorities was different.[61] Taking into consideration such tendencies, the Constitution regulates linguistic rights (Article 26.2). In comparison with the legislation, those rights are to be interpreted broadly. The Constitution of 1978 granted the right to enjoy one's native language, which included instruction and upbringing (Article 48), whereas that of 1993 guarantees the right to enjoy one's native language and to choose freely a language of communication, upbringing, instruction and creativity.

Article 68 of the Constitution indicates Russian language as official one ('the language of the State'). Its status is detailed in the Federal Law 'On the State Language of the Russian Federation' of 1 June 2005, as amended on 5 May 2014. However, the republics, like Federal Entities in Canada, India, US and South Africa, are competent to establish their own state languages, which may be used along with

60. L.V. Andrichenko, *Regulirovanie I zashita prav natsional'nikh men'shinstv i korennych malochislennych narodov v Rossiiskoi Federatsii* (Moskva: Gorodets, 2005); V.A. Kryazhkov, *Korennie malochislennie narodi v rossiiskom prave* (Moskva: Norma, 2010); A. Osipov, 'National Cultural Autonomy in Russia: A Case of Symbolic Law', *Review of Central and East European Law*, no. 35 (2010): 139–158.

61. L. Drobizheva, 'Sotsial'no-kul'turnaia distantsia kak faktor mezhetnicheskih otnoshenii', in *Identichnost' i konflikt v postsovetskih gosudarstvah*, ed. Olkott, Tishkov & Malashenko (Moskva: Tsentr Karnegi, 1997), 52.

Russian in government and local self-government bodies, as well as in the institutions of the republics. Furthermore, the right to retain languages and to create conditions for their study and development is guaranteed to all peoples living in the territory of the Russian Federation.

The Constitution stresses the necessity to ensure the rights of numerically small indigenous peoples in accordance with international standards (Article 69). Economic expansion and migration into the territories of their traditional settlement caused a substantial worsening of the ecological and demographic situation. As a result, the majority of persons belonging to those peoples are occupied in non-traditional branches of the economy and have no access to natural resources. Therefore, the protection of indigenous habitats and traditional ways of living of numerically small ethnic communities was included in the list of issues belonging to the joint jurisdiction of the Federation and Federal Entities (Article 72.1(l)).

Unfortunately, the constitutional regulation of the division of jurisdiction cannot be considered optimal from the viewpoint of the legislative technique, given that the federal governmental bodies have exclusive powers to regulate and protect rights of national minorities (Article 71(c)) while at the same time the protection of national minorities rights is indicated among the matters of joint jurisdiction (Article 72.1(b)).

The rights of national minorities basically are regulated by several laws – the RSFSR Law of 25 October 1991 'On Languages of the Peoples of the RSFSR' (Ved. RSFSR, 1991 No. 50) as amended on the Federal Law of 12 March 2014, the Federal Law of 17 June 1996 'On Cultural National Autonomy' (SZ, 1996 No. 25), as amended by the Federal Law of 9 February 2009, and the Federal Law of 30 April 1999 'On the Guarantees of the Rights of the Numerically Small Indigenous Peoples of the Russian Federation' (SZ, 1999 No. 18), as amended by the Federal Law of 5 April 2009. In 1998, the Russian Federation ratified the Framework Convention for the Protection of National Minorities (Federal Law of 18 June 1998).

§2. Language Rights

251. Under the provisions of the Language Law the people of Russia that do not have state or territorial units or that live outside of them have better possibilities to use their language in individual localities of their settlement. In that case their language may be used as an internal official language, as a language of office work and communication in industry, commerce, power engineering and communication, and as a language for the denomination of geographic entities and topographic and traffic signs. In accordance with the decisions of electoral commissions, in such localities the ballot papers for elections and referenda may be published in those languages which are not official ones. This rule is also applied to the protocols of the final results of the ballot.

Citizens of Russia have the right to receive secondary general education in their native tongue and to choose the language of instruction within the possibilities of the educational system. They may file recommendations, applications and complaints to the state bodies, institutions and associations in their national language, although the replies are given in the applicant's language or the official language. In court, persons who do not know the language of proceedings may participate through an interpreter and make statements and give explanations in their mother tongue or in any other language which they speak fluently. In the documents issued by the state bodies or in official registers personal names must be written in conformity with their national traditions.

§3. Cultural National Autonomy

252. According to the legislation of the Russian Federation, a cultural national autonomy is a form of national cultural self-determination, it may be deemed a public association of citizens who consider themselves belonging to a certain ethnic community and find themselves in a position of national minority on the correspondent territory formed to retain their identity and develop their national language, education and culture. The right to autonomy does not presuppose territorial self-determination. Cultural national autonomies as public associations may be formed at federal, regional or local levels. They are subject to registration at governmental justice bodies. By 1 January 2010 there were 18 federal, 205 regional and 524 local cultural national autonomies of 59 ethnic groups in Russia.

A cultural national autonomy has the right to represent the interests of the ethnic community before the government or local self-government bodies and get assistance from them; participate in the activity of international non-governmental organizations; and establish humanitarian contacts with foreign citizens and public organizations. It may retain and enrich the historical and cultural inheritance; have free access to cultural values; practice traditions and customs; develop handicrafts; establish educational, cultural and research institutions; and receive and disseminate information in its mother tongue through mass media established by it.

In the sphere of education those ethnic associations make recommendations dealing with the opening of classes, groups, state or municipal educational institutions with instruction in their national language. They may participate in the development of the state educational standards and model programmes for institutions, and conclude agreements with non-governmental organizations outside of the territory of Russia in the sphere of teacher's training, textbooks and other educational materials.

The Government of the Russian Federation defines a federal governmental body under which a Council with consultative functions to deal with issues of the cultural national autonomy, consisting of the delegates of federal associations of that type is formed (at present it is the Ministry of Regional Development according to the Order of the Government of the Russian Federation No. 527 of 17 April 2006). The Council coordinates the activity of autonomies, represents their interests before federal governmental bodies and participates in the elaboration of the federal programmes and draft laws connected with retaining and developing national cultures and languages.

§4. INDIGENOUS PEOPLES

253. According to the Federal Law 'On the Guarantees of the Rights of the Numerically Small Indigenous Peoples of the Russian Federation', mentioned above, peoples living in the place of their traditional settlement and safeguarding their original life-style and economy, numbering under 50,000 persons and identifying themselves as an independent ethnic entity, may be deemed numerically small indigenous peoples. An integral register of them is approved by the Government of Russia on the recommendation of the organs of state power of the Federal Entities. At present, in this register, there are forty-five peoples, forty of which live in the North, Siberia or the Far East of Russia (Order of the Government of the Russian Federation No. 536 of 17 April 2006, SZ, 2006 No. 17).

Those peoples have the right to possess, use and dispose of land gratuitously, control the utilization of the natural resources, and receive compensation for damages caused by the economic activity in the places of their traditional settlement. They may participate through their representatives in the decision-making process dealing with the protection of their habitat, original way of life and economy in the organs of state power and local self-government. They receive financial support aimed to reform the system of upbringing and instruction of the younger generation of indigenous peoples in accordance with their traditions. The law provides for an alternative to military service for those representatives of indigenous peoples who are occupied in traditional branches of the economy.

Chapter 4. Judicial Control of Administrative Action

I. Bogdanovskaia & T. Vasilieva

§1. Preventive Legal Protection

254. One of the main tasks of the Constitutional State based on the principles of democracy, the rule of law and the separation of powers, is to defend an individual from the unlawful activity of governmental bodies and officials. The relations of individuals with the executive power have become more complicated as a result of the strengthened role of the executive power as an instrument of the government of modern society.

255. The Russian Constitution of 1993 for the first time claims and regulates the access of the people to administrative documents and materials. This is indeed an important step to an open, or information, society that has developed democratic rule within itself. Article 24 of the Constitution obliges state and local government bodies and their officials to provide everyone with access to documents and materials directly affecting their rights and freedoms, unless otherwise provided by law. Because of the direct force of the Article any information, except data, containing the state secrets, information on the private life of a person, confidential information regarding the official, commercial, professional and inventive activity, must be accessible to a citizen, if the gathered documents and materials affect his rights and freedoms and the legislator does not provide for a special status of that information in accordance with constitutional principles, which substantiate the necessity and proportionality of its special protection (Decision of the Constitutional Court of 6 July 2000). It is necessary also to note provisions of the Federal Law of 9 February 2009 'On Providing Access to Information about State and Local Self-Government Institutions in the Russian Federation', as amended on 9 March 2016, and the Order of the Government of the Russian Federation of 12 February 2003 No. 98 'On Providing Access to Information about Actions of the Russian Federation Government and Federal Executives' These statutes contain a significant list of data covering these institutions organization, functions, electronic and postal address, point of destination, and procedure guidelines. The data must be located at its official sites. The demands of the list are completely comparable with provisions contained in analogous legislation in Western states. It indicates modernization and democratization processes taking place in Russian society and State.

256. At present, in Russia, there are different forms of control over administrative actions. For example, the President controls the acts of the Government and of the Federal Entities (Article 85); the Procurator's Office and Human Rights Commissioner also exercise controls powers. But the main form of control is the judicial one. Article 46 of the Constitution guarantees to everybody the judicial defence of human rights and freedoms. This means that an individual may appeal to the court even if the legislature does not foresee such a resolution of the conflict. According to the legal position of the Constitutional Court, exclusion of possibility of judicial control of administrative acts is an essential restriction of the human rights which is not acceptable in the democratic society and which contravenes the constitutional provisions (Judgment of 5 February 1993, VKS, 1994 No. 1).

§2. Curative Legal Protection

I. Historical Background

257. The Soviet legal doctrine rejected the possibility of a conflict between the Soviet people and the socialist State but admitted the existence of individual mistakes of officials. Judicial control was restricted while the administrative system prevailed. As a rule, in the case of a conflict with an official or administrative body, an individual was able to appeal to a higher standing administrative body. In practice this system was ineffective and unworkable.

The functions of control were exercised by the procurator's office whose position was strong. The procurator's office exercised review over legality, due enforcement of the laws of the Russian Federation by the federal departments and ministries, state bodies of the Federal Entities, local government, military government bodies and their officials, and review over the correspondence to the law of acts adopted by these bodies. If a procurator considered that an act or decision was unlawful he was able to lodge a protest with the executive body or official, demand the improvement of the situation concerning violations of laws, or institute proceedings against the executive body. The requirements of procurators were binding on all. The procurators took part in court proceedings in cases as required by specific laws, or on their own initiative, at any stage of the process if they found a violation of human rights. In criminal cases the procurators supported the state prosecution.

Judicial control was introduced in the Constitution of 1978. Citizens received the right to appeal against unlawful actions of the officials and state bodies and associations. But the Constitution had no direct enforcement means and an act detailing the constitutional provision was not adopted. Therefore this right was only on paper. Judicial control was developing slowly. The Act adopted in 1987 did not permit appeals against decisions of the collective bodies but this position was changed by the Law adopted in 1989. The present model of judicial review is regulated by the Russian Federationederal Law of 27 April 1993 'On Appeal in the Court against Actions and Decisions Violating Rights and Freedoms' (Ved. Russian Federation, 1993 No. 19), as amended on 9 February 2009.

258. The system of judicial review has become more democratic and in several respects more effective than the system established in previous years.[62] For example, in 1992 (before adoption of the present Federal Law on judicial review) there were only 9,965 appeals in the courts against unlawful actions (or non-action) of executive bodies and officials; in 1994 there were 27,767; and in 1995 there were around 34,000 appeals. The rise of appeals in absolute figures is spectacular. At the

62. N.U. Hamaneva, *Sudebni Control' za relizatsiei prav grazhdan v Sphere ispolnitel'noi vlasti* (Moskva: Institut Gosudarstva i Prava, 1999).

same time, taking into account the size of the population, the number of appeals for judicial review is still not high. Statistics show that about 75% of appeals were against decisions of officials of executive bodies. Another positive fact is that 70.5% of all the appeals (and 72% of appeals against officials) were successful. This means that the larger part of the Russian judiciary, for the first time in the century, support individuals' interests and dignity in their struggle against the unlawful activity of officials and bodies of State power.[63]

II. The Procedure of Judicial Review Against Unlawful Actions of Officials

259. Judicial review may be exercised by the Constitutional Court, the ordinary courts, and the arbitration courts. The Constitutional Court exercises review over normative acts of the state bodies enumerated in the Constitution and the federal constitutional law regulating its status. The Constitutional Court does not examine appeals against individual acts of the President. In such case, an individual may appeal to the ordinary court.

Individual appeal to the Russian Constitutional Court has some distinctive features. It is open to a citizen or a group of citizens whose constitutional rights and freedoms were violated by a law used in a concrete case. Previously an individual was able to appeal to the Constitutional Court only if all other judicial means were exhausted, that is only after the decision of the final judicial instance – the Supreme Court. At present an individual may appeal to the Constitutional Court if he or she believes that an act applicable in a case violates human rights and freedoms (even if the case heard by a Court of First Instance). The Constitutional Court is not the 'highest' or an 'exceptional' court, but one of the means of the defence of violated rights.[64] On receiving an appeal the Constitutional Court informs the executive body or official whose act is the subject of the appeal. This body may suspend the enforcement of the law until the decision of the Constitutional Court. If the Constitutional Court finds a law unconstitutional the corresponding bodies revise the case.

Ordinary courts are not able to examine cases within the competence of the Constitutional Court. The Supreme Court examines as a Court of First Instance, individual acts of the President, the Federal Assembly and the Government, and normative acts of the federal bodies of state power affecting human rights. The judicial review of normative acts of the state and municipal bodies in the field of entrepreneurial and economic activity is exercised by the arbitration courts which protect businessmen from unlawful activities or decisions of executive bodies affecting their rights and legal interests. Also, after abolishing the High Arbitration Court in 2014 during judicial reforms, the Supreme Court of Russia examines, as a Court of First Instance, normative acts of the President, Government, federal bodies of

63. *See* the Ruling of the Plenum of the Supreme Court of the Russian Federation of 21 of December 1993 No. 10 'On Consideration by Courts of the Complaints on Unlawful Actions Violating Human Rights and Freedoms', Bulletin of the Supreme Court Russian Federation, 1994, No. 3.
64. V.V. Lazarev, 'Grazhdanin i Konstitutsionni sud', *Rossiiskaia Federatsia*, no. 18 (1995): 56; U.L. Schulshenko, *Constitutsionni Control v Rossii* (Moskva: Institut Gosudarstva i prava, 1998).

executive power and individual acts of the Head of State, Government and Chambers of the Federal Assembly if they affect economic interests of human persons.

Under the provisions of the Russian Federation Law of 27 April 1993, as amended on 9 February 2009, actions and decisions of State and municipal bodies, institutions and enterprises, public associations and officials, either individual or collective, may be appealed against in a court in the case that those actions and decisions resulted in the violation of rights and freedoms of citizens, obstacles to their realization or illegally making somebody obliged or liable for '*pravonarushenia*' (delicts). Such appeals may also concern presentation of official information which was a basis for that action or decision. A citizen has the right and state and municipal bodies or officials have a duty to provide him access to documents and materials affecting his rights, if there is no federal law restricting the access to information therein. A complaint is examined in accordance with the rules of civil procedure with due regard for peculiarities provided for by the Russian Federation Law.

260. The current legislation establishes an easier procedure for an individual to appeal to a court. A citizen may appeal to the court within three months since he has known about the violation of a right, or one month since the day of the receipt of a written notice about the refusal to satisfy administrative complaint or since its filing, if he has not received a written reply. The complaint may be filled by the citizen whose rights were violated or by his legal representative. A person may not simultaneously file a complaint to a higher standing administrative body and to the court.

261. A citizen may choose the court. A complaint may be filed to a court in whose district the citizen lives or to a court in whose district the state body is situated. Military personnel may appeal to military courts against actions and decisions of military administrative bodies or officials. A citizen pays a limited fee or does not pay at all if the court decides so. An appeal is heard by the court within ten days. For that period the enforcement of the administrative decision or action which is appealed is suspended if the applicant asks the court to do so or if a court itself finds it necessary. The complaint may be examined by a single judge with the agreement of the applicant. If the respondent is not present, the court has the right to examine a complaint in his absence.

A citizen has to prove the fact of violation of his rights and freedoms, and the duty of the state or municipal body or official is to prove the legality of their action or decision (e.g., the refusal to give a visa to the applicant for going abroad, the establishment of additional taxes or fines, or the refusal to hold a meeting). The court makes a decision upon the foundations of the complaint and the legality of the administrative action.

262. If the judicial review finds an act unlawful, it is considered invalid. The decision of the court is binding throughout the territory of Russia. It is sent to a body or official and to the citizen who filled a complaint within ten days after it comes into force. The court and the applicant must be informed about the enforcement of that decision within thirty days after its receipt by the body or official. As a result, the violated rights and freedoms ought to be restored. This concerns not only the citizen who filled the appeal, but other persons whose rights were violated by this act.

§3. MISCELLANEOUS

263. The Declaration of the Rights and Freedoms of Man and Citizen of 22 November 1991 provided for the creation of the office of Human Rights Commissioner. This was in stark contrast to the whole previous Soviet legal doctrine and practice which claimed that human rights were protected enough by the Party, trade unions, Procurator's Office and the courts. According to the provisions of the Constitution, the Human Rights Commissioner is appointed and removed from office by the lower chamber of the Federal Assembly, State Duma. His status is regulated by a federal constitutional law (Article 103.1(e)). Even before this law was passed, the first Commissioner was appointed in January 1994 and performed his functions for a year. After the Federal Constitutional Law of 26 February 1997 'On the Human Rights Commissioner in the Russian Federation' (SZ, 1997 No. 9) (as amended on 31 January 2016 and now in force) the State Duma twice failed to approve the candidate, and only in May 1998 was the first Human Rights Commissioner appointed.

264. Under the provisions of the Federal Constitutional Law as amended on 28 December 2010, the Russian ombudsman facilitates the restoration of violated rights, the improvement of legislation in accordance with international law, the development of international cooperation, and legal education. Any citizen at least 35 years old having knowledge of human rights and experience in their protection may be nominated a candidate for this post. The candidates are submitted by the President, Council of the Federation, deputies of the State Duma and their factions. While a candidate must be approved by at least two-thirds of the total membership of the deputies of the State Duma to be included on the ballot paper, only a majority of votes is necessary for appointment. The Commissioner's term of office is five years, starting on the date the oath is taken before the State Duma. A person can serve a maximum of two consecutive terms.

The Commissioner is independent from other state bodies and officials. His post is incompatible with the status of a deputy of the State Duma or in the legislative (representative) body of any constituent entity, of a member of the Council of the Federation, any state service or other activity except teaching, research or creative activities. His political activity is restricted and he cannot be a member of any political party or social association pursuing political goals. The Commissioner enjoys inviolability during his term of office. He may not be subject to penal or administrative liability, detained, arrested or searched without the consent of the State Duma except in the case of apprehension in the commission of an offence. He may be removed from office prematurely on the following grounds: in the event of non-observance of the incompatibility rule, a final verdict of a court regarding a crime, or incapacity to perform his duties for at least four months.

265. The Commissioner examines the complaints of citizens, as well as aliens and stateless persons who are within the territory of the Russian Federation, against the State or local self-government bodies, officials and state servants if their actions were previously subject to judicial or administrative review. His activity does not extend to the decisions of the Chambers of the Federal Assembly and the legislative bodies of the Federal Entities. A complaint must be submitted within a year after the alleged infringement of the right has taken place. Any refusal to take up a case must be reasoned, and it may not be appealed. In the event of a massive violation of rights and freedoms, the Commissioner is competent to begin an investigation on his own initiative. He visits state institutions and bodies, and requests and receives information and explanations from all officials and state servants – except judges. After investigation, the Commissioner may petition the court in defence of the rights and freedoms violated, recommend actions against the official who violated the rights, petition the court or the prosecutor to investigate a decision, or initiate a proceeding in the Constitutional Court regarding the violation of constitutional rights and freedoms. In the event of a gross and massive violation of rights and freedoms, the Commissioner may present a report at the meeting of the State Duma, make a proposal to create a parliamentary investigation commission or hold hearings and take part in them. As a rule he submits annual reports to the President, the Chambers of the Federal Assembly, the Government, the highest judicial instances, the Procurator General and the Chairman of the Investigation Committee. Special reports may also be submitted to the State Duma (in 2008 the Commissioner submitted the report on the problems of protection rights of those persons who have sustained harm from crime).

According to the Annual Report for 2009 (RG, 28 May 2010) the Human Rights Commissioner received 32,043 complaints and applications, of which around 50% addressed civil rights and approximately 25%, socio-economic rights. The Commissioner highlighted the increase in the number of complaints regarding the non-effective functioning of the judicial system and the infringement of rights to judicial protection and to a fair trial. The greatest number of complaints was received from the Central (33.8%), Volga (17.2%), South (16.2%) and North-West (12.9%) Federal Districts.

Chapter 5. Legal Position of Aliens

T. Vassilieva

§1. Constitutional Provisions Regarding Aliens

266. The Constitution of 1993 establishes the 'national regime' for citizens of other countries and stateless persons except when otherwise provided by a federal law or an international treaty of the Russian Federation (Article 62.3). It contains few provisions which authorize a different treatment in comparison with Russian citizens. As mentioned above and below, these restrictions extend to political rights, land ownership, military service.

The Constitution also determines the basic guidelines for political asylum and extradition. The previous Constitution of 1978 granted asylum to aliens persecuted for the defence of the working people's interests and of peace, participation in revolutionary or national-liberation movements, or progressive socio-political, scientific and creative activity (Article 36). At present the approach for the granting of asylum is 'socially/politically neutral'. It may take place only in accordance with the generally recognized norms of international law (Article 63.1). As in many other countries, asylum is granted by the President (Article 89(a)).

Under the provisions of the Constitution the extradition of persons accused of committing a crime or the transfer of convicted persons to other countries to serve their sentence is performed only on the basis of a federal law or international treaty of the Russian Federation (Article 63.2). The extradition of persons persecuted for their political views or actions (omissions) not considered a crime in Russia is prohibited.

§2. Statutory Provisions Regarding the Status of Aliens

267. For a long period the Soviet/Russian society was a closed one. The process of democratization and the break-up of the USSR stimulated the intensification of the population's mobility and migration. According to data of census of 2012, no less than one million foreign citizens are legal residents of Russia. However, our country does not have a developed legislation in this field. Currently, the main issues are regulated by the Federal Law of 25 July 2002 'On the Legal Position of the Foreign Citizens in the Russian Federation' (SZ, 2002 No. 30), as amended on 30 December 2015 (often called 'Aliens Law'), Federal Law of 15 August 1996 'On the Procedure for Exit from the Russian Federation and Entry into the Russian Federation' (SZ, 1996 No. 34) as amended on 20 October 2016, Federal Law of 18 July 2006 'On Migration Control of the Foreign Citizens and Stateless Persons in the Russian Federation' (SZ, 2006 No. 30), as amended on 28 November 2015.

The 'Aliens Law' distinguishes three classes of foreign citizens – those temporarily staying and those permanently or temporarily residing in the country. As a rule, permanent residents enjoy rights and freedoms on an equal basis with citizens of Russia, but they may not be employed to the municipal service, be a commander of a civil aircraft, a crew member of a military air vessel or of a ship sailing under the Russian flag, be employed in the organizations whose activity is connected with the national security. For persons temporary staying or residing in Russia more restrictions are established. For instance, temporary residents may be engaged in labour activity which is compatible with the goals of their visit. Aliens are guaranteed the security of their persons and homes. They may apply to a court and other governmental body to protect their personal, family or property rights. Those who have committed crimes or offences on the territory of Russia are liable on general grounds. The aliens are subject to the migration control.

Furthermore, according to the Russian Federation Law 'On State Secrets' of 21 July 1993, as amended on 8 March 2015, aliens, as well as persons without citizenship, persons with double citizenship, emigrants and re-emigrants have restricted access to any State secrets as established by the Government of the Russian Federation (Article 21). Also aliens, persons without citizenship, foreign and international bodies and movements; non-commercial organizations fulfilling the functions of foreign agents are not allowed any activity concerning electoral campaigns (Article 11 of the Federal Law 'On the Election of the President of the Russian Federation').

It is necessary to mention that in some spheres there is a large gap between the legal position of aliens and existing practice. The activity of courts may bring improvements, and there are precedents in this field. In 1998, the Court of the Central District of Novosibirsk accepted the claim of a German citizen against an airline which had different ticket prices for Russian citizens and for aliens, admitted its validity and granted compensation.[65] The legislator recognizes specific relations with the compatriots residing abroad who maintain their connection with the State as a core of Russian culture. Under the provisions of the Federal Law of 24 May 1999 'On State Policy of the Russian Federation towards Compatriots Abroad' (SZ, 1999 No. 22), as amended on 23 July 2013, the compatriot's status is considered in the state-centred meaning and is not associated necessarily with ethnic origin. According to the Law, compatriots are those persons who were born in a certain state and have the characteristics of a common language, cultural heritage, traditions and customs, and their direct descendants. An alien may be deemed a compatriot if, residing abroad and belonging to the peoples which traditionally reside in Russia, he or she decides freely to maintain spiritual, cultural and legal contacts with our country. A person may be a former USSR citizen, residing in those states which were part of the Soviet Union, or an emigrant if her or his direct ancestors used to have citizenship in the Russian State, Russian Republic, RSFSR, USSR or Russian Federation. The recognition as a compatriot is an act of self-identification, confirmed by the social or professional activity which is aimed at the protection of the Russian language or the languages of the peoples of the Russian Federation, the development of Russian culture abroad, the strengthening of friendly relations between the country of residence and Russia, and support the public associations of compatriots. This status presupposes a right to acquire Russian citizenship in the simplified manner and to state assistance in the case of repatriation or a decision to receive education in the educational institutions of the Russian Federation.

65. *Izvestia*, 21 April. 1998.

I. Entry into Russia, Transit and Exit

268. Annually, between 350,000 and 550,000 foreign citizens (excluding tourists), the overwhelming majority of whom (around 90%) are citizens of CIS countries, enter Russia. In 2012, the figure was 417, 581; in 2013, 482, 241; in 2014, 590, 824; in 2015, 598, 617; in 2016, 575,158 persons[66] (the data for 2017 is not available). The Federal Law 'On the Procedure for Exit from the Russian Federation and Entry into the Russian Federation' of 15 November 1996, as amended on 20 October 2016, is applied both to citizens and to aliens. As a rule, citizens of other countries and stateless persons may enter Russia or exit from it on the basis of valid identification documents and visas issued by a diplomatic or consular mission of the Russian Federation (persons who have obtained a permit for residence in the country, under the residence permit, and those who are deemed to be a refugee in Russia, under a refugee travel document). A visa may be diplomatic, service, ordinary, transit or for temporary residence. Depending on the purpose of entry and stay of the person interested, ordinary visas are classified as private, business, tourist, student, working, humanitarian and for entry for asylum. As a rule, an ordinary business visa is issued for a term up to one year, an ordinary working visa, for the duration of the effective term of contract but not exceeding a year (three years, for qualified professionals). A visa for the temporary residence of a person is issued for a four-month term within the established quota. A foreign citizen who enters the Russian Federation fills in a migration card which must be returned at the border checkpoint at the time of exit. An alien may pass through the territory of Russia in transit, without the right of stopover. If he is forced to stay for more than twenty-four hours, there are necessary formalities to settle with the governmental bodies which exercise migration control at the place of the forced stay-over.

The right to entry and exit may be restricted for reasons connected with personal fault or misconduct, and the list of restrictions is vast enough. Entry may not be permitted if a person has violated rules regulating the crossing of the state border, customs and sanitary norms at the border checkpoints, if he has submitted false information or forged documents, if he has an unremoved or unexpunged conviction for a grave crime or if he have been held accountable for administrative offences in the territory of the Russian Federation twice or more times during three years. Entry is prohibited for reasons of national security, public order or health care protection. A person subjected to forced deportation during the last stay may not enter Russia during a period of five years after the deportation. The exit of an alien may be restricted as well if he was detained as a suspect or convicted for committing a crime or did not discharge his adjudicated liabilities or liabilities for taxes.

II. Sojourn or Residence

269. Under the provisions of the mentioned above Federal Law 'On the Legal Position of the Foreign Citizens in the Russian Federation', an alien may temporarily stay in Russia during the term of his visa's validity. If a receipt of visa is not

66. Arguments and Facts. 2018. No. 14.

required, a period of stay, as a rule, may not exceed ninety days. The term of stay may be prolonged in the case that a person is granted a work permit or patent. For those aliens who do not need visa the period of stay is no longer than a year (this restriction is not applied to qualified professionals). Persons temporarily staying in Russia must work within the boundaries of that constituent entity, where they were granted a work permit. It is necessary to note that the Government of Russia is authorized to increase to 180 days or decrease the term of staying for certain categories of aliens in order to ensure national security, gain the optimal balance of labour force taking into account the priority of the Russian citizens in the sphere of employment, or aims of the internal or external policy of the country.

A permit for temporary residence for a three-year term is issued within the quota established annually by the Government on the basis of the proposals of the regional executive authorities. This quota is not taken into account, if a foreigner has close contacts with the country or its residents (e.g., was born in Russia, has husband or wife, who is the Russian citizen, residing in the country), made investments in the Russian Federation, was enlisted for a military service or a participant of the programme of state assistance to the repatriation of compatriots residing abroad. A resident permit is issued for five years, and may be prolonged. As a rule, a person ought to live at least a year in Russia before the receiving of that permit (this rule does not apply to qualified professionals and members of their families). If a person violates the regime of sojourn – resides without documents or with invalid documents, fails to observe the rules of registration, sojourn or transit, or does not leave the territory in conformity with the residence permit – he may be subjected to a penalty under the provisions of the Administrative Code.

270. The Russian Federation Law 'On the Right of Citizens of the Russian Federation to Freedom of Movement and Choice of their Place of Sojourn or Residence within the Russian Federation' mentioned above was adopted in 1993, (Ved. Russian Federation, 1993 No. 32). Aliens enjoy a like right in accordance with the Constitution, laws and international treaties of the Russian Federation. It may be restricted in borderlands, closed military towns, certain administrative and territorial formations, zones of ecological disaster, and in territories where a state of emergency or martial law has been introduced. In the event of infection, disease, poisoning or a danger thereof, a special regime of residence and economic activity may be introduced. Under the provisions of the Aliens Law, freedom of movement is restricted if a special permit for entry to locality or organization is required according to federal legislation.

III. Deportation

271. In the event of deportation, different rules apply to aliens residing within the territory of the country legally and to those who cross the border without valid entry documents. If there are no grounds to initiate a criminal proceeding in respect of illegal migrants, the Federal Frontier Service may detain them and remove from the territory of the country. For instance, 39,000 citizens of other countries and stateless persons were detained for lack of entry documents in 1995. A foreign citizen ought to leave the country within three days, if his term of stay or residence is reduced, and within fifteen days, when his permit is cancelled. A person who does not follow this rule is subject to deportation. Aliens lawfully residing on the territory of the country may be deported only if their actions contradict the interests of national security and protection of public order, if their removal is essential for the safeguard of health and morality, rights and legitimate interests of citizens, or if they have violated laws.

A resolution on deportation may be issued by the officials of internal affairs, national security or the frontier service. This decision may be appealed against to a higher official and thereupon to the court. If an alien does not leave, he may be detained and subject to forced deportation. In the Judgment of 17 February 1998 (SZ, 1998 No. 9) the Constitutional Court held that an alien may be detained without a judicial decision for a period necessary for deportation but not more than forty-eight hours. Detention for a longer period may take place only upon a court decision in the event that the resolution on deportation cannot be enforced otherwise. Under the provisions of Aliens Law, persons subject to deportation are kept by court decision in the specially allocated premises of the internal affairs bodies or in the special institutions. They are recorded, photographed and subject to obligatory dactyloscopic registration, these data are transmitted to the central databank.

IV. Right to Asylum

272. The Russian law establishes three different legal procedures regarding to the right to asylum. Political asylum is granted by an edict of the President of Russia in accordance with the provisions of the Edict No. 746 of 21 July 1997 (SZ, 1997 No. 30), in the wording of 27 July 2007. This status is granted to aliens or stateless persons seeking asylum and protection against the persecution or a well-founded fear of becoming a victim of persecution in the country of their nationality or habitual residence because of their social and political activity and convictions, as well as to members of their family. The status of refugee and temporary asylum is granted upon a decision of the migration control bodies in accordance with the Russian Federation Law of 19 February 1993 'On Refugees' (Ved. Russian Federation, 1993 No. 12), as amended on 2 February 2014.

A person wishing to receive the status of refugee submits an application and may legalize his sojourn during its examination. A decision regarding the recognition as a refugee is taken on the basis of survey, individual interviews, verification of the authenticity of information and checking of the circumstances of his arrival to Russia.

A person who files an application undergoes a personal identification procedure, including mandatory fingerprint printout-. The status of refugee is granted in conformity with the international standards for a term up to three years, but may be prolonged annually. Decisions and actions regarding the recognition as a refugee may be appealed against. A complaint is filed within a month after the receipt of notification or within three months in the case that a person has known about the refusal to recognize as a refugee. Temporary asylum is granted to alien or a stateless person, if he may receive a refugee status, but does not apply for it or if there are no grounds for granting this status but humanitarian reasons prohibit his deportation. In the Decision of 30 September 2010 the Constitutional Court ruled that temporary asylum is an additional protective measure preventing deportation of those persons who do not have legal grounds but ought to stay in Russia because of their difficult vital situation of temporary character. According to the position of the Court, this institution has an extraordinary character and may not be interpreted as an alternative to the common procedure of granting a residence permit. According to the third Russian report pursuant the provisions of the Framework Convention for the protection of national minorities, in 2005–2008, 5,019 persons submitted application for temporary asylum, which was granted to 1,658. During that period 8,270 persons applied for refugee status, and 552 aliens and stateless persons received it.

§3. International Treaties of the Russian Federation

273. Citizens of the CIS countries have a special status in the Russian Federation, for free contacts and movement of citizens of the Member States is one of the goals of the Community proclaimed in its Charter. According to the Bishkek Protocol, these citizens may enter Russia on the basis of their internal passport. They do not need visa or a passport for travel abroad.

Under the provisions of bilateral treaties with Turkmenistan and Kazakhstan (BMD, 1997 Nos 10, 11) a special regime is granted to citizens of those countries permanently residing on the territory of Russia. In the case of Turkmenistan, this rule is extended only to conditions and procedures of entry, sojourn, removal or exit from the Russian Federation. Citizens of Turkmenistan and Kazakhstan may participate in the privatization of state companies alongside Russian citizens. Citizens of Turkmenistan permanently residing in Russia perform their military or alternative service in the country of residence, whereas the treaty with Kazakhstan provides for a special agreement in this field. In comparison with other CIS countries, Russia and Belarus have closer ties as members of the Union of two countries. At present, citizens of Belarus have equal rights with Russian citizens in such spheres as education, medical assistance and labour. As mentioned above, they may be granted electoral rights at the municipal level if they are permanent residents.

Part V. Specific Problems

T. Vassilieva

Chapter 1. War, Treaty and Foreign Affairs Powers

§1. National Defence

274. National defence issues belong to the federal jurisdiction (Article 71(l)). The powers of the federal governmental bodies extend towards such areas as defence and security; defence industry; determination of the manner of sale and purchase of arms, ammunition, military technology and other military goods; and the production of toxic substances and narcotics and the manner of their utilization.

Under the provisions of the Federal Law of 31 May 1996 'On Defence' (SZ, 1996 No. 23), as amended on 30 December 2015, the bodies of executive power of the entities of the Russian Federation ensure the enforcement of the contract obligations regarding the state of defence order, mobilization tasks and arrangements in the field of civil and territorial defence, organize the registration of citizens, the means of transport and technical equipment for military purposes.

I. Use of the Armed Forces

275. As a rule, the armed forces are used in the case of outside aggression or for the fulfilment of the international obligations of the country. The deployment of military units outside the territory of the country, their participation in the unified armed forces or their subordination to joint command is admissible only on the basis of an international treaty of the Russian Federation. But even in that case the Council of the Federation must give its authorization for their use outside Russian territory (Article 102.1(d) of the Constitution).

II. Martial Law and State of War

276. Martial law is introduced in the event of aggression against the Russian Federation or a direct threat thereof. The President issues an edict on the introduction of martial law, announces the general or partial mobilization and gives an order to the armed forces to begin military actions. The President is obliged to notify immediately both Chambers of the Federal Assembly (Article 87.2 of the Constitution), one of which – the Council of the Federation – has to confirm the presidential edict on the introduction of martial law (Article 102.1(b) of the Constitution). Under the provisions of the Federal Constitutional Law of 30 January 2002 'On Martial Law' (SZ, 2002 No. 5), as amended on 12 March 2014, the Chamber ought to examine edict within forty-eight hours after its submission, the decision is taken by the majority of votes of the members of the Council of the Federation. The regime of the martial law presupposes certain restrictions of the rights and duties of citizens, organizations and officials, and in the event of its introduction the President of the Russian Federation must inform the UN General Secretary and the General Secretary of the Council of Europe about the deviation from the international obligations regarding the restrictions of human rights.

A state of war is announced by a federal law. It may be adopted in the event of military aggression or the necessity to enforce the international treaties of the Russian Federation. A state of war exists until the cessation of conflict takes place.

III. Military Duty

277. The military duty for citizens in the peacetime (Article 59.2 of the Constitution) and the military transport duty for owners of transport vehicles are continues to exist in the Russian Federation. Under the provisions of the Federal Law of 28 March 1998 'On Military Duty and Military Service' (SZ, 1998 No. 13), as amended on 14 December 2015, males between the ages of 18 and 27 in appropriate health are subject to military service in the armed forces, as well as in border, internal, railway troops or troops of the Federal agency of governmental communication and information. Under the Federal Law 'On the Military Courts in the Russian Federation' of 23 June 1999, as amended on 3 July 2016, the Russian Federation, like several contemporary states (e.g., China), continues to maintain military courts and military Procurator Offices for the armed forces, in the peacetime.

Since 1 January 2008, the basic term of service in the armed forces consists of twelve months. The entrenching of that term means a considerable democratization and softening of conditions of conscription: in the USSR that term was between twenty-four months and thirty-six months, in various periods of peacetime. Call-ups to military service are announced by the name of the President twice per year – in the Spring between 1 April and 15 July, and in the Autumn, between 1 October and 31 December. Along with the process of civilizing the conditions of military service, it is possible to note that the share of volunteers enlisting (traditionally absent in peacetime in Russia/USSR) reflects currently a certain increasing trend.

Those citizens whose convictions and faith are at odds with service involving weapons have the right to a substitution of military service with an alternative civil service for (Article 59.3 of the Constitution). The Constitutional Court in its Judgment of 23 November 1999 (SZ, 1999 No. 51) pointed out that it is an individual right connected with the freedom of religion in its individual and not the collective aspect, and, therefore, it must be secured independently, weather the interested person is a member of a religious association or not. Under the provisions of the Federal Law of 25 July 2002 'On the Alternative Civil Service' (SZ, 2002 No. 30), as amended on 25 November 2013, this right also has those representatives of the small indigenous peoples who follow the traditional way of life. As a rule, the citizens do the alternative service outside of the territory the constituent entity of their residence, but the representatives of the small indigenous peoples may be employed in the organizations of their traditional economy. The term of that service is twenty-one months or eighteen months if a person serves in the organization of the armed forces.

IV. Military and Technical Cooperation

278. In the Russian Federation, the State has the monopoly in the area of military and technical cooperation. This entails the introduction of export control and licensing of exports and imports of that kind of production. Those measures are aimed to ensure the defence and economical stability of the country, protection of the internal market, fulfilment of international obligations regarding the limitation or liquidation of armaments, and non-proliferation of weapons of mass destruction. In accordance with the Federal Law of 19 July 1998 'On the Military and Technical Cooperation of the Russian Federation with Foreign Countries' (SZ, 1998 No. 30), in the wording of 21 July 2014 the basic principles of the policy in this field are the priority of the interests of the Russian Federation, state protectionism, protection of the rights and lawful interests of the legal entities connected with the elaboration, production and realization of military production, by the State. The President of the Russian Federation determines, upon the proposal of the Government, the types of military production and the countries to which such equipment may be exported. Nevertheless, the President may later restrict an export of certain types of production to individual countries included in the list.

§2. External Relations

279. Federal governmental bodies have predominant powers regarding contacts with other countries and international organizations. Among the areas of their jurisdiction are foreign policy and international relations of the Russian Federation, international treaties of the Russian Federation, questions of war and peace, external economic relations of the Russian Federation, and the determination of the status and protection of the state border, territorial sea, airspace, exclusive economic zone and continental shelf of the Russian Federation (Article 71(j), (k), (m)).

I. Treaty-Making Process, Negotiations and Conclusions

280. The treaty-making process is regulated by the Federal Law of 15 July 1995 'On the International Treaties of the Russian Federation', as amended on 12 March 2014. Negotiations leading to the conclusion of an international agreement are conducted by the state officials specified in the federal law or by authorized representatives. The President, the Chairman of the Government and the Minister of Foreign

Affairs have wide powers and opportunities to conduct negotiations and sign treaties, whereas the powers of other officials are limited. Federal ministers and heads of other federal bodies of executive power may conduct negotiations and sign interdepartmental treaties within their competence. Heads of the diplomatic missions in foreign counties or international organizations may conduct negotiations leading to the approval of a text of an international treaty with a State of their posting or within the competence of that organization.

II. Approval by the Federal Assembly

281. An international treaty is approved by statute in the following cases: if its implementation requires the adoption of a federal law or an amendment to it, or if the subject matter of a treaty belongs to one of the following issues: fundamental rights and freedoms, territorial delimitation of the state border, economic zone or continental shelf, defence potential of the Russian Federation, disarmament and international arms control or international measures for peace and security enforcement. The Federal Assembly must also approve peace treaties and agreements regarding collective security matters, and participation in interstate associations and unions or international organizations, in the event that such agreements provide for the transfer of state powers or for legally binding decisions of the bodies of those associations or organizations. If an agreement contains rules requiring the alteration of constitutional provisions, the latter takes place before the ratification of the agreement.

A federal law on ratification of an international treaty of the Russian Federation is subject to compulsory examination in the Counsel of the Federation (Article 106(d) of the Constitution). An instrument of ratification is signed by the President and countersigned by the Minister of the Foreign Affairs on the basis of that federal law. The denunciation of treaties ratified by statute must be approved by the Chambers of the Federal Assembly.

III. Publication

282. Treaties subject to ratification by statute are published in *Sobranie zakonodatel'stva Rossiiskoi Federatsii*, the official publication of the Federal Assembly, whereas interstate and intergovernmental treaties are published in the Bulletin of International Treaties. As for interdepartmental treaties, they may be published in the official publication of a federal body of executive power that concluded them.

IV. International Contacts of the Federal Entities

283. Under the constitutional provisions, coordination of the international and external economic contacts of the entities of the Russian Federation and fulfilment of the international treaties of the Russian Federation belong to the joint jurisdiction

(Article 72.1(n)).[67] In this field, Federal Entities act within limits established by the Federal Law of 4 January 1999 'On Coordination of the International and External Economic Contacts of the Entities of the Russian Federation', as amended on 13 July 2015, which applies to economical, commercial, scientific, technical, ecological, cultural and humanitarian relations with foreign partners. Constituent entities are empowered to conclude agreements with Member States or territorial units of the foreign countries, as well as with international organizations. If such agreements contravene the Constitution of the Russian Federation, federal laws, generally recognized principles and norms of international law or the international treaties of the Russian Federation, or violate legitimate interests of the other Federal Entities, they may be subject to court action. In that case the President of Russia may suspend the operation of that agreement until the termination of the proceedings and the final verdict of the court.

The Federal Entities may open missions outside the territory of the Russian Federation upon the consent of the Ministry of Foreign Affairs. These bodies are not considered diplomatic missions and cannot perform diplomatic or consular functions. Their employees do not enjoy diplomatic immunities or privileges, though a head of mission ought to be a citizen of the Russian Federation. By agreement with an authorized foreign partner, a mission of a Member State or a territorial unit of a foreign country may be opened in the territory of the constituent entity of the Russian Federation.

67. *See* I.I. Lukashuk, 'Legal Foundations of International and Foreign Economic Relations of Subjects of the Russian Federation', *Review of Central and East European Law* 21, no. 6 (1995): 545–563.

Chapter 2. Taxing and Spending Powers

§1. Taxing Powers

284. The federal Constitution does not contain many provisions regarding the principles of public finance and taxation. Most of them are developed through interpretations of the Constitutional Court[68] and detailed by the provisions of the first part of the Tax Code (SZ, 1998 No. 31). The Constitution of 1978 in its original wording included no article concerning the obligation to pay taxes, though the list of the constitutional obligations was an impressive one. It reflects the fact that in the socialist State taxes did not play a key role among state revenues. The formation of a new tax system began in 1992 after the adoption of the Russian Federation Law of 27 December 1991 'On the Fundamentals of the Tax System of the Russian Federation' (Ved. Russian Federation, 1992 No. 11). At present the tax legislation is codified and revised.

I. The Principle of Legality

285. Pursuant to the Constitution of the Russian Federation (Article 57), taxes and duties must be legally established. According to the Constitutional Court in its Judgment of 18 February 1997 (VKS, 1997 No. 1), 'legally established' may apply only to those taxes and levies that have been introduced in statutory form by the federal legislative body in conformity with the legislative proceedings established by the Constitution. These proceedings presuppose that draft laws on the introduction or abolition of taxes, or exemption from the payment of taxes, can be submitted to the State Duma only if an opinion of Government of the Russian Federation is presented (Article 104.3). Those laws, after being adopted by the State Duma, must be examined by the Council of the Federation (Article 106(b)). The mere fact that individual taxes or levies are mentioned in budget laws is not enough since those laws do not contain any substantial elements of fiscal obligations. In its Judgment of 21 March 1997 (VKS, 1997 No. 4) the Constitutional Court expanded the application of the principle of legality to the regional level. It pointed out that taxes might be considered as legally established if introduced by the legislation of the entities of the Russian Federation in accordance with the general principles of levying taxes and levies defined by federal law.

Under the provisions of the Tax Code it is necessary to define all the elements of taxation, the legislative acts on levying taxes and duties must contain comprehensive rules in order that everyone may have an exact knowledge of which taxes (levies), when and in what amount he ought to pay. In accordance with the principle of legal certainty legislative acts on taxation take effect not earlier than a month after the date of their official publication and not earlier than the first day of the next tax period for the corresponding tax. The Code includes as well the presumption of

68. *See* G.A. Gadziev & S.G. Pepel'aev,. *Predprinimatel'- nalogoplatel'shik – gosudarstvo. Pravovye pozitsii Kostitutsionnogo Suda Rossiiskoi Federatsii* (Moskva: FBK-PRESS, 1998).

innocence of the taxpayer, according to which irresoluble doubts, contradictions and vagueness regarding the legislation on levying taxes and levies are interpreted in the favour of a taxpayer.

II. Non-retroactiveness of Fiscal Laws

286. The general constitutional rule concerning possible retroactive force of law (Article 54.1) is specifically emphasized in the field of taxation (Article 57). In the Russian case, this provision is important, for there were examples of granting a retroactive effect to some laws in this field. In accordance with the Tax Code, legislative acts establishing new taxes and levies or new obligations for taxpayers, increasing tax rates, establishing or aggravating liability for tax law infringements may be classified as laws worsening the position of taxpayers. At the same time, the Code admits the retroactive effect of laws abolishing or mitigating liability or establishing additional guarantees for the protection of the taxpayers' rights and does not exclude the possibility of granting such effect to laws abolishing taxes and obligations of taxpayers or decreasing tax rates. The Constitutional Court expanded the application of this principle towards laws of the entities of the Russian Federation in its Judgment of 8 October 1997 (VKS, 1997 No. 5) and to those cases where a tax law does not contain a special rule in the text, but in its substance is retroactive or when such effect is provided for by an act of interpretation or by the law-enforcing practice.

III. Principles of Equality and Non-discrimination

287. According to the Constitutional Court, as formulated in its Judgment of 12 October 1998 (RG, 20 October 1998), the constitutional right to equality of different types of taxpayers is derived from the provisions of Articles 19.1 and 57 of the Constitution. As far as the constitutional obligation to pay legally established taxes and levies is applied to all taxpayers, the constitutional principles and guarantees are expanded, when possible, to legal persons. According to the Code, tax legislation must have a universal, equal, non-discriminatory and non-arbitrary character. Those laws cannot be applied differently on the basis of social, racial, ethnic, confessional or other similar criteria. Different rates of taxes and levies or tax privileges cannot be established or granted on the grounds of the form of property, citizenship or the place of origin of capital.

In its Judgment of 4 April 1996 (VKS, 1996 No. 2) the Constitutional Court stressed that the principle of equality requires the consideration of the capability to pay tax from the point of view of legal principles of justice and proportionality in order to ensure the regulation of taxation in conformity with the Constitution. Taxation paralyzing the exercise of constitutional rights must be deemed disproportional (this rule was later included into the Tax Code).

§2. Budgetary System of the Russian Federation

288. The Constitution of 1993 devotes little attention to the budgetary system of the Russian Federation and inter-budgetary relations. This approach was not typical for the previous Constitution. The Basic Law of 1978, in its original wording, contained a special chapter on the state budget of the RSFSR. At that time the state budget, which was an integral part of the state budget of the USSR, was drafted on the basis of the state plans for the economic and social development of the USSR and the RSFSR and the state budget of the USSR (Article 161). The general indexes regarding the implementation of the state budget were published for general information purposes (Article 162). The present budgetary legislation is codified and revised. The Budgetary Code (SZ 1998 No. 31) came into force on 1 January 2000 (as amended on 30 November 2016). Before 2000, the process of formation of a budget was regulated by a special federal law which was adopted annually.

289. The budgetary system of the Russian Federation consists of three levels of budgets: the federal budget and the budgets of the state extra-budgetary funds (those funds are aimed to ensure the enjoyment of the constitutional rights of citizens to pensions, social insurance and social security); budgets of the Federal Entities and budgets of the territorial state extra-budgetary funds; and, finally, local budgets. Those budgets are adopted by the representative bodies of the appropriate level in the form of the federal (regional) statute or local normative act. An annual budget is approved for each fiscal year (which coincides with the calendar one). All the budgets are drafted in conformity with the common budgetary classification and principles determined by the Budgetary Code. Among those are the unity of the budgetary system and the independence of budgets. In its Judgment of 23 April 2004 (SZ, 2004 No. 18) the Constitutional Court ruled that the federal law on federal budget does not establish or abolish rights and duties and as *lex posterior* it may not change the provisions of the other federal laws regarding taxes or expenditures of the Russian Federation.

§3. Federal Budgetary Process

290. According to the Constitution, the Government of the Russian Federation drafts the federal budget, submits it to the State Duma and ensures its implementation, as well as submits a report on the implementation of the federal budget (Article 114.1(a)). The other participants and the schedule of the budgetary process are established by the Budgetary Code.

According to the Code, the President determines the basic guidelines of the budgetary policy for a fiscal year in the Budgetary Message which is submitted to the Federal Assembly not later than in March. The Government must submit a draft law on the federal budget based upon the Budgetary Message, the prognosis for the socio-economic development of the country and the basic guidelines of the budgetary and tax policy to the State Duma by 1 October. It is necessary to mention that now the Budgetary Message is drafted for three years (e.g., 'On the Budgetary

Policy in 2014–2016') and the federal budget – for the next fiscal year and two subsequent years (e.g., – for 2014 and planned period of 2015–2018). The Council of the State Duma submits it within three days to the Council of the Federation, other subjects of the legislative initiative, committees of the State Duma and the Audit Chamber.

The draft law contains the basic characteristics of the budget – the total amount of the expenditures and revenues, as well as the deficit. In addition, the Government submits draft laws regarding the amendment of tax laws, the budgets of the state extra-budgetary funds, the suspension or abolition of those federal laws that provide for expenditures from the federal budget which are not planned for a next fiscal year, and a report on the implementation of the federal budget.

According to the Budgetary Code, the basic characteristics of the federal budget and each section of the budget classification must be examined by at least two committees of the Chamber, one of which is the Budgetary Committee. The draft law on the federal budget is examined by the State Duma in three readings. A first reading takes place within twenty days after its submission. During the first reading, the Chamber hears the report of the Government, the supplementary reports of two parliamentary committees, as well as the report of the Chairman of the Audit Chamber. If a draft law is approved in the first reading, the Chamber is not empowered to increase the expenditures and the deficit of the federal budget without the consent of the Government. When the State Duma rejects a draft law in the first reading, it may either submit it to the conciliatory commission, return it to the Government for further improvement or entertain a motion of non-confidence. A federal law on the federal budget adopted by the State Duma is subject to compulsory examination by the Council of the Federation (Article 106(a) of the Constitution) which may vote for its approval as a whole. The Chamber must examine the law within fourteen days after its submission and send it to the President of the Russian Federation within five days after the approval. A federal law on the federal budget is subject to official publication within five days after its promulgation. A federal law on the federal budget may be amended during a fiscal year, a draft law is examined extraordinary within twenty-five days in three readings.

Chapter 3. Emergency Powers

§1. Constitutional Provisions

291. The Constitution of 1993 regulates very thoroughly the procedural aspects of the emergency powers and the admissible restrictions on human rights under a state of emergency. This regime may be introduced by the President of the Russian Federation over the whole territory of the country or in individual localities, but the general rules regarding a state of emergency are determined by a federal constitutional law. The President is obliged to notify immediately the Federal Assembly (Article 88). Furthermore, the presidential edict on the introduction of a state of emergency is subject to compulsory examination by the Council of the Federation and must be confirmed by the Chamber (Article 102.1(c)).

A state of emergency presupposes restrictions on certain fundamental rights and freedoms,[69] the extent and term of their duration are instituted in conformity with federal constitutional law (Article 56.1). Those measures are aimed to ensure the security of citizens and the protection of the constitutional order and set some limits on the activity of governmental bodies in extraordinary situations. These restrictions are not applied to certain rights (Article 56.3), the list of which is substantially wider than in the European Convention for the Protection of Human Rights and Fundamental Freedoms. Among these constitutionally protected rights are the right to life (Article 20), the right to dignity (Article 21), the right to inviolability of private life, family and personal privacy, the protection of honour and good name (Article 23.1), the right to information (Article 24), freedom of conscience and religion (Article 28), the right freely to use one's abilities and property for entrepreneurial and other economic activities (Article 34.1), the right to housing (Article 40.1), and procedural rights (Articles 46–50).

292. The previous Constitutions, including the Constitution of 1978 in its original version, contained no provisions regarding emergency powers. These powers ought to be implemented under the discretion of executive bodies of State power. The revision of 21 April 1992 led to the creation of new Articles, some of which regulated the relationship of federal and regional authorities in the event of introduction of a state of emergency. As a rule, federal governmental bodies were empowered to introduce a state of emergency over the whole territory or in individual localities, but republics could declare this regime in their territory upon notification of the President and the Supreme Soviet of Russia. Such a decision of federal governmental bodies had to be made in concert with an interested constituent entity, in the case of republics beforehand. As a rule, the governmental bodies of the Federal Entities were not so eager to give their consent, and the federal authorities could not ensure adequate measures in time.

69. *See* A.V. Pchelintsev, *Problemi ogranichenia prav i svobod grazhdan v usloviah osobyh pravovyh rezhimov* (Moskva: Norma, 2006).

§2. STATUTORY PROVISIONS

I. State of Emergency

293. Under the current Federal Constitutional Law of 30 May 2001 'On the State of Emergency in the Russian Federation' (SZ, 2001 No. 23), as amended on 12 March 2014, a state of emergency may be introduced only in the 'special circumstances', including attempts to alter the constitutional system by force, to seize or take over power, an armed uprising, mass riots, acts of terrorism, blockade or taking over of especially important installations or individual areas, training and operation of illegal armed formation, ethnical, interconfessional and regional conflicts accompanied by acts of violence; natural or technology-induced states of emergency, emergency ecological situations. The edict of the President of the Russian Federation on the introduction of the state of emergency specifies the circumstances which served as the grounds for its introduction, arguments to justify the introduction of a state of emergency, borders of the territory in which it is imposed, forces and means to ensure this regime, a list of emergency measures and their limits, including an exhaustive list of temporary restrictions of the human rights and freedoms, state bodies and officials responsible for implementation of these measures, effective period of the state of emergency. A state of emergency may be declared over the whole territory of the country for thirty days, or in individual localities for sixty days. This regime presupposes specific forms of government, certain restrictions of rights and additional duties for citizens and legal persons. Under a state of emergency, the governmental bodies may provide for total or partial suspension of the powers of executive authorities of the Entity (Entities) of the Russian Federation and local self-administration bodies; establish a specific procedure for entry and exit from the territory and special forms of protection of public order; restrict the enjoyment of freedom of movement and traffic, individual types of financial and economic activity; ban or restrict assemblies, meetings, rallies, demonstrations, strikes and other forms of mass activity. But those measures cannot have a discriminatory character. In its Judgment of 17 September 1993 the Constitutional Court of the Russian Federation has ruled that the ethnic affiliation of a citizen cannot be a ground for temporary limitations of human rights and freedoms under a state of emergency (VKS, 1994 No. 6).

If a state of emergency is introduced in connection with attempts to alter the constitutional system, an armed uprising, mass disorder, interconfessional or ethnic conflicts and siege of individual localities, the governmental bodies may impose a curfew, document inspections, searches of persons and of housing and means of transport; introduce censorship and restrict the freedom of press and the mass media; suspend the activity of political parties and public associations; and prohibit the sale of arms, alcohol and toxic substances. When it is caused by a natural calamity, epidemic, epizootic, or serious accident threatening the life and health of the population, the governmental bodies may organize temporary evacuation, utilization of the governmental material reserves, declare quarantine, mobilize the resources of organizations regardless of their legal status and forms of ownership, alternate their work regime, make changes in their production and commercial activity, or in exceptional cases provide for the mobilization of the population and utilization of transport vehicles of citizens for emergency, rescue or other urgent operations.

II. Emergency Situations of Natural and Technogenical Character

294. Emergency situations of natural and technogenical character are connected with accidents, dangerous natural phenomena, catastrophes, natural calamities or other disasters. The Federal Law of 21 December 1994 'On the Protection of the Population and Territory Against Emergency Situations of Natural and Technogenical Character' (SZ, 1994 No. 35), as amended on 23 June 2016, provides for the creation of the state system for prevention and liquidation of such situations and the state examination of the drafts of especially dangerous, technically complicated and unique establishments, as well as defence or security establishments in order to prevent emergency situations. According to the provisions of this law, citizens of the Russian Federation must be informed of the risk to their health and life in certain localities. They have the right to protect their life, health and property, and to receive compensation for damage. The bodies of the state power and local self-government must give trustworthy and operative information regarding the adopted measures in such situations.

III. Existing Practice Regarding a State of Emergency

295. After the adoption of the Constitution of 1993, a state of emergency was introduced only in individual localities of the North Caucasian Republics – Ingushetia and North Ossetia. Though the interethnic armed conflict between Ingushs and Ossetinians took place in October and November 1992, the state of emergency was proclaimed several times in 1994 because of the existence of violence and terror and in order to ensure the return of the forced migrants and refugees to their places of residence. In February 1995 the Council of the Federation failed to approve presidential edicts on the introduction of a state of emergency in those localities. As a result, the Temporary State Committee for the reparation of the after-effects of the Ingush-Ossetian conflict was established and restrictions connected with the state of emergency were abolished in accordance with the Presidential Edict No. 139 of 15 February 1995.

296. In 1991–1994 an extraordinary situation arose on the territory of the Chechen Republic where the validation of the federal Constitution and laws was denied; the system of legitimate bodies of power was destroyed; regular unlawful armed formations were created and widespread violation of human rights took place. In November 1994 the President of Russia gave authorization for use of armed force to restore constitutional legality and legal order in the territory of that Republic. The Council of the Federation and the State Duma lodged applications to the Constitutional Court concerning the constitutionality of several presidential and governmental acts.

The Constitutional Court in its Judgment of 31 July 1995 (VKS, 1995 No. 5) concluded that it was impossible to introduce a state of emergency in the Chechen Republic in accordance with then RSFSR Law of 17 May 1991 'On the State of Emergency' (Ved. RSFSR, 1991 No. 22). That law was not applicable to extraordinary situations where the federal bodies were opposed by forces relying on unlawfully established armed formations with modern military equipment. According to the Constitutional Court, it did not follow from the Constitution of the Russian Federation that state integrity and constitutional order in such extraordinary situations could be ensured only by the introduction of a state of emergency or martial law. At the same time, the Court stressed that the Federal Assembly should settle the legislation on the use of the armed forces and on the regulation of other conflicts and matters arising in extraordinary situations.

Chapter 4. The Constitutional Relationship Between Church and State

§1. Constitutional Provisions Regarding the Freedom of Conscience

297. Under the provisions of the Constitution of 1993, Russia is a secular State where no religion may be declared a state or compulsory religion (Article 14.1).[70] The relationships between the State and different confessions are based upon two principles – the separation of religious associations from the State and their equality before the law (Article 14.2). The creation and activity of those social associations whose aims and actions are directed towards the stirring up of religious dissent, propaganda and agitation exciting religious hatred or religious superiority are prohibited (Articles 13.5, 29.2).

The State guarantees the equality of the rights and freedoms of man and citizens irrespective of their attitude towards religion and bans any restrictions of the rights on the basis of religious affiliation (Article 19.2). Under the constitutional provisions, the guaranteed freedom of conscience and of religion includes the right to profess any religion individually or together with others or not to profess any, and to choose, hold and disseminate religious and other convictions freely and to act in accordance with them (Article 28), as well as the right to the substitution of an alternative civil service for military service for those citizens whose convictions and faith are at odds with military service (Article 59.3). The right to freedom of conscience and of religion is among those rights which are not subject to restrictions if a state of emergency is introduced.

298. The provisions of the Constitution of 1993 regulating religious beliefs and the interests of believers must be analysed in a historical context. After the socialist revolution of 1917, atheism was made an official ideology of the country, and a large part of all church property was nationalized. The status of church institutions as legal persons was abolished. During the period of democratization, the provisions of the Constitution of 1978 regulating freedom of conscience were changed twice: in 1990 and in 1992. An examination of the constitutional amendments makes it possible to follow the transformation of the position of the legislator. Under the provisions of the Constitution of 1978, relations between the State and religion presupposed the separation of the Church or religious associations from the State, as well as the exclusively secular character of the educational system. The definition of freedom of conscience was not stable. Originally, it included the right to maintain atheistic propaganda (Article 50 of the Constitution 1978); later it meant only the right to choose whether or not to profess any religion, as well as the right to act in accordance with convictions which are in conformity with the law (Article 50 as amended in 1990 and Article 44 as amended in 1992). The principle of equality of religions and religious associations was declared only in 1990.

70. *See* A.V. Pchelintsev, *Svoboda religii i prava veruiushikh v sovremennoi Rossii* (Moskva: Jurisprudentsia, 2007); A.G. Zaluzhnyi, *Pravovye problemi gosudarstvenno-konfessional'nykh otnoshennyi v sovremennoi Rossii* (Moskva: Institut kompleksnykh social'nykh issledovanyi RAN, 2004).

The Basic Law of 1978 provided for certain guarantees concerning the enjoyment of the freedom of conscience. The original version contained a ban on incitement to hatred and hostility in connection with religious convictions. In 1990, the rule on inadmissibility of restrictions to the rights of citizens on the basis of their attitude towards religion was added. The Constitution, as amended in 1992, included another provision: insults against the personal convictions of citizens were made punishable under the law. The Federal Law of 29 June 2013, as amended on 1 July 2017, and Article 148 of the Criminal Code of Russia have added provisions about criminal punishment for 'purposefully insulting feelings of believers' that does not comply with the constitutional principle of equality of all citizens and leads to reasonable misunderstanding and dissatisfaction of non-believers and agnostics. Between 2013 and 2017 several citizens were prosecuted and sentenced to terms in prison under that provision. On the other hand, on 12 July 2016, the Law was amended to permit preaching only within the precincts of churches (of any confession). Officially is the explanation is a necessity to counter extremist menaces and non-traditional foreign confessions like Mormons, and so on.

§2. Statutory Provisions

299. During the period of democratization, the legislation regarding the freedom of conscience and religion was not stable. The RSFSR Law of 25 October 1990 'On the Freedom of Religion' (Ved. RSFSR, 1990 No. 21) was a liberal one, but its concept presupposed the regulation of the activity of atheist associations as well as religious ones. Besides, the common opinion was that this law made possible the activity of totalitarian sects of foreign origin in the Russian Federation. The Federal Law of 26 September 1997 'On the Freedom of Conscience and on the Religious Associations' (SZ, 1997 No. 39), as amended on 6 July 2016, was supported by the Russian Orthodox Church. At the same time it was severely criticized in Russia and abroad for the non-observance of the principle of equality of religions and religious associations, and because of restrictions regarding the rights of religious minorities and religious activity of aliens in Russia.[71] In 1999, the Human Rights Commissioner of the Russian Federation O. Mironov submitted to the Committee on the activity of social associations and religious organizations of the State Duma his opinion on the conformity of the provisions of the Federal Law with the international obligations of the Russian Federation (RG, 22 April 1999). The Commissioner came to the conclusion that some of them were in conflict with the principles established by international instruments.

I. Relations Between the State and Religious Associations

300. Under the Federal Law of 26 September 1997, the key principle determining relations between the State and religious associations is non-interference. The

71. *See* Filatov (ed.), *Zakon o svobode sovesti 1997 g.: mezhdunarodnye normy i rossiiskie traditsii* (Moskva: Moskovskii obsh'estvennyi nauchnyi fond, 1998).

State is neutral to the activity of religious associations when it is in conformity with the law. Religious associations cannot perform any functions of governmental and local self-government bodies, and those bodies do not perform religious ceremonies in their activity. The State or local self-government officials and military men cannot use their position to favour or hinder any religion.

Religious associations do not participate in elections, in the activity of political parties or movements either, and cannot support them. Governmental bodies may (but not obliged) announce that a religious holiday is a non-working day in a certain territory upon the request of the religious association. Although the education in public or municipal institutions is secular, the administration of these institutions may grant an opportunity to teach religion outside the framework of the educational programmes upon parental request (particularly, at the high schools/colleges) and after consultation with the local self-government bodies.

The Federal Law recognizes the existence of traditional religions and identifies them in its preamble. Then Human Rights Commissioner O. Mironov considered that provisions stressing the specific role of Orthodoxy in the history of the country, expressing respect for Christianity, Islam, Buddhism, Judaism and other religions that belong to the historic inheritance of Russia, may be classified as the establishment of a privileged position of certain religions within the territory of the Russian Federation. At the end of the last century, the State began the process of transferring to the religious associations of the buildings, structures of worship and other property for religious purposes which have been confiscated by the Soviet authorities. The Government issued several decrees concerning the procedure of transfer of such property (the latest one is the Decree No. 490 of 30 June 2001, SZ, 2001 No. 28), and the Federal Assembly adopted the Federal Law of 30 November 2010 'On Transfer to Religious Organizations of the Property for Religious Purposes which is in the Federal or Municipal Ownership' (SZ, 2010 No. 49), as amended on 23 June 2014.

II. Religious Associations

301. A religious association may be created by citizens and permanent residents in the form of a religious organization or a religious group. Their creation is prohibited in governmental or local self-government bodies, state bodies or institutions, military units, and state or local self- governmental organizations. Foreign religious associations may have representations on Russian territory but these representations cannot ensure religious activity or enjoy the status of religious association.

The Federal Law of 26 September 1997 has imposed a division of religious associations between religious groups (a new term for Russian legislation) and religious organizations. A religious group is a non-registered religious association, which does not enjoy legal personality and can be created freely. Only those religious groups which will subsequently apply for the status of religious organization must inform the local self-government bodies about the beginning of their activity. Those groups may practice their ceremonies and ensure the religious education and upbringing of their followers. A religious organization is an association enjoying legal personality subject to registration at the Federal organ of state registration or at its territorial agency. In accordance with the territorial sphere of their activity, religious organizations may be classified as local or centralized. A local religious association is created by at least ten persons, not younger than 18 years old, that permanently reside in the same locality. A term of 'permanent residence' is not indicated. It must submit a document issued by the local self-government bodies confirming that it has existed in the individual locality for not less than fifteen years, or a document issued by the centralized religious organization of a certain confession confirming that it belongs to that organization. The status of centralized organization is granted to those organizations which have at least three local religious organizations belonging to their community. A centralized organization which has functioned legitimately on the territory of the Russian Federation for not less than fifteen years at the time of application for state registration may use words 'Russia' or 'Russian' in their denominations. According to the data of the Federal registration service, 22,866 religious associations (among them 454 centralized and 21,550 local) were registered in the Russian Federation on 1 January 2008. Only registered religious organizations have the right to establish and maintain religious buildings and other places of worship, to manufacture and distribute religious literature and materials, to create cross-cultural organizations, educational institutions and mass media, to own property and hire employees. The Human Rights Commissioner O. Mironov considered that provisions regarding the different status of religious groups and organizations and the activity of foreign religions in Russia may cause discrimination of certain confessions.

The State may reject the registration of an organization upon the following grounds: its aims and activity are not in conformity with the Constitution or legislation of Russia; it is not recognized as religious; its founders are incapacitated or documents contravene the legislation; an organization with the same denomination already exists in the state register of legal persons. The dissolution of a religious organization may take place by court order. The Constitutional Court ruled that the registration of a religious organization could not be made conditional on the fulfilment of requirements that were introduced by the Federal Law 'On the Freedom of Conscience and on the Religious Associations' and which had not legally existed when the organization was founded. A court could only decide on the dissolution of an organization which had failed to bring its documents into compliance with the Law if it was duly established that the organization had ceased its activities or had engaged in unlawful activity (Decision of 7 February 2002, SZ, 2002 No. 9). Under the Federal Law of 25 July 2002 'On the Counteraction of Extremist Activity', as amended on 23 November 2015, a religious organization may be dissolved, while the activity of a religious group may be banned by court order for the exercise of extremist activity on the basis of a statement of the Procurator General or a procurator, as well as of the federal registration body or its territorial agency. In particular, by way of example, the Supreme Court of Russia in 2015 has found one of the local organizations of the Jehovah Witnesses as an extremist one.

III. Freedoms of Conscience and Religion

302. The Federal Law contains a constitutional definition of the freedoms of conscience and religion and certain guarantees concerning them. It prohibits different approaches towards persons based upon their religious beliefs, as well as public actions insulting religious feelings which take place close to objects of religious cult. The law stresses that no one is obliged to disclose, or compelled to determine, his attitude towards religion, and guarantees the secrecy of confession.

Selected Bibliography

T. Vassilieva

1. Constitution – Text and Commentaries

Chetvernin (ed.). *Konstitutsia Rossiiskoi Federatsii. Problemnyi Kommentaryi.* Moskva: Tsentr Konstitutsionnykh Issledovanii Moskovskogo Nauchnogo Fonda, 1997.

Zor'kin, L. (eds). *Kommentaryi k Konstitutsii Rossiiskoi Federatsii.* 2 izd. Moskva: Eksmo, 2009.

Lazarev, L. (ed.). *Kommentayii k Konstitutsii Rossiiskoi Federatsii.* 3 izd. Moskva: Novaya pravovyya kultura, Prospekt, 2009.

2. Casebooks

Konstitutsia Rossiiskoi Federatsii v. resheniiah Konstitutsionnogo Suda Rossii. Moskva: Institut prava i publichnoi politiki, 2005.

Lazarev, L.V. *Pravovye Poz0itsii Konstitutsionnogo Suda Rossii.* 2 izd. Moskva: Formula Prava, 2008.

3. Doctrine

General Studies

Avak'ian, S.A. *Konstitutsionnoe pravo Rossii.* Moskva: Norma, 2010.

Bondar, N.S. Ekonomichesky konstitutionalm v Rossii: ocherki teorii i praktiki. Moskva: Norma, 2017.

Bykova, E.V. *Sovremennye protsessy sblizneniya i razmezhevaniya pravovykh System.* Moskva: Jurtlitinform, 2012.

Chirkin, V.E. (ed.). *Konstitutcia v XXI stoletii: sravnitelno-pravovoye issledovanie.* Moscow: Norma, 2014.

Kleandrov, M.I. *Mechanizm eticheskoy orvetstvennosti sud'y: problem formirovania.* Moskva: Norma, 2017.

Kravets, I.A. *Formirovanie rossiiskogo konstitutsionalisma. Problemi teorii i praktiki.* Moskva-Novosibirsk: UKEA, 2001.

Kutafin, O.E. *Rossiiskii konstitutsionalism.* Moskva: Norma, 2016.

Nersesyants, V.S. *Pravo i pravovoi zakon. Stanovlenie i razvitie.* Moskva: Jurist, 2009.

Novikova, E.V (ed.) *Verkhovenstvo prava kak factor ekonomiki.* Moskva: Mysl, 2017.

Pigolkin, V.A. & Tikhomirov, Yu.A. (eds.) *Globalizatsia i razvitie zakonodatelstva: ocherki*. Moskva: Jurist, 2004.
Rybakov, O.Yu. Pravo, otchuzhdeniye i soglasie v sovremennom Rossiyskom gosudarstve. Moskva: Gorodets, 2009.
Vitruk, N.V. *Vernost' Konstitutsii*. Moskva: RAP, 2008.
Volkov, V.V. et al. *Pravo i pravoprimenenie v Rossii*. Moskva: Jurist, 2010.
Zorkin, V.D. *Konstitutsionno-pravovoye razvitie Rossii*. Moskva: Norma, 2016.

Institutions

Abrosimova, E.B. *Ocherki rossiiskogo sudoustroistva: reformi i resultati*. Moskva: Institut prava i publichnoi politiki, 2009.
Baglai, M.V. *President v Soedinennych Shtatakh Ameriki i v Rossiyskoy Federatcii*. Moskva: Norma, 2008.
Dorozhkov, V.V. *Sovremennoye sostoyanie pravosudia*. Moskva: Statut, 2017.
Golovko, L.V (ed.) Sud i gosudarstvo v Rossii, Moskva: Statut, 2017.
Habrieva (ed.). *Pravitel'stvo Rossiiskoi Federatsii*. Moskva: Norma, 2005.
Kleandrov, M.I. *Pravovaya organizatciya mechanizma pravosudia Rossiyskoy Federatcii: problemy sovershenstvovania*. Moskva: Norma, 2018.
Koniuhova, I.A. *Sovremennii rossiiskyi federalizm i mirovoi opyt: itogi stanovlenia i perspektivi razvitia*. Moskva: Gorodets, 2004.
Kolokolov, N.A. et al. *Istoria sudebnoy sistemy v Rossii*. Moskva: Unity-Dana, 2016.
Michailovskaya, I.B. *Sudy i sudii: nazavisimost'il upravliaemost'*. Moskva: Prospekt, 2016.
Smirniagin, L.V. (ed.). *Sovet Federatsii: evolutsia statusa i funktsii*. Moskva: Institut prava i publichnoi politiki, 2003.
Tikhomirov, Ju.A. *Gosudarstvo. Preemstvennost i innovatsii*. Moskva: Jurisprudentsia, 2011.
Vitruk, N.V. *Konstitutsionnoe pravosudie. Sudebnoe konstitutsionnoe pravo i protsess*. 3 izd. Moskva: Norma, 2010.
Volkov, V.V. et al. *Kak sudii prinimayui reshenia: empiricheskie issledovania prava*. Moskva: Statut, 2012.

Fundamental Rights and Freedoms

Ebzeev, B.S. *Lichnost' i gosudarstvo v Rossii: vzaimnaia otvetstvennost' i konstitutsionnie obiazannosti*. Moskva: Norma, 2016.
Lukasheva, E.A. (ed.). *Prava cheloveka*. Moskva: Norma, 2009.
Vitruk, N.V. *Obshaia teoria pravovogo polozhenia lichnosti*. Moskva: Norma, 2008.

Index

The numbers here refer to paragraph numbers.

Index